"From Eritrea to Wakanda to Palestine to the church pew, *Imagine Freedom* reminds us of the interconnectedness of all those oppressed—our pain *and* our refusal to be erased. A book that demands unapologetic truth-telling as we excavate our histories and durable hope, as we expand our collective imagination for healing. On the journey to liberation, Tesfamariam is a dauntless and honest guide."

— **Cole Arthur Riley**, creator of Black Liturgies

"*Imagine Freedom* confronts global anti-Blackness with a poetic narration of a theo-political ethics that aims to nourish Black life. Tesfamariam gives us poignant analysis on Black activism, an urgent plea for renewed links between Africa and America, and a compelling theological vision. Her unique journey across continents, faith, and the academy deftly tracks hip-hop, media, and social movements. Both love letter and prayer, this book is exquisite food for the mind and sustenance for the soul!"

— **Andre C. Willis**, Brown University

"Tesfamariam has devoted her life to global liberation struggles and spiritual awakening. With her characteristic grace, soul, and fire, she invites us to dream our world anew."

— **Imani Perry**, National Book Award winner

"Tesfamariam's poetic and prophetic voice brilliantly surveys the fractured American social and spiritual landscape to help us all reimagine freedom, dignity, and human thriving. Part spiritual reflection, part memoir and Baldwin-esque essay, this thoughtful and beautiful publication will be quoted, studied, and referenced by future generations."

— **Otis Moss III**, Trinity United Church of Christ

"*Imagine Freedom* is a deep dive into trauma. The reader emerges cleansed, renewed, and transformed. It is a balm for the angst we feel living in a world of war, chaos, and indifference to our pain and the pain of others. Read it, gift it, and let's use it to collectively move forward with greater intention and imagination."

— **Medea Benjamin**, cofounder of CODEPINK

IMAGINE FREEDOM

Transforming Pain into Political
and Spiritual Power

Rahiel Tesfamariam

AMISTAD

An Imprint of HarperCollins*Publishers*

For my daughter, Zamara Azaria Msazurwa,
my angel sent by God to watch over me.

As I "[walked] through the valley of the shadow of death,"
your presence anchored me;
your joy and unconditional love comforted me.

May you and your generation experience freedoms
that we can only imagine today.

HarperCollins books may be purchased for educational, business, or sales promotional use. For information, please email the Special Markets Department at SPsales @harpercollins.com.

FIRST EDITION

Designed by Nancy Singer

Library of Congress Cataloging-in-Publication Data has been applied for.

ISBN 978-0-06-325308-7

23 24 25 26 27 LBC 5 4 3 2 1

Contents

Introduction

◆

A Freedom Journey

The evolution of *Imagine Freedom* is bookended between the birth of my daughter and the deaths of four of my matriarchs. Between infinite hope in the unborn future and ineffable experiences of suffering.

This book is my generational love offering, a compilation of conversational letters, prayers, and philosophical explorations of Black liberation, written during personal seasons of trauma and rebirth. As I was navigating my own journey, I felt intimately connected to the pain and power of people of African descent worldwide. Through *Imagine Freedom*, I seek to examine how our quests for freedom and healing are knitted together. It is my belief that freedom and healing are not destinations but instead journeys to the past, present, and future. To actualize freedom, we must be able to reimagine ourselves, our communities, and our relationship to Africa. But there are also freedoms and ways of being that require reclamation and decolonization.

In March 2020, as COVID-19 began the havoc it would wreak in our communities, causing us all to shelter in place, I learned I was pregnant with my first child. As I nurtured life in my womb, I joined the global chorus of people enraged by viral videos of police brutality. I watched in shock as George Floyd took his last breaths while a police officer kneeled on his neck for more than eight minutes. In response to this, the largest mass protests in United States history would unfold with "about 15 million to 26 million people"[1] participating. As $200 billion was committed to racial justice organizations,[2] debates ensued about what it meant to defund the police and abolish prisons. Black liberation had taken center stage with corporations and celebrities feeling compelled to release public statements in defense of Black life. Many civil rights leaders were working tirelessly to keep the momentum going, fearing that progress would stall as it had so many times before. It was from this historic and critical moment in U.S. history, as well as my transformative personal experiences that overlapped with it, that the idea for this book came to be.

Imagine Freedom's release in 2024 marks a decade since the Ferguson Uprising, which inspired political awakening for many within my Black millennial generation, deepening an awareness sparked by the 2012 killing of Trayvon Martin.[3] While many of us were forever changed by the movements those historical moments birthed, nothing has shifted the fact that we continue to suffer from the ills of capitalist oppression, white supremacy, and police brutality. In the aftermath of all that has happened, we stand at a generational crossroads asking questions individually and collectively: Who are we called to be? How should we move forward? What should we do? I wrote this book because I seek to be in conversation with freedom seekers, particularly millennials, who are asking these timeless questions.

Throughout the pages of *Imagine Freedom*, my writing seeks to honor the intellectual, spiritual, and cultural traditions that make me who I am. The chapters weave together political and social analysis, theological reflection, and personal storytelling. As a community organizer, journalist, and public theologian, I have cared deeply about liberation my entire life. For the past two decades, I have committed myself to political and theological education. This has included academic pursuits, mentorship by elders, and participation in several U.S. and Africa-based "freedom schools" in which I was educated by community organizers and liberation-centered scholars. I am a student of the movement. At the same time, I have trained thousands of people all over the globe and organized alongside hundreds of social justice organizations.

As a minister, I have wrestled with our generation's questions about faith and freedom for decades. Spirituality is alive and ever-present to me. Although my framework is Christian and Jesus is my spiritual center, I invite you to approach this book with your own worldview. My beliefs are grounded in liberation theology,[4] which asserts that God is fundamentally for the poor and oppressed and that the Bible can be read through a lens of liberation by all subjugated people. The liberating power of faith was crystallized for me while on a delegation to Darfur, two years prior to attending seminary. When I asked a destitute Sudanese boy what was causing him to smile so much, he responded: "Because I know Jesus loves me." As Black people have for generations, he possessed the capacity to break chains by wielding God's unconditional love. Having witnessed African and Black American women do this my entire life molded me into a womanist[5] who has a deep spiritual love for Black women and is committed to uplifting our unique stories and struggles, as I do throughout this book.

Through my experiences, I came to know that people are

longing for insight, vocabulary, and narratives that will help them make sense of their pain and what is happening in this moment. This has always been made evident on my speaking tours. In 2019, most memorably, an African American male college student asked me: "Why am I here [on earth]? And if I am here for a purpose, then why does it hurt so bad?" His question poetically expressed the yearning for healing and wholeness that I had heard from hundreds of college students through the years. Their tears remain with me to this day, filling me with an immense sense of urgency. I am reminded of them whenever I read that depression and suicide rates are increasing among young people.[6] The unforgettable conversations I have had with them cement my belief that in order for the U.S. to heal from racialized trauma and cultivate the freedoms our ancestors so desperately longed for, this nation must first acknowledge and then work to mend the wounds of Black pain and multigenerational trauma.

As a child of war-torn Eritrea who was an undocumented immigrant in the United States for a decade, I was raised to see this country as a place of refuge. It took living here and leaving for a period of years to understand that the brand of the U.S. is very different from the reality of what it is. While our government is willing to invest billions into the armed forces of Israel and Ukraine, it refuses to provide its own citizens with universal, free healthcare. The Republican Party demonizes our very existence, and the Democratic Party is failing to advance the political will of Black America. We are left tragically bound to this failed two-party system and suffocating daily from the reality and pain of life without holistic freedom.

While some may fear being perceived as anti-American for being critical of the U.S., many of us understand that the most American thing we can do is hold this country accountable to its self-professed democratic ideals. In *Notes of a Native Son*, James Baldwin writes, "I love America more than any other country in the world, and, exactly for this reason, I insist on the right to criticize her perpetually."[7] I hope that more of us begin to think as Baldwin did, especially those of us who are immigrants and/or internationalists. Many of our native countries became unbearable due to political conflicts, regimes, and socioeconomic conditions brought about by Western intervention. We have every right to critique the United States. We have every right to hold this country accountable for its neocolonial foreign policy agenda toward African nations. We do this not only from a place of righteous anger but also with an acknowledgment of the freedoms and opportunities afforded to us by the U.S. that should be extended to others around the globe and defended.

On the day that Donald Trump was inaugurated as president of the United States, I landed in Johannesburg, South Africa. What was supposed to be one year of residence and organizing throughout the continent ended up being three years. It was a life-altering experience, as I learned about Pan-Africanism from contemporary African thought leaders and freedom fighters engaged in a myriad of liberation struggles. There were many moments where my Americanization revealed individualism, privilege, ignorance, and arrogance. But whenever I was invited to and it was appropriate to do so, I rolled up my sleeves to co-organize with them and offered whatever skills I had to their various causes.

Together, we imagined a new world and unraveled what it would take to build it. We chanted protest slogans daily and held weekly culture nights. We sang freedom anthems like "Azania," which speaks of reclaiming African land "from Cape to Cairo, from Morocco to Madagascar." We dissected the legacies of African anti-apartheid and anti-colonial luminaries like Albertina Sisulu, Chris Hani,

Julius Nyerere, Jomo Kenyatta, Miriam Makeba, Nelson Mandela, Patrice Lumumba, Steve Biko, Thomas Sankara, and Winnie Madikizela-Mandela. Constantly juggling theory and praxis, we immersed ourselves in the works of Amílcar Cabral, Antonio Gramsci, Frantz Fanon, Karl Marx, Kwame Nkrumah, W. E. B. Du Bois, and others. My time on the continent cemented my political knowledge of precolonial and postcolonial Africa. It also reconfigured how I understood, talked about, and envisioned Black liberation throughout the diaspora. I began to *truly* imagine freedom.

During that time, I watched from afar, with a new lens, as social justice organizations focused their energies on resisting Trump's leadership. Domestic terrorism was on the rise, as neo-Nazi and right-wing extremist groups felt emboldened by Trump's racist rhetoric. The wounds of the past were being scraped open once again by his reactionary, fascist "law and order" policies. It was under Trump's watch that we would see barefoot children, wearing diapers, running from tear gas fired by U.S. border patrol agents.[8] For the first time in U.S. history, "zero tolerance" polices punished migrants through immediate family separation.[9] Nearly half a million migrant children were held in detention during his presidency.[10] A leadership vacuum was created in this country that sucked away most remnants of hope. The four years he was in power were some of the most turbulent times that many of us have ever lived through.

Months prior to my arrival in South Africa, I had traveled to occupied Palestine and Israel as part of an Indigenous and People of Color Delegation organized by Eyewitness Palestine (formerly Interfaith Peace-Builders). We learned about the 1948 mass displacement of Palestinians, the Occupied Palestinian Territories, illegal settlements, the demolition of Palestinian homes, mass human rights violations, the Palestinian right of return, and the role of the U.S. government in financially supporting the occupation. While meeting with Palestinian and Jewish activists, we were told about modern-day resistance efforts, including the Palestinian-led Boycott, Divestment, Sanctions (BDS) movement. One Palestinian organizer told us that our American tax dollars fund the ethnic cleansing of Palestinians. Prior to that delegation, I had been traveling back and forth to St. Louis to offer media-strategy support to organizations in the aftermath of the Ferguson Uprising. These experiences forever altered my relationship to the United States, shifting me away from the immigrant idealism that had defined much of my life.

Like many of us, I was also retraumatized every time a new viral video of police officers torturing and killing African American men and women was released. Our collective grief, the psychological toll of daily despair, and the dangerous role of mainstream media were undeniable. I would never be able to relate to the U.S. in the same way again. These experiences transformed my understanding of what it meant to be an American and categorically shifted my perspective on the American Dream. More than at any other point in my life, I began to think critically about global State violence, unbridled capitalism, profit-driven media, and other tools of suppression.

I came to understand that we are living through a crisis of leadership. When we reflect on the leaders of the Civil Rights and Black Power movements, we are reminded of their prophetic and global perspective. They held the Black American liberation struggle in balance with Africa's anti-colonial struggle. Whether explicitly or not, Pan-Africanism was woven into the fabric of their political ideology. Understanding that the Jim Crow South held a mirror to the brutality of the apartheid regime in South Africa, they combatted racial oppression in the U.S. while also giving voice to what was happening in Africa.

Today, we don't tend to make the same connections. Our tunnel vision often leads us to think that domestic issues are most important or all that matters. While on a delegation to France to unite Ferguson and Paris community organizers, we were told: "We know the names of your victims of police brutality, but you do not know ours." If we look beyond these borders, we will see a world full of pain and suffering. Doing so will not only inform us about how racial terror plays out globally but also create opportunities for us to be inspired by the past and present freedom struggles of people worldwide. The *Nueva Canción* political and artistic movement of Latin America, the 15-M anti-austerity movement of Spain, the civil rights struggle of Australia's Aboriginal people, labor unions in South Africa, land occupation in Brazil, and countless other movements for social change all have something to teach us.

So many of us are hungry for a map to guide us through the wilderness that is the United States. Others of us are yearning for a meaningful pathway that reconnects us to Africa. This book is born out of my deep love for Black people and my prayerful desire to see us healed of racialized suffering. I do not claim to have the answers, but I do care deeply about the questions.

Woven throughout Black America's historical legacy of resistance to oppression, there has been a belief in and connection to the spiritual realm. This is why I write about trusting in a higher power that can propel us toward the future we seek. History has shown that generations of Black people have leaned on Christ to help guide them through the freedom struggles of their time. As younger generations are increasingly rejecting this spiritual inheritance from their ancestors, I believe it is important to remind them that they descend from prayer warriors, spiritualists, and wounded healers: a subjugated people whose resilience defied the barbarity of slavery. Through faith, they took worship songs intended to bind them in chains and remixed them into the Underground Railroad's pathway. They curated a new Black theology. Black people took the meek white Jesus and transformed him into Christ the revolutionary Liberator. They lost their identities, languages, and families but evolved into a culture that imprints every corner of the globe today. It is impossible to write about Black freedom without recognizing faith as a powerful weapon on our past and present battlefields.

How do we seize what we have lost and what has been stolen from us? What is our birthright and inheritance as children of Africa? One of those promises is that death will not have the final word. And that fear does not have to be our master. By resisting the oppressive forces that seek to destroy us, we begin to overcome spiritual strongholds in our lives. The journey we are embarking on is one that challenges us to decolonize our conceptions of faith, love, and self-determination in our quest toward liberation.

Yet, the discussion does not stop at Black trauma, since offering hope and inspiring tenacity is a matter of generational urgency. The bruised capacity that traumatized people have to imagine a new way forward and the "failure of imagination" on the part of the American democracy to alleviate Black suffering have led us to this critical moment. As Proverbs 29:18 (KJV) warns, "where there is no vision, the people perish."

There is immense internal and collective work to be done. We are at a pivotal juncture in United States history. Race is at the forefront of daily discourse and current affairs. Not since the 1960s (some argue since the Civil War) has our nation been this racially divided. The myth of a post-racial U.S. has been completely debunked. White supremacy prevails as America's Achilles' heel—a debilitating moral failure preventing the nation from actualizing the ideals it boasts of. The U.S. is particularly divided over what defines America's greatness and its treatment of Black people. There is no question that we are living through one of the most politically and racially polarized moments in modern history.

The imprints of our subjugation always come to the surface. For centuries, people of African descent have fought to survive and thrive in the face of unimaginable circumstances. We are the "walking wounded." A four-hundred-year reservoir of trauma from the shores of the Atlantic Ocean to the Ninth Ward in New Orleans. Filled with the blood, sweat, and tears of African ancestors. Manifested through modern-day poverty, disease, mass incarceration, and early death. A historical stream of suffering that connects us to the global struggle of oppressed people on every continent. Today, we see it play out as emotional and psychological exhaustion amplified by mainstream media, social media, and celebrities. In the aftermath of the police killing of Jacob Blake, Doc Rivers, who was the Los Angeles Clippers coach at the time, said, "We keep loving this country and this country does not love us back."[11]

Through their merchandise, the Florida-based student-led organization Dream Defenders has popularized this question: "Can we dream together?" It's a powerful and underrated invitation to collective dreaming. It not only suggests that dreaming is a part of liberation work, but it also compels us to dream as a community. Sadly, many freedom struggles focus on what we stand in opposition to. They cultivate reactionary responses to our sources of systemic oppression. And, too often, we are divided by ideological tribalism and generational differences. But organizations like the Dream Defenders are calling on us to imagine a better world—together. Have we yet envisioned what a futuristic Black America could look like? Can we see, smell, hear, touch, and taste that dream?

Dreaming is not always a foreshadowing of the future. At times, dreaming is a call to the past. It may draw us back to a time, place, or former part of ourselves that no longer exists. Dreaming can be the catalyst to reclamation and restoration. Dreaming together requires us to lay down all our opinions, ideologies, and schools of thought to picture the seemingly impossible. Dreaming together is how we begin to imagine freedom in ways that will transform us, our families, and our communities. Black people have always been pregnant with, birthing, and nurturing visions of liberation. Some of us come from a tradition that encourages writing a vision down, making it plain, and faithfully waiting for it to manifest (Habakkuk 2:2–3). Throughout this book, I name countless individual, organizational, and community-based models in hopes that *Imagine Freedom* can serve as a resource guide—a wellspring of information and inspiration.

The three parts of this book—Resilience, Resistance, and Redemption—are inspired by the scriptural account of the children of Israel journeying through Egypt (a site of trauma), the wilderness (a site of rebellion), and the Promised Land (a site of divine fulfillment). This was a multigenerational freedom journey against oppressive forces, which is why chapter 1 focuses on the reclamation of what has been lost and stolen. This is where the yearning for liberation may call us into remembrance. Who were we before foreign ships arrived at African shores? What were our villages like before arbitrary borders divided us? How deeply did we love? How simple was our way of life before oppressors sought to turn us into human machines engineered for perpetual labor? For some, reclamation means reconnecting with Kemet, ancient Egypt. For others, it means doing genealogy and DNA testing. Then, there will always be those who yearn to touch down on African soil for the first time.

This is, of course, not a mandate to physically return to Africa in search of stolen identity, history, and culture. This is an invitation to reclaim the Eden within our own mind, body, and spirit. To heal our inner child who was born free but was socialized to fear, envy, and distrust. I do not know what has been stolen from you personally, but you do. You know how the constant need for validation and the endless pull toward relevancy are draining you of every ounce of joy and peace. You know what parts of you were lost to our culture of instant gratification. You know the difference between childlike you and adult you, what caused the divide, and how the gap between the two is so wide that you barely recognize this version of yourself.

In chapter 2, I write about trauma and the need for healing rituals. For centuries, people of African descent have engaged in never-ending balancing acts of life and death. In the past, this looked like the "slave patrol" and apartheid police. Today, it doesn't look that much different, with the endless media looping of Black death at the hands of police officers and vigilantes. We are the hardest hit by countless chronic illnesses, and as we all know, COVID-19 unfairly ravaged our communities. Blackness has a painful intimacy with death and trauma that is incomprehensible. And this is why the disposability of our bodies has become so normalized.

So much of our freedom is based on our capacity to defy the grip of trauma—both personally and communally. As I write this to you, I am reminded of what Matthew W. Williams, former president of the Interdenominational Theological Center (ITC) in

Atlanta, once said to me about his healing journey from cancer: "To live in healing is not to deny the war. There is a war. But to live in healing is to take on a different type of weaponry." In African and Black American cultures, there are infinite indigenous and inter-generational pathways to healing—herbalism, warrior-like prayers, rites of passage, and "breaking bread" to name a few. In an era when social media celebrates superficiality and gives us a false sense of human connection, many of us have lost touch with the rituals and diasporic lessons on healing that have empowered our people for generations.

In chapter 3, I write about how living in a capitalist society leaves us open to constant harm and convinces us that our worth is defined by our labor. In late 2016, when I was at the peak of my professional success, I made one of the most difficult decisions of my life: to leave everything behind, including the home of my dreams and my well-paying speaking career, and move to the continent. In the end, it was undoubtedly one of the best decisions of my life, but it instantly stripped me of everything that I *thought was important*. I don't expect everyone to walk away (not all of us have the privilege, capacity, or desire to), but I hope that you have the same mental shift, nonetheless. That you begin to know, if you don't already, who you are independent of any job title, ac-colade, or monetary value. Together, we can redefine "enough" so that younger and future generations will not be confused about measures of self-worth and contentment.

Freedom is deeply tied to our capacity to resist inhumane and unjust systems. Our survival depends on it. Like so many within my generation, I have had to recover from my disillusionment about the American Dream. There are more life-giving ways of navigating the world. We can reclaim ancestral wisdom. Freedom begins in the mind with our commitment to self-transformation. It is a journey of constant learning and unlearning. Decolonizing our psyche can alter our entire reality. Freedom is a quest for intellectual, moral, and spiritual elevation that never ends but instead constantly regenerates itself. By breaking free from the shackles of the grind culture, we declare that profit-driven oppressors will not kill us in the millions once again through new tools of annihilation like burnout, anxiety, and depression. And they will not strategically deter us from imagining freedom by keeping us on the hamster wheel.

Chapter 4 shifts our focus to the power of U.S. mainstream media and the need to detoxify from destructive propaganda. White hegemonic culture dictates who is celebrated and who is criminalized. It decides the lies that render us inferior and the racial myths that define us as violent and savage. I grieve for our daughters who endure pressure to conform to European standards of beauty. In this chapter, I write about the rich legacy and ongoing need for the Black press. As mainstream media actively attempts to co-opt Black cultural production, we continue to create multidimensional, countercultural, and futuristic depictions of Blackness.

This chapter also examines how social media is shaping millennials. For me, it had become an unhealthy tool of escapism and avoidance. The endless scrolling was a way to disassociate from reality—to not have to think about or feel anything. It felt harmless in comparison to other possible coping mechanisms. You have your own ways of numbing pain, but they all come at a price. Going down the rabbit hole of information-seeking on social media tricks us into believing we are being empowered and distracts us from authentic engagement with the world around us. All the healthy living and inspirational content can disillusion us into thinking that we are on the path to wholeness. But screen time takes away from real-life practices of self-rejuvenation. Yes, we may benefit from newfound knowledge, but the obsessive-compulsive behavior will ultimately deplete us. To free ourselves from unhealthy practices, we begin by shifting away from endless consumption (of information and products) toward intentionally *being* (fully experiencing the present moment).

It has been a never-ending life project, for many of us, to break free from these systems of control. As we know, fear is often weaponized in many of our communities (and homes) to ensure obedience. During the Ferguson Uprising, our country witnessed Black millennials engaged in fearless acts of resistance, which I highlight in chapter 5. That helped many of us to reimagine what courage, strength, and power can look like for our generation. We witnessed Canfield Drive, a site of trauma, transform the city and country into a battleground for freedom. Undeniably, Ferguson protestors helped birth, challenge, and sustain larger movements. But they also taught us many lessons about the price freedom fighters are often required to pay.

The Ferguson Uprising's legacy of resistance is now embedded in the DNA of a generation that has witnessed real-time revolution. While the American empire may want us to unsee Ferguson, the images are etched in our communal memory forever. Now, will we stay on watch for other models of defiant audacity? I name a few of those examples in this chapter. For purists who believe victory can only be claimed after the total dismantling of broken systems, our liberation movement will be regarded a lost cause. But we would be remiss not to define survival and success on our own generational terms.

With a focus on Pan-Africanism, chapter 6 highlights multi-generational, diasporic efforts to unite the anti-colonial struggle of Africa with the Civil Rights and Black Power movements of the U.S. Many of us will already know these stories of intercontinental solidarity, but for countless millennials, these historical Pan-Africanist examples are needed now more than ever. Europeans have controlled how we view one another and sought to prevent us from uniting our struggles. Yet, the freedom arc transcends geography. Deep down inside, we know that our fate is eternally linked.

Too often, our connection to one another is rooted in cultural admiration. While ours is a shared heritage, appropriation is possible when there is no acknowledgment, contextualization, and political thoughtfulness. There's a difference between paying homage to the identity of a people and simply adorning oneself with their culture for personal benefits. In the United States, we tend to focus on the cultural aesthetics of Africa. There are many African Americans who wear African print clothing and adinkra symbols as jewelry. For some, Africa is a patch on a bag, a pendant on a necklace, or a pair of brass earrings. The late Nigerian musician and political activist Fela Kuti is revered by millennials who were introduced to him through the rising popularity of Afrobeat. And many contemporary African artists have become infused into the fabric of Black American culture.

Similarly, throughout Africa, American hip-hop and pop artists are in heavy rotation in bars and nightclubs. Millions of African youth living in cities like Johannesburg and Dar es Salaam are carbon copies of African American urban youth in Brooklyn and Atlanta. Netflix's *Young, Famous & African* depicts a group of young African influencers who could easily be starring in a Los Angeles–based reality TV show. The show's stars are obsessed with high-end European designers, maintaining a luxurious lifestyle, and building their brands. We do our people a tragic disservice by glorifying and/or co-opting the other's cultural aesthetics without tangible Pan-African political consciousness and commitment.

Countless barriers stand between oppressed people and self-determination, which is the focus of chapter 7. Today, repressive conservative policies threaten many freedoms we have enjoyed (and perhaps taken for granted) for so long. Throughout the chapter, there are several models of how we, as a people, are seizing hold of our agency. When we are told what we can and cannot do with our bodies, we go in search of autonomy. When attempts are made to suppress our voices and disqualify our votes, we mobilize and declare that nothing will silence or stop us. And when our communities face food apartheid and environmental injustice, we create cutting-edge solutions that meet the needs of our people. But through it all, it is our responsibility to awaken ourselves and the masses to the possibility of political and spiritual power. Collectively armored with the weaponry of resilience, resistance, and redemption, our people stand at the gates of self-determination ready to seize freedom once and for all.

But what is the value of freedom in a loveless land? Love is the forgotten revolution that has the power to regenerate us. For centuries, our cohesion and communalism have been under attack. I write in chapter 8 about how love in the American context tends to be transactional. The romantic aspirations of millennials are too often shaped by "power couples." The glitz and glamour mask the fact that what is marketed as love is often capitalism in disguise. Can we reimagine what twenty-first-century love looks like for Black people? What does it mean to love and protect Black women fiercely in a post–Sandra Bland and Breonna Taylor era? How do we shield the men we love from being terrorized by the reality described by

Michelle Alexander in *The New Jim Crow*?[12] What does healing look like for Black families crushed under the weight of State violence?

Revolutionary love is both an individual and a collective project. Ideally, we would love ourselves enough to acknowledge when we need help and have the humility to seek it out. The struggle needs our whole (total and self-actualized) selves. Not perfected selves, but open, willing vessels ready for deep listening and emotional stretching. The more Black culture honestly reflects the conditions of our people, the more inspired we will be to take our battles head-on. Let our writers, performing and visual artists, and filmmakers give us new ways to envision Black liberation. In defiance of white supremacy's desire to extinguish the flames of our shared Pan-African love story, what are our collective dreams for Black love? What would it take to create the conditions and set the terms for revolutionary love? What does this mean in your own life?

If there is anything oppressors have manipulated to keep us subjugated, it is our image and understanding of God, as I write about in chapter 9, the last chapter. This is why theological decolonization should run parallel to any freedom journey. Eurocentricism has shaped our understanding of the spiritual realm. When we question our intrinsic value, we are simultaneously questioning the magnitude of our God. Individually and collectively, we can unlearn every theological lie we have ever been told about our Maker. There's also power in reimagining darkness as part of God's grand, good creation. We can be the generation that shifts from a punishment-centered theology to one that mothers our deepest wounds.

I make no assumptions about your beliefs. You may be Muslim, Buddhist, atheist, agonistic, a spiritualist, an Indigenous practitioner, or none of these. But we can't speak about Black liberation without considering the historical and present-day role of faith in shaping understandings of bondage and freedom. Our people took an imperialistic religion intended for domination and repurposed it for liberation. Black people's reconfiguration of Christianity is one of the greatest acts of resistance in human history. How necessary it is to declare and believe without a doubt in our minds that God loves *us*, the African people of the world. As the most consequential freedom fighter to ever live, how can we reimagine Christ for the diaspora?

Throughout these pages, we embark on the difficult but necessary work of decolonization. This book offers new ways to imagine self, community, nation, and world, but, most important, a new way to imagine and actualize freedom. All anti-colonial liberation efforts require spiritual excavation and a return to a more indigenous way of life, begging the questions: How do we individually and collectively heal while constantly being retraumatized? And what did we value and believe in before we believed in the promises of the American Dream?

The United States, which has always been a predominately Christian nation, has never truly adhered to the second commandment to "love your neighbor as yourself" (Mark 12:31, NIV). American history reflects a State and civilian obsession with defining who is not considered a neighbor. Yet, our African-centered beliefs—that there is intrinsic worth in all human beings and that the well-being of the village is top priority—uplift all humanity. In the same way that the psychological and emotional wounds of one individual can negatively affect the collective, communal healing and restoration have the capacity to transform every person within their reach.

The possibilities are endless. We can combat internalized self-hatred by being radically compassionate and intentionally affirming our community. New imaginative ways of speaking will be needed. In the age of self-talk, communal talk can usher in deliverance from the internal and external demons preventing us from experiencing the freedoms we so desperately seek. What are the sacred secrets of resiliency that have yet to be told? What are the safely guarded stories younger generations should hear? Daily, our language can actively challenge our most closely held beliefs, starting with how ingrained individualism is embedded within us. First, we learn to love (not idolize) self, then we return to that spirit of communalism that compels us to serve others.

This is where the church has power in challenging each of us to "not be conformed to this world but be transformed by the renewing of [our] mind[s]" (Romans 12:2, NKJV). While this verse comes from the Bible and is directed at Christians, it can be useful to anyone on a freedom quest. Imagination equips us to see beyond the natural, material realm. It creates the conditions for transformation, as we begin to think and act in new ways, which has its own ripple effects.

I do not claim to have the prescription to remedy hopelessness and fear. However, I wrote this book to reframe how we understand oppression and imagine freedom. I have straddled an African and Black American identity my entire life. The two worlds have taught me a lot about the colonial, systemic, psychological, and spiritual strongholds that prevent us from loving one another and experiencing freedom.

As in the preaching tradition, allow me to offer an illustration to guide you in picturing what I mean. In the 2004 hit movie *The Notebook*,[13] Allie's mother conceals the love letters written to Allie by her working-class lover, Noah. For years, she interferes with their bond and prevents them from being together, leaving both to feel rejected and forgotten by the other. It is a ruthless act of class division. As a result, they turn to other lovers and unhealthy coping mechanisms to distract themselves from the union their hearts desperately seek and need. When Allie and Noah finally discover the barrier that Allie's mother built between them, they defiantly choose unity. Together, they go on to write their own legendary story of unconditional, restorative love. A bond determined to sustain itself against all odds. A bond that transcends trauma and death. A bond rooted in indestructible cohesion.

For centuries, white supremacy has stood in the way of African diasporic freedom. Revolutionary love letters between the continent, Black America, and the diaspora have been intercepted by white oppressors for generations. This has often suppressed our hopes, dreams, and yearnings for freedom. It has prevented some of us from truly loving ourselves and our people. Yet, we have always defiantly self-loved and self-affirmed.

Now is the time for us to pen intercontinental and intergenerational visions of liberation, to memorialize our shared dreams and diasporic solidarity. Our freedom struggles are intricately connected. Together, we can rekindle the political and spiritual flames burning between Africa and the diaspora. Only by uniting our struggles can we break free from the iron-fisted grip of white supremacy and capitalism on the lives of our people. I invite you to join me on the journey ahead—a journey that hopefully inches us closer and closer to liberation with each turning page.

◆

PART ONE

RESILIENCE

Egypt: A Site of Trauma

The chapters in this part illuminate the importance and positive effects of resilience through vivid personal and collective accounts of pain, grief, endurance, and survival in the face of trauma. While resilience is often problematically depicted as Black people's superpower, we, children of Africa, cannot deny that our individual and collective resilience is how we have made the best out of soul-taxing situations. Today, it is about what gets us "up and out" in the morning despite feelings of hopelessness, attack, and defeat. Resilience reinforces our survival strategies, meaning-making, intrinsic wit, and strength as we sit by the rivers of Babylon weeping, remembering Zion, and wondering how we will "sing the Lord's song in a strange land" (Psalm 137:1, 4, KJV).

1

❖

Reclamation

The Lost and Stolen

*Another world is not only possible, she is on her
way. On a quiet day, I can hear her breathing.*
—Arundhati Roy

Regardless of our socioeconomic circumstances and social
positioning, we are all born free. At birth, we possess an
awe-inspiring degree of freedom within our bodies. Through the
carefree, fearless movements of infants, you can witness unmitigated
joy and unconditional, unmerited love. Infants have no worries
about tomorrow. They have no insecurities about how they look and
whether they measure up. Trusting in their parents for protection,
infants have no regard for the complex world surrounding them.
They are not yet burdened by thoughts of race, class, and gender.

My toddler daughter is not yet aware of what it means to be
African or a dark-skinned Black girl living in the United States.
She is not burdened by stereotypes and colorism, nor does she yet

know anything about how Black women face inequities in employment, unjust medical practices, and a lack of representation in the media. She does not yet carry the burden of identity on her shoulders. She is sheltered from power dynamics, evil, and knowledge of how society is constructed to oppress her. She is a free Black girl.

As part of my daughter's daily ritual as an infant, she used to crawl into my bedroom, push the exercise ball I intended as a barrier out of her way, and then joyfully look into the full-length mirror propped against the wall. She never got tired of doing this, as made evident by the huge smile on her face each time. And her reaction never changed regardless of what she was wearing or how untamed her hair was. The pleasure derived from this activity was matched only by looking at pictures of herself on cell phones. It was obvious that seeing her own reflection brought her an immense sense of happiness and fulfillment. I always find it to be enviable— the noncritical, nonjudgmental gaze of an infant that is drenched in admiration and love. It's completely untainted and generously offered to caretakers.

From early on, my daughter protested swaddles designed to constrict her movement while sleeping. We went through several brands before we finally found one that gave her freedom of movement while still limiting her "startle reflex." She resisted anything that attempted to constrain her. As I would lift her up to place her in activity centers or playpens, she would lock her legs and grab hold of my clothes, refusing to be placed where she didn't want to be. My daughter, like many babies, took the greatest joy in roaming aimlessly around our home. Watching her, I would often think about how her world was a glorious one full of curiosity and simplicity.

Her freedom made me think critically about how we are gradually brought into bondage. It also made me want to unlearn everything life had ever taught me and to reclaim the innocence and powerful self-acceptance that we are born with. We come into the world with freedoms that throughout our adult lives we spend so much time trying to regain—trying constantly to break free from the world's definition of who we are and the constraints placed on us. The quest for freedom is tied to reclamation, taking back what has been lost or stolen from us.

ZOMBIES AND BATTERIES

So often, we feel that inner tug toward a different way of life that reminds us that this is not how we were intended to live. In the U.S., in the name of work and productivity, we are like machines wired to be efficient. If left unchecked, our society's capitalistic and corporate-driven emphasis on production can turn us into "zombies." Afrobeat pioneer Fela Kuti warned against the capacity to become a tool of the State and lose one's humanity in the 1976 protest song "Zombie" that *OkayAfrica* described as "a scathing attack on the Nigerian military that uses zombies as a metaphor for soldiers mindlessly following orders."[1]

Waking up every day to the sound of an alarm, we are programmed to make the most out of every waking moment. We rush to get dressed, then robotically make our morning commute to work either on packed public transportation or congested highways. For some, more than forty hours of a week are spent in a small cubicle in front of a computer screen with minimal human interaction and almost zero time experiencing the joys of nature. From sunup to sundown, we measure our worth by how much we accomplish that day.

No wonder the "Great Resignation" swept through the United

States in the aftermath of Americans working remotely at home during the COVID-19 pandemic. According to the Pew Research Center, "The nation's 'quit rate' reached a 20-year high" in 2021 due to "low pay, a lack of opportunities for advancement and feeling disrespected at work."[2] The trend continued the following year when "about 50.5 million people quit their jobs in 2022, beating out the 47.8 million in 2021, according to [a] Job Openings and Labor Turnover Survey" reported in CNBC.[3] Ironically, it took us all being isolated at home to question whether we were truly benefiting from or finding value in our careers. This disruption changed our perspective, and with it we began to challenge the status quo in unprecedented ways.

The profit-over-people system we are trapped in is contrary to what has been taught and preached for centuries. Almost all religious traditions have a Sabbath, a day of rest and restoration. In Christianity, God declared the need for a Sabbath even for God's self. Otherwise, the threat of burnout looms. Journalist Jill Lepore explains this perfectly in the *New Yorker*: "To be burned out is to be used up, like a battery so depleted that it can't be recharged. In people, unlike batteries, it is said to produce the defining symptoms of 'burnout syndrome': exhaustion, cynicism, and loss of efficacy. Around the world, three out of five workers say they're burned out. A 2020 U.S. study put that figure at three in four."[4]

We have bought into the myth of financial independence, believing that we can work our way toward holistic freedom and a happier life. Yet, when we examine the lethal combination of systemic racism and a society driven by corporate profits over all else, we realize that freedom is an ever-shifting goalpost in the United States. It's a mirage that we thirst after but have no way of grasping. The reality is that freedom is elusive in this country.

The inner, hopeful flame that burns within us all is being extinguished daily.

As a result, individuals have become increasingly wary about their own sense of self-worth. These "survival of the fittest" times of uncertainty are undoubtedly mentally and spiritually exhausting. Communities of color and young adults are the hardest hit by constant burnout. Journalist Sean Illing poignantly writes in *Vox*, "It's what happens when you live without any margin for error, when you're always one accident or illness away from bankruptcy or eviction. Living so close to ruin saps the joy from nearly everything because there's no security, no peace of mind."[5]

Capitalism is dependent on us working for wages. This is why everything from our society's educational system to corporate media, our cultural norms, and our government policies reinforce the idea that our identities are defined by our labor. Capitalism convinces us that our productivity (rather than our intrinsic humanity) is what gives us a sense of purpose. In many ways, public discourse about purpose has become tethered to capitalism. This is why our best is never good enough. And we are often apologetic about needing rest: we are apologizing for not fulfilling our perceived purpose. This is also why we introduce ourselves based on what we do ("I'm a writer and speaker") rather than who we are ("I'm an immigrant and mother"). For capitalism to thrive, it's required that we continuously produce and consume. So, when we're not working, we are often buying. The beast's insatiable appetite must be fed one way or the other.

Reclaiming our freedom is deeply tied to reclaiming everything that capitalism has taken from us—our time, peace of mind, sense of security, and joy. I long for the day when we, as a society, prioritize deep human connection. The day when our basic human needs (housing, food, education, healthcare, etc.) are met without requiring that we work endlessly for them. As life in the U.S. stands today, capitalism is at fault for many of our misconceptions about worth and value. In its current iteration, success is defined by material possessions like houses and cars, as well as measures of status like having a college education and a well-paying job. Capitalism cares nothing about our character and how we may have treated others as we were climbing the corporate ladder. It doesn't hold us accountable to helping build the "beloved community,"[6] suggesting that what we achieve individually matters infinitely more than who we are.

This current system has proven that it is incapable of quenching our appetite for freedom. It will always fall short because it distorts our understanding of liberation and steers us away from obtaining it. Still, we refuse to succumb to hopelessness and a defeated mindset. Reclaiming what was lost and yearning to return to a time and place where we were truly free demands that we seek a freedom that comes without condition. This is a twenty-first-century freedom that rips off the shackles of performance, emancipates us from the need to prove our worth, and restores our human dignity. It's a freedom that declares that we are more than enough.

A FANTASTIC VOYAGE TO A BLACK EDEN

This leads me to think about freedom within the context of Eden, the setting for the early chapters of the book of Genesis. The story tells of how we fell out of God's grace when Adam and Eve were disobedient by eating from "the tree of the knowledge of good and evil" (Genesis 2:17, KJV). Their banishment from Eden disconnected us from the earthly paradise that God sought to offer, leaving us forever cursed and destined to grow old and die. Countless volumes have been written about our exile from Eden and have explored what a "return to Eden" would look like. Dismissing the possibility of a physical return to Eden, many have focused on other conduits (whether spiritual, psychological, or emotional) to earthly paradise.

In *Postcolonial Imagination and Feminist Theology*, theologian Kwok Pui-lan writes, "The New World and the tropical islands had a strong attraction for European men, for they had projected onto these distant lands the images of the lost Garden of Eden or the much-sought-after Paradise to ease the social and psychic ills of Europe."[7] Pui-lan suggests that the search for Eden, particularly for Europeans, has often been tied to escapism and conquest. Indigenous people suffer due to European claims to territory that is not their own. Historically, colonizers have carved out an Eden for themselves in every corner of the globe, leading to institutionalized cruelty.

In contrast, the Black claim to Eden is not a colonial endeavor. It is about reconceptualizing freedom in our collective dreaming. As we seek to constantly redefine what human liberation means to us, Eden can be envisioned through a lens of Afrofuturism.[8] This allows us to be the architects of our own Black future, designing and constructing an unborn, glorious world on the terrain of infinite imagination. Eden then becomes the epicenter of freedom. And we all become authors, inventors, and animators of a fantastical reality unlike anything in our past or present. As a people and generation with a legacy of prophecy and poetic imagination, what are our Afrotopian[9] daydreams? How would we narrate our vision of an ideal Black world? What is the Afrofuturistic backdrop of our most precious prayers for Black life?

Eden does not have to be a specific destination that we return to or voyage toward, but a state of individual and collective being—a symbolic "place" devoid of all forms of oppression. May the day come when we reclaim a paradise where we are not imprisoned by other people's opinions of who we are meant to be, what we should do, and how we look. There is an earthly and internal haven we can create where we have forsaken the tricks and traps of capitalism and white supremacy. Eden is the site of refuge where we can draw a line between an inner, affirming voice and the judgmental, controlling voices of society. In Eden, our minds are not bound by fear and anxiety and our bodies are not subjected to judgment and condemnation. We instead understand our bodies as instruments of purpose, power, and pleasure.

Eden is where the most whole and free versions of us reside. It is where vulnerability comes easily because transparency, integrity, and trust are the foundation of every bond. In Eden, we love ourselves and others in the purest way. Agape love, rooted in transcendent self-sacrifice, is the law of the land. Intimacy, in all its forms, is sacred and soul-feeding. We are givers and receivers of everything that is nourishing and righteous. Untainted by the systemic, psychological, emotional, and spiritual pollution of our modern times, Eden offers a vision of Black people being unconditionally free.

We do not have to be kings and queens to have worth in Eden. Royalty is not the measure of our value. Our value is intrinsic. There is nothing we can do to earn it; it is freely given to us by God. Material goods do not define us, nor does the quest for them drive us. We are not slaves to consumption and production. Biological clocks are not a looming hindrance because our fruitfulness is not solely evaluated by work and childbirth.

We have clarity of vision and are capable of birthing heart-filled and soul-saving concepts and ideas into the world. We live and move without fear, trusting that our basic needs will be met. Eden allows us to simply *be* rather than to constantly *do*. Eden

 how

does not require perfection and achievement from us; it instead celebrates our vulnerability and utter dependance on the Creator. When we turn to the source of all life, we understand more clearly who we are and what our purpose is.

The voyage to Eden is a return not only to the Maker and the highest versions of ourselves but also to Mother Earth. Regardless of where our Afrofuturistic vision takes us, like the "Prodigal Son," we should humbly reimagine our relationship to this land that has been neglected by us. This desecrated land eagerly awaits repair and restoration, "for we know that all creation has been groaning as in the pains of childbirth right up to the present time" (Romans 8:22, NLT). Nothing short of restorative environmental justice can reconnect us to the soil that we, as Americans, have viciously harmed, ravaged, and exploited. Reconciliation with the land requires that we acknowledge our human greed, confess our sins of materialism, and atone for our rampant waste. We should ask for divine forgiveness for having abused what was never ours to begin with. The United States government should repent for having stolen this land and for having committed genocide against Indigenous peoples. Land restoration should be a moral and political priority.

THE ENEMY: DEMONIC AND SYSTEMIC

It must be understood that a return to or arrival at an imagined, unborn Eden is unnecessary without the reality of a very dangerous, ruthless, and strategic enemy. Christians have historically defined this enemy as Satan, the devil, or Lucifer. The enemy can operate alone or in legions of demons. Often changing like a chameleon, the enemy adapts to its surroundings and takes the form of earthly vessels to catch us off guard and defenseless. But in every situation, the enemy's mission remains the same: a thief that "comes only to steal and kill and destroy" (John 10:10, NIV). Depicted as a serpent in the Garden, the enemy seeks to disrupt the harmony within us and our relationships with others, our environment, and God. In her book *Your Inner Eve*, author Susan Newman states that the enemy's "main agenda that day was to upset the equilibrium in Adam and Eve's Garden."[10] While designed as a paradise, Eden became a site of trauma where God's people experienced demonic intervention and enemy occupation for the first time.

Today, there are countless empires and socioeconomic systems of oppression in place that are an enemy to justice-loving people. These systems, sustained by humans, lead to communal disruption, discord, and multigenerational harm. Then and now, oppressive forces thrive on deception and take advantage of our vulnerability by leading us to believe that our best interests are at heart. Just as the serpent tempted Eve to eat from "the tree of the knowledge of good and evil," we are tempted to question the goodness in our lives and to believe that what society glorifies is better than what God has intended for us.

Worst of all, this systemic enemy encourages us to question our human dignity, the worth we have as God's children. Newman argues that "the result of such encounters is always a breakdown in our spirits, our growth, and our self-worth."[11] In the end, we are introduced to a theology of scarcity, advancing the lie that we are not enough, we don't have enough, and that even our God is insufficient. For so long, we have been fed the myth that there is not enough food, land, or other natural resources for us all. It's hard to worship a God you believe is intentionally withholding goodness from you. When we buy into these lies of depravity, our joy and faith are shattered. This is why it is imperative that we reclaim our joy and decolonize our spiritual beliefs.

Just as the serpent lured Eve into destruction through her ego, oppressive systems attempt to do the same with us, convincing us that more is always needed and that we should be willing to do *anything* to get it. We are seduced into believing that life is about instant, continuous self-gratification and not an eternal destiny. This will ultimately result in feelings of inadequacy or a sense of emptiness because the ego is incapable of delivering on its promises. Living up to his role as "the accuser," the enemy causes us to constantly fault ourselves. Systems do the same. Whenever we conspire with "the father of lies," self-blame is inevitable. Our perceptions of ourselves, the world, and God become distorted. This is a vicious cycle intended to deny the deep harm being inflicted upon us, shrink our capacity for freedom, and alienate us.

There is tremendous power in understanding our battles in life through a lens of spiritual warfare. The spiritual realm (heaven and hell) carries out its will in the world by using human beings as vessels of good and evil. Reclaiming our freedom means breaking free from the grip of demonic and systemic strongholds. "For our struggle is not against flesh and blood, but against the rulers, against the authorities, against the powers of this dark world and against the spiritual forces of evil in the heavenly realms" (Ephesians 6:12, NIV).

Like many of us, I've spent a lifetime combatting negative external messaging to fully experience the freedom of knowing I am enough. As an immigrant, this has not been an easy feat. I had to free myself from the lie that my résumé tells the most complete story about my life. On the other side of that lie, freedom awaits. Freedom awaits when we detach ourselves from capitalistic conceptions of value and achievement. Freedom awaits when we resist the urge to engage in self-validating busyness and allow ourselves space to do nothing. Freedom awaits when we refuse to be defined by societal measures of success but instead believe in the intrinsic worth of all human beings.

We are deserving of a freedom that silences the anxiety in our heads and compels us to "be still and know that I am God" (Psalm 46:10, KJV). This type of freedom promises peace. Are we ready for a freedom that reprioritizes how we spend every minute of our day and ensures that we put first things first? When we reclaim this freedom, we reclaim both our individual and collective purpose in the world. We begin to ask ourselves: How do my personal dreams intertwine with God's dreams for the world?

ALL ROADS LEAD TO AFRICA

From a Pan-African worldview, a return to Eden has historically been understood as a reconnection to Africa, our ancestral "land of milk and honey" with abundant natural resources. This has either meant a physical relocation (as was the case with the founding of Liberia in the nineteenth century) or an ideological repatriation. It has meant a return to our communal ways of being in which extended family members live together, share everything they have, and strive to ensure that everyone's basic needs are met. It is a forsaking of the nuclear family model we have come to know and an embrace of the village system that sustained our people for generations. Without Africa, we have lost our inheritance and legacy as Black people.

Robin D. G. Kelley's powerful book *Freedom Dreams* speaks extensively about Africa's role in our collective liberation. He writes, "'Freedom' even became a kind of metonym for Africa—the home we never knew, the place where we once enjoyed freedom before we were forcibly taken in chains across the sea."[12] From Marcus Garvey's Black Star Line (one intention of which was to physically transport African Americans back to Africa), to the Pan-African ideology of W. E. B. Du Bois, to Molefi Kete Asante's scholarship on Afrocentricity, intellectuals and activists have long understood Africa's significance in Black liberation.

While most Americans are uninformed on the complex realities of life in the massive continent of Africa, Black Americans have always imagined an African existence beyond the ubiquitous negative portrayals of starving children. Many believe that Africa affords Black people the freedom to be self-actualized without the constant, debilitating presence of white supremacy. This is because postcolonial Africa grants us the power to govern ourselves and, in some cases, own land.

Africa is understood as the pathway to reclamation. It is a recouping of the lost self, defiled cohesion, untold history, and dismembered land. It is a recovery of the agency that existed before our self-reliance was forcibly and deceptively shattered. Reclamation is rooted in a sacred knowledge of who African people were and the potential of who they could have become before experiencing diasporic trauma and economic bondage for centuries. Before the branding of naked Black bodies, "enforced labor camps,"[13] lynching trees, Jim Crow laws, police brutality, and the school-to-prison pipeline. Reclamation refuses to allow pain and suffering to be the end of our story.

Freedom is very much about peeling back layers of multigenerational harm, returning us to life before catastrophic encounters with the enemy. For Africans and Black Americans, it's a question of who and how we were before encountering Europeans. What was Africa like before colonization and imposed borders? What would Africa have become had it not been for the transatlantic trade of enslaved persons?

Freedom is about reclaiming who we were before we were taught to hate ourselves, as Malcolm X said in a 1962 speech. Malcolm asked the following questions of the Black audience: "Who taught you to hate the color of your skin? Who taught you to hate the texture of your hair? Who taught you to hate the shape of your nose and the shape of your lips? Who taught you to hate yourself from the top of your head to the soles of your feet?"[14] Malcolm was simultaneously naming the demons of white supremacy and Black internalized self-hatred. Today, we are still fighting that same twofold war of anti-Blackness externally and internally.

In *Freedom Dreams*, Kelley writes about Revolutionary Action Movement (RAM) activists who linked the reclamation of African values by Black people as being essential to Black liberation. According to Kelley, they "agreed that 'a fundamental cultural revolution or re-Africanization of black people in America was a prerequisite for a genuine black Revolution.' They spoke of 're-Africanization' in terms of a rejection of Western materialism in favor of an essential African communalism, humanism, and spiritualism that, many insisted, was intrinsic to traditional African society."[15]

Reclamation is not limited to individual decisions about reconnection to Africa. It's embedded in the Black cultural and media framework. We see it in the popularity of African print clothing, DNA ancestry tests, and group travel to Africa. We see it in the films *Black Panther* and *Coming 2 America* that connect us to the Afro-utopian, fictional countries of Wakanda and Zamunda. We see it in the cultural aesthetics of Beyoncé's film *Black Is King* and in the depiction of African women warriors in *The Woman*

King. The years 2018 and 2019 were particularly unique in the cultural reclamation of Africa when you consider the global popularity of declaring #WakandaForever in 2018 and Ghana hosting the "Year of Return" in 2019, described by the United Nations' *Africa Renewal* e-magazine as "a year-long [program] of activities to commemorate the 400th anniversary of the arrival of the first recorded enslaved Africans in the state of Virginia in the United States."[16]

REMEMBRANCE AS RESILIENCE

For over four centuries, Black Americans have lived between these two worlds: the land of African ancestors and the land of historical subjugation, the United States. Stripped of language, religion, and culture, memory defined the distance between the two. While it is greatly debated exactly how much enslaved Africans were able to retain, we know that memory has always been the bedrock of Black resilience. Eugene D. Genovese, author of *Roll, Jordan, Roll*, writes about the retention of religion: "In ways indirect, distorted, ambiguous, and even confused, the spiritual experience of the slaves took shape as part of a tradition emanating from Africa."[17] Genovese goes on to say "that a significant thrust in black culture emanated from the African tradition."[18]

Robert Farris Thompson's classic book *Flash of the Spirit* illuminates the influence of African cultural traditions from artistry to burial of the dead on "New World" descendants, focusing on how five African civilizations have imprinted Black culture within the United States and throughout the African diaspora.[19] The Netflix series *High on the Hog: How African American Cuisine Transformed America*, inspired by a book written by culinary historian Jessica B.

Harris, is a window into how even African American culinary traditions reflect the power of African cultural retention. Enslaved Africans were adamant about their remembrance of Africa. As one episode of *High on the Hog* makes clear, okra is as much a staple in Southern dishes as it is in West Africa. Keeping the traditions alive reflected individual and collective resilience.

In 2017, I traveled to Dakar, Senegal, and stood at the edge of the Door of No Return at Gorée Island. Staring out into the Atlantic Ocean, I felt an intense anger as I thought about the millions of African ancestors who were kidnapped, shackled, and placed on ships. It's said that those who survived the journey of the Middle Passage were the strongest, and millions more died, were killed, or committed suicide along the way. The ineffable degree of trauma experienced during that era of capture, commodification, and deculturalization is incomprehensible.

Efforts have long been made to combat historical erasure and to reclaim the remembrance of this history for communal grieving and healing purposes.[20] "More than fifty locations"[21] throughout the U.S., primarily at Black churches, host annual commemorations for the Maafa. Mount Aery Baptist Church in Bridgeport, Connecticut, which hosts an annual weeklong Maafa Influence, defines Maafa as "a Kiswahili word, used to describe real calamity, catastrophe, tragedy or disaster."[22] Reverend Dr. Johnny Ray Youngblood, along with his then-congregation at St. Paul Community Baptist Church in Brooklyn, pioneered the "transformative theatre or sacred psychodrama"[23] when he hosted the inaugural Maafa Suite in 1995. A steadfast theme of the commemoration for many churches is "the way out is back through"[24] and has included, among other methods, cleansing rituals, dancing, drumming, blessing ceremonies, and paying homage to ancestors.[25]

RESTORATION: MAY GOD HEAL OUR LAND

It's of course about more than just diasporic reclamation of Africa; it's also about reclaiming the glory of Africa for Africa herself. Even before 1884, when arbitrary borders were drawn up at the Berlin Conference to divide up Africa among Europeans, "the ideas of Africa as a playground for outsiders" had already existed, suggests Al Jazeera writer Patrick Gathara.[26] He argues that the conference laid the groundwork for the "Scramble for Africa," when the continent began to be dominated by Europeans, looted of its natural resources, and denied self-determination.

Reclaiming and restoring Africa's vast richness is well overdue, which has led to much discussion about the return of African cultural artifacts to Africa. At the time of this writing, French president Emmanuel Macron had recently returned to Benin twenty-six pieces of African art. In an article reporting on the return of the artwork looted 130 years ago, Al Jazeera states that "experts estimate that 85 to 90 percent of African cultural artifacts were taken from the continent."[27] Restoring to Africa what belongs to her is the bare minimum of postcolonial redemptive efforts for European nations to partake in.

Journalist Joy-Ann Reid perfectly summed up the complexities of restoration for Africa when she wrote, "Tied up in the [*Black Panther*] film is the notion that you can't go home—that for the descendants of enslaved Africans, the continent of our ancestry is in fundamental ways lost to us, and we are lost to it."[28] Out of sheer resilience, the descendants of enslaved Africans not only survived the brutality of the institution of slavery, but they also birthed a new (African American) culture into the world. This newfound culture has now touched every corner of the globe through music, fashion, cuisine, sports, and cinema. Through the birth of this culture, a new resilient people were born who are now strangers to the land of their ancestors.

Similarly, those indigenous to Africa have been reconfigured by the multigenerational trauma of colonization and postcolonial forces. Precolonial Africa is no more; we are left with the reality of modern Africa. We cannot deny that the European domination of Africa and imperialistic U.S. intervention persists in many countries through indebtedness, land grabbing, brain draining, resource depletion, and causing political conflict. Too often, Americans have very limited knowledge about the continent and the strong-arm postcolonial tactics that sustain Africa's plight.

Mainstream media undermines our possibilities for internationalism by offering little to no coverage of the continent, primarily sharing stereotypical narratives about war, disease, and scarcity. Reid challenges us to "contrast Wakanda with the Africa of today, a continent too often depicted in movies and the scant Western news coverage it receives as nothing more than a collection of backward and impoverished nations ruled by corrupt regimes and ripped apart by colonialism and dictatorship; what the [then] current American president called 'shithole' countries."[29] Rarely can the stories of African nations be quickly and fairly told, as our histories are multilayered and complex. Too often, the human side of our struggles are not widely known. Similarly, the suffering of our people often gets overshadowed by internal and external politics.

As Black people, we all have origin stories, whether or not we yet know them, that link us to Africa. Reclaiming those stories helps reconnect the children of Africa back to their ancestral land. My origin story, tragically narrated through a lens of war, begins in

Asmara, Eritrea. Due to its border access to the Red Sea, Eritrea has always been a target of colonialism and imperialism.

As the United Nations was considering statehood for Italy's colonies in Africa, the United States, motivated by its own political self-interests, advocated for the UN federating Eritrea with its ally, Ethiopia.[30] While this went against the will of the Eritrean people, the UN complied with this recommendation and later did not punish Ethiopia for its 1962 annexation of Eritrea, which was a UN agreement violation.[31] These events led to one of the longest wars in African history. From 1961 to 1991, Eritrea engaged in a war of independence against Ethiopia. Eritrea's resilient, valiant armed struggle against a superpower-backed regime is an important and inspiring story of African claim to self-determination.

I had not yet been born when my eldest brother left home for combat training, trading in his teenage years for guerrilla warfare. Eritrean rebel fighters like him fought tirelessly for the national liberation movement. My mother was pregnant with me when her eldest child, my sister, left for Khartoum, Sudan. She had been providing basic medical treatment to wounded soldiers. Stories like theirs, of walking through the desert to reach Sudan as refugees, are common within the Eritrean diaspora. As the war has left us scattered across three continents till this day, my mother never had her eight children gathered in one room before her death in 2022. For both Eritrean and Ethiopian civilians, the wars, ongoing border conflicts, regional upheavals, and political persecution have ripped through the soul and soil of each country leading to mass casualties, refugee crises, atrocities, and devastating consequences to every facet of life.

Much of what I believe about freedom is connected to the independence struggles of African countries, their ongoing quest to assert sovereignty, and the unimaginable sacrifices of African people, particularly our martyrs who died so that liberated African countries could be born. As an Eritrean, my concept of freedom has always been rooted in the prayerful hope that God will heal our land. I continue to pray that better days are ahead of us—rather than the brutal era of colonization, ever-present political and economic turmoil, and mass human rights violations that have defined our country's history.

In 2013, a shipwrecked boat on the Italian island of Lampedusa made international headlines with a reported death toll of over 360 people; the boat was believed to have been carrying migrants (primarily Eritrean and Somali asylum seekers) from Libya to Italy.[32] Twenty-eight at the time of his death, my cousin Dahlak was one of countless Eritreans to die in overcrowded boats headed to European shores. Three years later, in 2016, while on a delegation to occupied Palestine and Israel, I met and spoke with young Eritrean refugees at Holot, a now-closed Israeli detention center for African asylum seekers. When I asked them their reason for fleeing Eritrea, they all pointed to the economy and policies of the government. They told our delegation that, as asylum seekers, they were given two options: return to your country of origin or remain in Israel under indefinite detention. They decided on detention in Israel over a return to their homeland.

BREAKING POSTCOLONIAL STRONGHOLDS

The *Black Panther* film, a timeless cultural phenomenon, leads us to fantasize about and envision an independent African nation that has not yet been scarred by European-inflicted trauma. We deserve to relish in an Afrofuturistic, escapist portrayal of Africa. We deserve to imagine Black superheroes and futures beyond the limitations of facts and history. But our fantasies of Africa threaten to perpetuate an ideal that makes it difficult to contend with modern-day realities.

Africa continues to bleed out, having to bandage herself up day by day because the wounds are too deeply embedded. Only when we are willing to confront Africa's majestic glory *and* her incomprehensible trauma will we be able to marry our explorations and visions of freedom with Africa's dreams for herself. We should also acknowledge that, as it relates to gender equality, LGBTQIA+ rights, and destigmatizing mental illness, many countries in Africa have a long way to go before they can be viewed as beacons of hope. Illusions can steer us away from what we truly seek—diasporic healing, empowerment, and liberation.

While in Johannesburg in 2017, I had two conversations (one with a Zulu man and the other with an African American man) during which it was argued that South Africans have proven themselves incapable of self-governance and would be better off under the leadership of Europeans. Their opinions infuriated me, as they spoke fondly about economic and infrastructure advancements made by Europeans in Africa during colonization. Sadly, these beliefs are unknowingly shared by many whose fond remembrance of Africa's "glory days" is in fact romanticization of domination. Many struggle to envision an Africa without foreign aid dependency, ignoring the indebtedness and destabilization it often causes. We do a disservice to the global community when we become apologists for neocolonialism.

Neocolonial apologists remind me of the biblical children of Israel. As told in the book of Exodus, they roamed the wilderness for forty years after having been delivered out of slavery in Egypt by Moses. They were caught between the world left behind and the world ahead of them. Their newfound liberation led them to look back on Egypt with fond nostalgia. They spoke of how good life was there, forgetting their enslavement and oppression under the Egyptian pharaohs. Formerly, they feasted on the meat and resources provided by their captors. Later, they were surviving day by day from "manna" from the heavens, questioning the benefits of liberation.

Freedom is not always found in the past, in turning back to a time and place deemed liberating. Freedom is often about exodus—departure or forward movement. Our yearning for freedom may compel us to seek a drastic shift in our lives by leaving behind what is familiar and safe in search of the unknown. For the children of Israel, the forward journey to the Promised Land was the pathway to freedom. Turning backward would mean returning to enslavement and bondage. A return to Egypt would have meant a return to subjugation and oppression under Pharaoh. Yet, the children of Israel, like many traumatized people healing from the deep scars of the past, still looked back at Egypt with romanticization. Michael Walrond, pastor of First Corinthian Baptist Church in Harlem, once said, "It took God one night to get the people of God out of Egypt, but it took forty years to get Egypt out of the people of God. It took forty years to sever the dysfunctional addiction to captivity."[33]

Egypt is symbolic of ways of thinking, habits, and addictions that prevent us from living a life free of bondage—an abundant life that God desires for us. It represents the mental blocks we can never seem to escape. Egypt is that toxic relationship that we are reluctant to end because we are terrified of being alone or, even worse, believe that we are undeserving of something better. It's that painful memory that mentally and emotionally imprisons us. Egypt is whatever person, place, or thing that stands between us and our holistic freedom. As we seek to flee Egypt, we balance surviving the present and fixing our eyes on a liberated future.

When I imagine, I envision an Africa and Black America that have yet to be actualized. I grasp hold of an Afrofuturistic vision of a new day for both. An Africa completely free from foreign indebtedness and influence. A Black America liberated from racial subjugation and trauma. I see a people that have healed from centuries of brutality and exploitation. I imagine Africa gathering all her children together from across the diaspora and uniting them under one umbrella of Pan-African unity. Nourishment is intrinsic to her. She provides for all her children from her bare bosom, yet she simultaneously has her own needs met by them. I envision an Africa that can finally be what African Americans want and need her to be. Too often, we obsess over the link between Africa and Black America without considering that much of Africa is still on a postcolonial journey of self-discovery.

Just as there is no going back to a utopian Eden, there is also no going back to the Africa our ancestors knew. Those two worlds are gone forever. What remains of them is the vision they give us of not only what has been but also of what is possible. Our imagination serves as evidence that there is more to life than the world we know today. When we are told that exploitation and degradation are the only way, we can look to the birthplace of civilization to remind us of a time when communalism was the way of the land. We have the power to reclaim who we were before the enemy's arrival, while simultaneously building the future of our dreams.

2

Trauma

Healing Rituals

The Devil whispered in my ear: "You're
not strong enough to withstand the storm."
I whispered back: "I am the storm."
—Adharanand Finn

With a feeling of deep dread, I whispered: "God, why is this happening? Please don't let this happen! Please don't let me lose my baby."

I stood up, looked in the toilet bowl, and saw hefty droplets of bright-red blood. This was the moment that pregnant women dread, and this moment had come for me minutes before midnight on my due date. Unexplained bleeding was the culmination of a day filled with intense pelvic pressure, an indescribable lower-abdomen pain, and a sudden internal "pop" sensation. Walking had become an impossible feat, but none of that was worrisome until the show of heavy bleeding. As I called out for my husband, nine months of maternity flashed before my eyes. I remembered the two positive home pregnancy tests (the second taken minutes after the first out of disbelief), all the ultrasounds, the nausea, the growing bump, the joy of loved ones, my COVID-avoidant virtual baby shower, the glamorous maternity photo shoot, and the nursery that awaited a newborn's arrival.

A call to a twenty-four-hour advice nurse line confirmed what we already knew: we had to make our way to the hospital as fast as possible. We scrambled to get dressed and grabbed the packed bags that had sat by the front door for weeks. In it were several copies of a carefully crafted "birth plan" that in no way accounted for a constant flow of blood. After we checked in at the emergency department of a hospital, a nurse brought out a wheelchair for me and escorted my husband and me to the labor and delivery unit. Despite my reluctance and fear, I agreed to be medically induced, because they were unable to determine the cause of bleeding and what they referred to as the baby's heart rate "acting up." For the next twenty-eight hours, the doctors and I journeyed through a series of tough medical decisions to safely bring my daughter into the world.

Induced labor commenced with an intensity that immediately shattered my fantasies of an unmedicated, "natural" birthing experience. From the onset, my contractions were coming four (and sometimes two) minutes apart. As more and more Pitocin entered my body through an intravenous line, the pain felt as if a tsunami of shock waves was battering the walls of my uterus. As my legs trembled, I frantically gripped my husband's body for comfort and balance. The intensity of my pain was affirmed by having dilated four centimeters in four hours. The white female doctor on duty entered my room periodically to perform vaginal exams and accidentally ruptured my water sac while doing so. Throughout the process, she was cold and matter-of-fact in her dialogue with me, seemingly lacking any degree of empathy.

Over the course of the next sixteen hours, my daughter and I danced together in the sacred, ancient ritual of childbirth. Somewhere in between that age-old rite of passage, my temperature climbed to 102 degrees due to chorioamnionitis (an infection of the uterus), requiring antibiotics. Murphy's Law was in full effect in my birthing story, with one challenge following quickly after the next. At some point, the doctor came to tell me that it was time to begin pushing because the baby was distressed. An emergency C-section loomed as a threat. For fifty-five minutes, I pushed and pushed some more. Finally, her head crowned and there was an immediate end in sight. The moment I, thirty-nine years old at the time, had been waiting for finally arrived at 3:55 a.m. My daughter was born. But she came into the world limp, silent, and apneic with a temperature of 101.7 degrees. A T-piece resuscitator was needed to clear her lungs in her first two and a half minutes of life.

With every inhale and exhale, I came closer to birthing her. But I also came closer to one of the many fatal possibilities the doctors kept warning me about. I was terrified, and my fears had merit when you consider the alarming Black maternal mortality rates in the U.S. The Centers for Disease Control and Prevention (CDC) reports that "Black women are three times more likely to die from a pregnancy-related cause than White women. Multiple factors contribute to these disparities, such as variation in quality healthcare, underlying chronic conditions, structural racism, and implicit bias."[1] And this, of course, is not unique to North America. When congratulatory messages came from my husband's homeland of Zambia, his family's matriarch praised me for surviving. In their African cultural understanding (due to Zambia's own high maternal mortality rates), when she is pregnant, a woman straddles life and death, and I had succeeded in remaining in the land of the living.

VIRAL BLACK DEATH AND RACIALIZED TRAUMA

Nothing better illustrates the lack of freedom that Black people have in the United States than the various balancing acts of life and death that we are forced to engage in daily. Whether it's unwarranted stop-and-frisk incidents or deadly "mistaken identity" tragedies, the price for racial bias and white paranoia is paid seemingly every day by Black Americans. Institutionalized racism and racial profiling are literally killing us at every turn. We can't seem to do *anything* without someone calling the police on us and without facing the threat of death. So much so that news articles and social media memes have been created to identify all the ways Black people have been racially profiled and, more tragically, killed while engaging in the most basic, routine activities. From going to the store to buy snacks (Trayvon Martin) to playing with a toy gun in a park (Tamir Rice) to driving to a new job (Sandra Bland) to sleeping in a car in a fast-food restaurant's parking lot (Rayshard Brooks) to walking home (Elijah McClain).

One case that hauntingly illustrates our life-and-death balancing act is what happened in Louisville, Kentucky, on March 13, 2020, when Breonna Taylor, a twenty-six-year-old African American medical worker who was in bed with her boyfriend, was killed by plain-clothes police officers with a no-knock warrant. In the months that followed, her death led to much national discussion about all the freedoms Black people lack in America. Taylor, who was killed one week before I learned I was pregnant, led me to think a great deal about what protection looks like for Black women in this country. If a woman can't be safe in bed next to her lover, then where can she ever be safe? Tragically, the officers were not charged with murder, but instead one officer was charged with wanton endangerment in the first degree for bullets that entered the apartment next door. The *Beaverton*, a satirical news coverage site, published an article titled "Wall Adjacent to Breonna Taylor's Apartment Grateful for Justice to Have Been Served."[2]

Through video footage, we have too often witnessed police officers adamant to capture Black people, particularly Black men, by any means necessary. It's eerily reminiscent of an era in which patrols had the power to seize us "dead or alive." But this phenomenon is not limited to State violence. White women weaponizing tears, social status, and accusations have a long history of being a threat to Black freedom, with countless Black men and boys like Emmett Till paying the ultimate price. In recent years, this phenomenon led to the social media trend to collectively nickname white women behaving this way as "Karen." On May 25, 2020 in New York's Central Park, for example, Amy Cooper warned Christian Cooper (no relation) before calling 911 that she would tell police "an African-American man is threatening my life."[3] Prior to that, bird-watcher Christian Cooper, a board member of the New York City Audubon Society, which protects birds, had simply asked that she leash her dog in adherence to park rules.[4]

One of the most haunting images we have ever seen of white supremacy happened on that same day in Minneapolis, Minnesota. Unarmed George Floyd was killed by a cop pressing his knee on his neck as he repeatedly cried out that he could not breathe. Officers were called because Floyd was believed to have used a counterfeit

$20 bill in a convenience store. The video of Floyd's final moments alive looped repeatedly on all the major cable networks. We collectively normalize State violence and public lynching to the extent of them being aired on television and shared on social media daily. How barbaric the images have become of Black death. So often, these images have a debilitating effect on us. And that's exactly what white supremacy wants—to immobilize us. To prevent Black escape. Because Black escape represents Black humanity, liberation, self-determination, self-governance, and, most dangerous of all, Black power. The act of stopping a Black escapee is equivalent to putting an end to their audacity to affirm their human dignity, rebel, seek liberty, and assert agency. Hasn't death always been the price that freedom seekers must be willing to pay for liberation?

Amid the record-breaking number of protests that followed in the aftermath of Floyd's murder, a viral image emerged of a white woman holding up a sign that read: "All mothers were summoned when George Floyd called out for his momma." I did not yet know the gender of my child as I watched all of this unfold. But the image of a grown Black man calling out for his deceased mother in his final moments on earth led me to hope, in that moment of utter sadness, that I was not having a boy. My soul was tender from the thought of bringing a Black male child into the world who could one day be murdered with his face pressed against sidewalk concrete as he called out for me in desperation.

Black Americans were not only being killed with terrifying frequency at the hands of police officers but were also the hardest hit by the pandemic. In March 2020, days before I learned that I was pregnant, the United States began to lock down due to COVID-19. While life was growing in my womb, the nation and world were combatting a pandemic that gripped us all with fear. As I would count the weeks of gestation, news networks broadcasted the daily virus infection rates and death tolls.

In major cities throughout the United States, African Americans were dying from COVID-19-related causes at disproportionately higher rates than other racial groups. CNN reported that while African Americans only make up 30 percent of the population in Chicago and 32 percent in Louisiana, they accounted for 72 percent of the COVID-19-related deaths in Chicago and 70 percent in Louisiana.[5] According to the *Guardian*, a study conducted by the Office for National Statistics in the United Kingdom found that "black people are more than four times more likely to die from COVID-19 than white people."[6] It is an undeniable fact that socio-economic and racial disparities played a critical role in the alarming infection and death rates we witnessed throughout the country and world.

In a *Washington Post* op-ed titled "Essential Workers Don't Need Our Praise; They Need Our Help," labor organizer Kim Kelly writes about low-income workers who do not have the privilege of working from home. She argues that they "work in industries that often lack labor protections; are not and have not been paid a livable wage; still cannot access affordable health care; and are still disenfranchised by a deeply flawed system that places people of color and those who are not documented at increased risk whether there's a pandemic raging or not."[7]

How can Black people ever actualize freedom if we are constantly being traumatized by this nation? Social inequality is only half of the equation. The systemic trauma we are subjected to is in tandem with the personal trauma very few of us have been immune to. Being human comes with its own experiences of suffering. We all know that it's trauma to the soul and psyche that so often does the most long-term damage. But many of us may not even know we have had traumatic experiences, normalizing what should have never happened.

Trauma is unwanted touches and uninvited intimacy. Trauma is bearing a lifelong secret that smothers the soul. It's never having enough or feeling like enough. Trauma is wounds of loss, betrayal, violation, and inexplicable grief. It's the absence of someone or something that leaves a void nothing else can fill. Trauma is and will always be empty cabinets that lead to empty stomachs, for what is poverty but endless trauma? Trauma is anything and everything that hurts the human spirit as much as birth pangs hurt the body. And just as the postpartum period has lingering effects on a woman's mood and physical well-being, trauma to the soul also reconfigures the anatomy and foundation of who we are.

The long-term effects of trauma, whether personal or systemic, can manifest in catastrophic ways in the lives of survivors. In his book *Race Matters*, Cornel West describes nihilism as "the lived experience of coping with a life of horrifying meaninglessness, hopelessness, and (most important) lovelessness."[8] He continues, "The frightening result is a numbing detachment from others and a self-destructive disposition toward the world. Life without meaning, hope, and love breeds a coldhearted, mean-spirited outlook that destroys both the individual and others."[9] The deep psychological and emotional wounds of trauma often stir up distrust, attachment issues, insecurity, self-blame, and collective shame. The ripple effects can be costly to individuals, families, and communities.

People of African descent have existed in a continuum of collective trauma. We must link historical and modern-day diasporic injustices to the State-sanctioned killings of African Americans and the poor. We cannot disconnect the institution of slavery from the millions confined in U.S. prisons today. These intersections are necessary to help us fully grasp the multigenerational psychological and emotional assault on Black Americans that researcher and educator Joy DeGruy argues has led to survival "adaptations" or "Post Traumatic Slave Syndrome."[10]

Today, the medical world classifies racial trauma, also known as race-based traumatic stress (RBTS), as a "mental injury" rather than a mental disorder.[11] According to Mental Health America, racialized trauma "can come as the result of a direct experience where racism is enacted on you, vicariously—such as where you see videos of other people facing racism—and/or transmitted intergenerationally."[12] Not surprisingly, the American Psychological Association reports that communities of color "experience higher rates of posttraumatic stress disorder (PTSD) as compared to White Americans."[13]

GENERATIONAL CYCLES OF TRAUMA

Systemic trauma affects us at every level and in every generation. During pregnancy, I surveyed every inch of my body and my conscious mind, every physical scar and every psychological wound, praying that my child would never know the trauma that I had experienced. I did not want her to know the abandonment, betrayal, and abuse I came to know as early as childhood. I committed to fiercely discerning who I allowed to have access to me (and therefore her). I knew that I could not shield her from everything I went through, but I could take intentional responsibility for what she would be exposed to and when. It wasn't about perfection but instead protection. Life would inevitably happen, but

I did not want her to be overexposed, as I had been while growing up in the South Bronx and Washington, DC.

Coming of age in low-income neighborhoods during the height of the crack epidemic, I was among a generation of youth who had proximity to drug dealers, pimps, and prostitutes. Crack vials littered my downtown DC neighborhood and I frequently saw criminal activity in the alley behind our building. I was exposed to too much too young too fast. As I began my journey toward healing and wholeness, I found there was a tremendous amount of unlearning I had to do. The "hard-knock life" I had would require me to do a lot of soul-searching to regain what socioeconomic hardships, adultization, and a traumatic childhood had taken from me. The bruises left me with a body, mind, heart, and spirit in need of periodic regeneration.

Since my husband's life experiences were equally rooted in poverty, parental loss, and wounds caused by others, I wondered whether there was a way to ensure that our daughter would not "inherit" our trauma. Was there a way for her to embody our work ethic, creativity, and analytical minds without the depravity and survival needs that often accompany those gifts? My fear was that my daughter would not only be genetically embedded with her parents' gifts but that our unresolved baggage would also be transmitted to her. I refused to be a carrier of generational trauma, passing on unmerited suffering to my innocent child. It may seem like an unwarranted fear, but we, particularly Africans and African Americans, have long been warned about the power of generational curses (or "cycles," as I prefer to call them).

These beliefs have biblical origins, built on God's punishment for Adam and Eve in Genesis 3:14–19. Their disobedience, which Christians believe introduced sin into the world, would have ghastly implications for all of humanity: excruciating pain during childbirth, male domination over women, the perpetual need to ensure survival through labor, and the ultimate penalty of death. This "generational curse" is what led to the need for the coming of a messiah who would be crucified but resurrected, offering redemption and salvation to all who believe in him.

Today, commonly held misconceptions about generational "curses" are largely rooted in the socioeconomic conditions of marginalized people. Put simply, we often blame poor and oppressed communities for the cyclical nature of race and class-based subjugation. In worrying about the genetic transmission of trauma, I had to first acknowledge that my daughter would be spared from the trauma that poverty often inflicts. As a native-born American, she would not have the same fears that come with being undocumented on foreign soil, as both of her parents were for over a decade. She would have all her needs met by a community of family and friends investing in her well-being while she was still in the womb. Having an Ivy League graduate as a mother, she may find that the notion of "legacy" can take on tangible meaning in her life. More importantly, her parents have curated lifelong stories of resilience, spiritual and political awakening, and Christ's love that we will happily share with her one day, as heirlooms for her to store up as treasures on earth.

None of us are born immune to trauma. And despite our efforts at prevention and suppression, it will often make its way into our lives. Burying it in our psyche or adopting habits of escapism is futile because trauma will always demand acknowledgment. It is always better for us to unearth and release trauma on our own terms than for it to force its way to the forefront of our lives. In my late thirties, it became clear to me that if I did not evict the trauma that was living rent-free in my psyche, it would hold me hostage as a prisoner in my own body. As feminist theologian Meggan Watterson once said to me, "The greatest pilgrimage we can go on is to that deepest place within—where the body has been traumatized."

PATHWAYS TO HEALING

Despite efforts to dissociate from trauma, the day comes when all the coping mechanisms, avoidance, suppression, and methods of distraction can no longer overpower the reality of chronic health problems. We are finally confronted by a body that has suffered for far too long. Neuroscientist and trauma expert Bessel van der Kolk explains in *The Body Keeps the Score* that "the memory of trauma is encoded in the viscera, in heartbreaking and gut-wrenching emotions, in autoimmune disorders and skeletal/muscular problems."[14] Our bodies are paying an unbearable price for personal and systemic trauma. At some point, everything we have spent a lifetime running from begins to catch up with us and demands our undivided attention.

As written on the Survivor's Sanctuary section of the Me Too Movement's website, "The body is wise, it holds our joy, contains our stories, and is the first site of our liberation."[15] This is why the movement, founded by Tarana Burke to raise awareness about sexual violence and offer support to survivors, calls for integrative healing, which they define as "having an awareness of mind and body and applying this awareness (embodiment) to healing pursuits."[16] All parts of us must be healed, including our understanding of our pain.

In preparation for labor, the doctor or midwife may make it clear to the mother that she cannot bring a baby into the world without experiencing a high degree of pain. The more we physically suffer, the closer we get to holding our baby. Birthing forces us to be flexible in our physical and psychological capacity for pain if we are going to give life to the miracle and gift planted within us.

Pain is also a natural component of lived experiences. As the thirteenth-century Muslim theologian and poet Rumi once said, "The cure for pain is in the pain."[17] I cringe whenever I hear someone speak about "the gifts of trauma" but the call to not run away from our pain directly coincides with all the trauma experts who write about how facing our trauma has the capacity to transform us and make us more resilient. It was also Rumi who offered the hope that "the wound is the place where the Light enters you."[18]

Suffering remakes us. It takes us to the edges of hell and dares us to find our way back home. There are those of us who are tired of carrying resilience around as an individual and communal trophy. But perhaps the point is to say that the pain we endure does not have to be meaningless. The pain, repurposed through our resilience, can bear transformative personal, communal, and societal fruit. As James Baldwin says in *The Fire Next Time*, "People who cannot suffer can never grow up, can never discover who they are."[19] He goes on to say that "if one is continually surviving the worst that life can bring, one eventually ceases to be controlled by a fear of what life can bring; whatever it brings must be borne."[20]

Freedom looks like us healing from both personal *and* communal trauma. It means we are no longer forced into the constant loop of grief and shock over these modern-day lynchings of Black people. Freedom is us having space and agency to be fully human with all the messiness, mistakes, and complexity that comes with it. We deserve access to the full range of human experience—in real life as well as in media portrayals.

There is no Black freedom without Black healing. Our pain cuts too deep to think that we can simply put institutional and legal

Band-Aids on our trauma. Freedom is best experienced holistically, touching every inch of our minds, hearts, bodies, lives, and communities. And we must be active participants rather than reactive bystanders. This is why healing rituals are essential in our journey toward freedom.

Throughout the pandemic, I tried to combat the mainstream cycles of death by clinging to life. I did this through the routines I shared with my husband, the tranquility I found in the isolation, and the food that reminded me of the joys of breaking bread with friends. The ritualistic stillness within itself was deeply healing; it taught me that slowing down may be our single most transformative act of self-care. We are worthy of the time it takes to cultivate wholeness. Stillness is not passive. It strategically arms us with sufficient mental space to explore the best practices that our cultures and communities have to offer. It ensures our bodies are given the recovery time needed to heal. And it frees our souls to experience the serenity that productivity often suffocates. Stillness is a radical act of time reclamation, opening the door to a more peaceful and grounded life.

On countless nights during the national shutdown, I knelt at the foot of my bed to pray that the past reality so many of us had taken for granted would soon be normalized again. But it was in our habitual immersion in nature that I felt most at peace. I did not know at the time that we were engaging in a form of mindfulness and "ecotherapy" known as "forest bathing," a "term [that] emerged in Japan in the 1980s as a physiological and psychological exercise called *shinrin-yoku*."[21] This is, of course, not a new phenomenon. Cultures throughout the world, especially Indigenous and African ones, have known and valued the healing and medicinal powers of nature for centuries.

It was also in nature that I felt surrounded by the undeniable, loving presence of a majestic God. Whenever we look within ourselves and on high to the Divine, solitude (at least temporarily) becomes inevitable. We have no choice but to draw closer to silence to hear the messages our bodies and the Spirit are whispering to us. At times, this may mean carving out a few minutes for a meditation practice or a weekend for a silent retreat. Other times, we may feel called toward breathing, stretching, moving, and other body-centered or embodiment practices like yoga or somatic therapy.

This process of self and Spirit discovery almost always leads to purging, as we are compelled to release what is no longer serving us. It is important to explore the healing dimensions of spiritual and material purging. It is the internal work of cleaning out old ways of being, thinking, feeling, seeing, and hearing. The sweeping out of harmful thoughts, patterns of behavior, and, yes, even people and belongings. Those elements that do not serve any useful purpose in your life must fade away for there to be a renewal of purpose and intent. Space must be made for that part of us that has yet to be born. This is why purging, often manifested as literal cleaning, is a natural and powerful component of the nesting stage during pregnancy—the mother is preparing not only to birth but also to be born anew. Rebirth and regeneration help break cycles of trauma.

RECLAIMING OUR VOICES

In healing from trauma, as with surviving childbirth, the key is release, knowing what to hold on to and what to surrender. Yet, never pushing prematurely. Knowing when and how to breathe. Mastering the rhythm and timing of inhales and exhales. Inhaling your own strength and courage. Exhaling your anxiety and rigidity, for fear has an immobilizing effect. Not everything can go where your spirit, body, and Maker are trying to take you.

Rarely do people speak of the trauma associated with birthing. Think back to 2020 and the controversy over the Oscars and ABC rejecting a Frida Mom ad that was to air for postpartum recovery products depicting the numerous challenges faced by new moms in the "fourth trimester." Trauma, like that ad, is perceived as "too graphic."[22] So instead of collectively knowing and sharing in the reality of the agony, the one experiencing it is left with a sense of isolation and shame. Left to carry secrets about what was experienced and harbor resentment toward those who seem to be living trauma-free lives.

Trauma can often have a silencing effect on us. Abusers may even demand that their victims not speak of what has happened and threaten harm if they do. Telling the truth of our victimization has the capacity to free us from the shame and self-blame that trauma often perpetuates, especially if we have a compassionate listener and nurturing community. As a child and teenager, my love of writing and oratory practically saved my life. It put me on a healing journey before I could even articulate my brokenness. Reclaiming our voice and being able to identify our triggers, a process that may take years, counteracts the muting effects and suppression that trauma often initiates.

Before Jesus cast out demons that were oppressing people, he demanded that the demons tell him their name. Jesus would then determine the method of exorcism, deliverance from demonic strongholds, based on the type of demon he was dealing with. Two thousand years later, naming endures as an integral part of the healing process.

For some, true healing will only come by way of telling the

perpetrator of the harms they have caused (if it is possible and safe to do so), keeping in mind that they may have willful amnesia or be in denial. For others, telling *any* person of the harm is enough to bring about a sense of relief. But it is always important to discern safe space. The sacred truth of what has happened to us in life should only be entrusted to those who will protect and honor our stories. I am reminded of Matthew 7:6 (NKJV): "Do not give what is holy to the dogs; nor cast your pearls before swine, lest they trample them under their feet, and turn and tear you in pieces."

After more than four hundred years, this country has yet to name and atone for its original sins of genocide against Native peoples and enslavement of Africans. As part of our collective healing, it is imperative that we properly name the systemic demons that haunt us daily. We too easily let those who perpetuate racialized trauma off the hook with our language. We discuss "white privilege" but shy away from "white supremacy." We often analyze "white fragility" when "white nationalism" should be our focus. We speak of "white apathy" rather than "white complicity." Our language should accurately reflect what we are enduring and confront the grandiose delusions that so many hold about whiteness. It's an inability or unwillingness to see others as equal and therefore deserving of the same rights, protections, privileges, and benefits. Let us speak boldly and regularly about the incomprehensible damage that white supremacy has caused throughout human history. Not to shame white people, but to instead hold space for transformative truth-telling and create opportunities for restoration.

In her 1988 book *A Burst of Light*, Audre Lorde wrote, "Caring for myself is not self-indulgence, it is self-preservation, and that is an act of political warfare."[23] The commercial popularity of this quote often erases the fact that Lorde penned these words while living with liver cancer, after previously having breast cancer, and succumbed to the disease in 1992.[24] Using metaphors such as "battle" to describe illnesses like cancer is not ideal as it creates a dichotomy of "winners and losers" and tells patients they must "achieve 'victory' over [an] 'enemy,'" according to a podcast episode from the Dana-Farber Cancer Institute.[25] This is a powerful reframing, as "death and life are in the power of the tongue" (Proverbs 18:21, KJV). However, Lorde, a Black lesbian who aligned herself with the working class, intentionally used the militaristic language of "warfare" while describing her cancer journey to draw parallels to her fight against systemic oppression. "Battling racism and battling heterosexism and battling apartheid share the same urgency inside me as battling cancer. None of these struggles are ever easy, and even the smallest victory is never to be taken for granted," she wrote.[26]

NO MORE HIDING: BEING HEALED IN COMMUNITY

We, as Black people, are often led to believe that our communal trauma is our fault, as opposed to it being linked to institutionalized racism and white supremacy. We are led to believe that all our suffering is personally inflicted, versus seeing our plight in a larger systemic context. This perpetuates feelings of guilt, as we buy into the lie that we brought the pain upon ourselves. Trauma can often be a forced, inhumane hiding place. In *All About Love*, bell hooks writes: "Rarely, if ever, are any of us healed in isolation. Healing is an act of communion. Most of us find that space of healing communion with like-minded souls. Other individuals recover themselves in their communion with divine spirit."[27] It often takes a tribe of intergenerational healers to help us tend to our physical, emotional, and psychological wounds.

The day comes when solitude can no longer serve us and we need others to help us tend to our wounds because we acknowledge our own limitations. In community, we can be nourished and replenished, which is critical to healing. As the angel of the Lord directed the prophet Elijah, "Arise and eat, for the journey is too great for you" (1 Kings 19:7, ESV). Those parts of us that trauma emptied out need replenishment; collectivism creates the possibility for sustenance. Recognizing that solidarity often ushers in greater healing, Sybrina Fulton, mother of Trayvon Martin, created Circle of Mothers "for mothers who have experienced the loss of children to senseless gun violence to engage in experiential restoration activities that will equip them to self-manage their coping and healing process."[28] Restorative justice practices, which bring victim and offender together for truth-telling and reconciliation, are another powerful example of how healing happens in community.

In the days following my daughter's birth, there was a multiethnic and multigenerational team of women who taught me the day-to-day rituals of postpartum healing and restoration. These nurses tended to my wounds and taught me how to do the same for myself. They taught me to cleanse my vagina, which had become a site of trauma, with water to prevent infection, to apply wet strips infused with witch hazel for relief and soothing, and to use medicated sprays as needed to numb the pain. Passing on survival strategies, they taught me to monitor and respond to my levels of discomfort and bleeding. These strangers cared for me in the most intimate, delicate, and sacred way possible.

My postpartum experience taught me that healing is a sustained, collective journey and not a quick, personal arrival at a destination. Just like the six weeks of bleeding that a woman often goes through after vaginal delivery, healing takes time. Celebrity narratives that glorify instant physical restoration can be harmful to mothers. When you factor in how new moms often struggle with their mental health in the postpartum stage, "snapback" culture is a myth that underplays the trauma of birthing. The real "bouncing back" is staying in your right mind as a first-time mom. Many of us discover that it's not about getting back to where we once were; it's instead about being at peace with the reality of our new normal.

In the same way that healing from childbirth requires a daily cleansing ritual, trauma requires that we cleanse ourselves of its imprint on our psyche. Rehearsing and reliving the agony only serves to retraumatize us. In the words of the late theologian and mystic Howard Thurman, "I will make of my remembering a High Priest of Truth. I purpose in my heart that I shall not use my memory to store up those things which fester, poison, and destroy my living, my life, or the living and life of others."[29] We do this by taking inventory of everything we internalize and mediate on (our conversations with people, the media we consume, the books we read, the images we see, the places we go, etc.). Peace of mind comes by way of setting clear boundaries and filtering out and, at times, blocking certain thoughts—and people. It doesn't happen by chance.

Not all healing can be self-generated or entrusted to loved ones, particularly when it comes to matters of mental health. Like mental disorders, some trauma requires the help of a professional trained in psychotherapy, CBT (cognitive behavioral therapy), EMDR (eye movement desensitization and reprocessing), and/or medicine management. Because I have endured the long-term effects of trauma and know how fragile mental wellness can be, I have utilized all these resources at one time or another in my adult life.

Post-traumatic stress disorder (PTSD) is not limited to war veterans; countless traumatized people unknowingly or silently suffer from it. My therapist says I have had varying iterations of PTSD for over twenty years. It has manifested in different ways at different times, including recurring nightmares, heart palpitations, insomnia, and hypervigilance. I am not alone, as PTSD prevalence is highest among Black Americans compared to whites, Latinos, and Asians, according to a 2010 study published in *Psychological Medicine*.[30] There are countless women and millennials like me who are delicately navigating life in the aftermath of traumatic experiences.

For anyone seeking to be free, societal stigmas surrounding mental illness should never stop you from getting potentially life-saving help. There is no shame in needing medicine to treat a chemical imbalance, shift your outlook on the world, and regulate your emotions. Sadly, mental disorders often go undiagnosed, and people silently suffer without knowing that another way of being is possible. Our minds can be reprogrammed. How often have we demonized people in our communities as evil, messy, problematic, weird, or "off" when therapy, diagnosis, and/or medication could have set their lives on a different path?

Healing is the diligent work of slowly reassembling our lives piece by piece, person by person, place by place, thing by thing, and thought by thought. Healing is about surrender but also self-actualization. It is a refusal to let despair and death be victorious. Healing is also about breaking cycles of cultural shaming that prevent individuals from seeking resources, support, and treatment. By pushing back on social stigmas, millennials are boldly creating new paradigms for us to imagine holistic healing.

Despite my prayers and preemptive efforts, trauma was awaiting my daughter from the beginning. It was in the womb, the birth canal, and even in her first few minutes of life. The reality is that trauma is inevitable in this fallen, sin-sick world. Yet, she survived it all even as an infant. My daughter made her way to me and into the world against all odds. Despite the fever, worrisome heart rate, and non-breathing. Even as a baby, she possessed the power of resilience within her.

In *My Grandmother's Hands*, psychotherapist Resmaa Menakem writes that resilience, like trauma, is transmitted through bloodlines and "can ripple outward, changing the lives of people, families, neighborhoods, and communities in positive ways."[31] He goes on to explain that "resilience is both intrinsic and learned" and "manifests both individually and collectively."[32] Resilience is our greatest act of resistance in the face of trauma. We are reborn whenever we resist a premature call to death and demand that we shall have life and have it more abundantly.

The pain I underwent in labor was repurposed as love the second my daughter came into the world. The nearly yearlong pregnancies that we endure as women prepare us for the moment when we morph into a mother focused on sourcing the breast milk her baby needs. Similarly, we have the capacity to convert our trauma, transforming what almost killed us into a source of strength and inspiration for others. It takes seeing beyond our own pain and connecting with the needs of others. Not merely for altruistic reasons, but because our own survival demands that we turn our attention away from our agony long enough to find reasons to keep going. We have the power within us to bravely run toward life. As Andy (played by Tim Robbins) said to Red (played by Morgan Freeman) in *The Shawshank Redemption*, "I guess it comes down to a simple choice, really. Get busy living or get busy dying."[33]

THE POWER OF COLLECTIVE MOURNING

Death is always lurking at every corner. If not a physical death, a steady social, psychological, and spiritual death. But as a proclaimer of the "Good News," I hold on to the belief system that tells me that death has already been defeated and that the victory has already been won. As the popular millennial saying coined by Nipsey Hussle goes, "The marathon continues."[34] Despite death's sting. For centuries, Black people have been busy living despite the ever-present threat of death. We have made a mockery out of mortality, constantly evading it. We are survivors in every way imaginable. Out of the ashes, we rise to our feet. From the belly of the beast, we sing a war cry. We are a resilient people. Within us exists the capacity to repeatedly heal and be born anew. This is because healing is not a place that we strategically arrive at after having fixed and perfected everything within us and around us. Healing is instead an ever-evolving state of mind and way of being that has the power to liberate us from fear, nihilism, and subjugation.

It wasn't until my mother's death, which happened just one month prior to my writing this, that I came to understand how death and healing are sometimes intricately connected. My siblings and I watched our mother endure immense suffering in her final days on earth. We watched her breathless, voiceless, and seconds away from death—return, revive, and say "amen" after hearing the prayers of a priest. We watched a woman who is the mother of eight, grandmother of thirteen, and great grandmother of three have nothing left to give but her body and soul back to her Maker. Healing, in her case, did not mean the restoration of her body back to health. It meant permanent departure from it. It was no longer equipped to house her soul. Healing meant perishing for the sake of transitioning toward the spiritual realm.

But, surprisingly, my mother's death also became a pathway for the healing of my family. God allowed her legacy as a peacemaker to live on through us. While restoration is rarely instantaneous, I witnessed firsthand that God can break generational cycles of unforgiveness in a single night. My mother's death taught me that unforgiveness is a form of psychological and emotional bondage that we must liberate ourselves and others from. It is poisonous and venomous, threatening to destroy our minds, relationships, and eternal standing. I pray that you and your loved ones would be freed from the soul-crushing weight that unforgiveness places on the psyche and heart.

While my mother was one of the most humble and self-sacrificial individuals I ever knew, her death revealed that she was powerful and loved beyond our comprehension. On the day she passed, I drove at lightning speed from New York to Washington, DC, to make it to her before the funeral home arrived to take her corpse away. I pulled my car up to her senior living facility at the same time as the van from the funeral home. Holding my toddler daughter in my arms, I cried out in anguish as I saw my eldest brother directing two funeral home workers and a stretcher onto the elevator. As we stepped off that elevator, my daughter was taken from my arms by my sister. The women of my family who were piled into my mother's living room, bedroom, and hallway were wailing uncontrollably. I was brought to my knees in anguish, as I kissed my mother on her forehead one last time.

The two funeral home workers then transported her in a black postmortem bag from her apartment to the lobby of her building. Two of my brothers, my niece, and I were on the elevator with them and the stretcher carrying my mother when the elevator doors opened to the lobby. Awaiting her were nearly thirty elderly Eritrean and Ethiopian women with *netelas* (a traditional headscarf) wrapped around their heads. In a unified chorus of mourning, they cried out for my mother along with my family members and me. We all poured out onto the sidewalk and wailed endlessly as her body was put into the back of the funeral home van. I will carry these images with me for the rest of my life. My mother had a village that loved her deeply.

Our community's rituals of collective mourning (*hazen*, in our native language, Tigrinya) had begun. During *hazen*, friends and family came from near and far to gather with us as we physically sat still for days in the reality of our anguish. My mother was mourned widely and excessively across three continents. My father's body was exhumed from a burial site in Asmara, Eritrea, after thirty-seven years so that they could be buried together in his native village. When the mourning period ended, a feast celebrating her life took place.

A month later, my family would repeat the same cultural and religious rituals for my eldest sister, who passed away after a heroic battle against pancreatic cancer. Two months after that, a woman who was a lifelong maternal figure and best friend to me transitioned as well. As I gathered with her sons and their community in the South Bronx, I was struck by the similarities in African and Black American mourning rituals. When trauma and death comes, the Black community provides for one another. Food and nourishment become a village endeavor. We do our best to repair woundedness and restore joy to traumatized people.

After caring for, losing, and helping to bury three matriarchs in the span of four months, I was not only enveloped in grief, but I also had a newfound understanding of what exit out of this world looks like. It is often so much more tragic and gruesome than what we are led to believe in popular culture and storytelling. With death, as in birth, it becomes clear that our bodies are simply limited vessels experiencing the best and worst that life has to offer. It's the resiliency of spirit that lives on beyond trauma and death. Throughout the entire process, I found myself serving as "a conduit between the living and the dead," as my longtime friend Gregory C. Ellison II described.

These events taught me that collective mourning, although it won't feel like it in the process, can also be a ritual of healing. When done in community, it unites those grieving, affirms their pain, and gives them a renewed sense of purpose to honor the dead. It creates space for remembrance and thoughtful reflection. It can also have the power to purge you (over time) of sorrow, despair, and hopelessness. Other examples of collective mourning are protests, memorials, candlelight vigils, prayer nights, and moments of silence.

There are soul-nourishing lessons to be learned from loss. During periods of mourning, there may be outbursts. The body and mind may resist what's happening. But ultimately the living are called to repurpose their pain into power and find the strength to carry on. As Black people in America, we go through collective rituals of mourning almost daily. We perpetually grieve Black trauma and death. Let our collective mourning over the plight of our people not be in vain. May it transform us, laying the groundwork for our resistance.

PART TWO

❖

RESISTANCE

The Wilderness: A Site of Rebellion

When we move beyond survival, we begin to yearn for radical change. Chapters in this section on resistance show how hope and courage dare to transform a bad situation into a better one and how to define reality on one's own terms. It is about pressing against limits and simultaneously creating new opportunities for the seemingly impossible. We've seen it play out through the Civil Rights and Black Power movements; in the vernacular, fashion, and music of the post–Civil Rights generation (the hip-hop generation); and, most recently, through the Movement for Black Lives. Every generation of young Black people has dared to imagine and seize freedom.

3

✦

Capitalism

Awakening from the American Dream

*Capitalism is but the gentleman's
method of slavery.*
—Kwame Nkrumah

In 1985, when I was four years old, my father passed away, leaving our mother behind as a young widow with eight children in a country ravaged by war. The loss of our patriarch shattered our family in ways that still affect us to this day. Months after his death, my eldest sister invited my mother to the United States for her wedding. My mother agreed to come only on the condition that she could bring me, her youngest child, along with her. While her two oldest children had arrived as refugees seeking political asylum, my mother and I arrived at John F. Kennedy International Airport in New York City in 1986 on six-month tourist visas.

During that time, we lived in a building in which the residents were primarily Eritrean and Latino immigrants. Our days were spent sightseeing and making wedding preparations. When our time in the U.S. had come to an end, my mother began packing our clothes for our return home to Eritrea. I told her not to pack mine, because I wasn't returning. Shocked, my mother and siblings heard my adamant refusal to return to Africa, which I described in our native language as the land with "dirt on the ground." My eldest brother prepared a one-way return ticket for me, nonetheless.

Three decades later, on my wedding day, he spoke of these early years of my life in his remarks at the reception. "When Mom went to the gate for her flight back home, I thought Rahiel would follow. She stepped back and said, 'Bye, Mommy,'" he said in front of the guests present, as he choked up. "That was the best choice she made in her life. And that choice was strong. It scared me. I remember looking at her as I drove back to our apartment, and she acted like nothing had happened. I said to God that day: 'I hope You have a plan for this one, because I surely don't.'"

That moment at JFK caused my mother to make the toughest decision of her life. She chose to leave me, her baby girl, in the United States in the care of my siblings to save me from the fate of growing up in a hostile war zone. My departure from Eritrea was supposed to span only six months. However, I would not see my mother again until nearly a decade later. And it took nineteen years before I would return to my homeland as a visitor. I would come to understand this decision as a defining moment in my destiny—ordained by God— that set the stage for everything to come. Although I was only a child, I was willing to be without my mother to live in the U.S. I believe this was my first attempt in life to grasp hold of the American Dream— even if I could not yet give voice to it.

My early years in the U.S. were not easy. Having come with no understanding of English, I was desperate to communicate with other children. At first, I struggled to learn the language. With an expired travel visa, I became undocumented and had no legal status in the country. As a child, I was warned to never speak about this and was guided on how to respond if ever asked specific questions. I always feared that someone at school would discover my immigration standing and that I would be deported. Although I went without "papers" for ten years, I was able to attend public schools in the South Bronx and the District of Columbia without detection. When my eldest sister gained U.S. citizenship, she adopted me as her daughter and successfully secured my status as a legal permanent resident. It wasn't until my senior year at Stanford University that I became a U.S. citizen. In the years that followed, my mother, three siblings, two nieces, and a nephew arrived in the country as new immigrants. For the past four decades, my family has been entangled in the United States' immigration system in one way or another.

In Washington, DC, I grew up within a community of Eritrean hotel housekeepers, taxicab drivers, hot dog stand owners, and parking lot attendants. The immigrant men and women in my childhood worked tirelessly but had little to show for all their efforts. They rented apartments rather than owning homes. They took public transportation rather than driving cars. And I never knew them to travel anywhere for leisure purposes.

As an undocumented African, I knew that my education was the only pathway I had to escape a life of poverty. This fostered an almost obsessive relationship with academic and professional progress. If my life was going to be any different than what I grew up seeing, then I had to pour the totality of myself into educational pursuits. Some may not see anything wrong with this, but I was looking for a gateway out of poverty as if my own personal striving was the only factor. I didn't yet know about the racial inequality and systemic failures that were contributing to everything I was witnessing.

THE AMERICAN IMAGE VS. THE REALITY OF LIFE

For so many outside the country, the United States is pictured as a socioeconomic and cultural utopia. It is regarded as a place where high-paying jobs are readily available to the masses, no one worries about when or where their next meal will come, and people are not burdened by the lack of development and the political chaos that plague other countries. The American marketing machine brilliantly portrays a facade of perfection that masks horrific social ills. We can't fault people for believing the messaging they get from Hollywood and mainstream media. Through culture, the U.S. exports its values and way of life out into the world daily. This in turn births generations of noncritical "fans" of America whose only connections to life in the U.S. are shows like *NCIS*, *The Big Bang Theory, and The Bold and the Beautiful*.[1]

Couple that with the two-term presidency of Barack Obama and the election of Kamala Harris as vice president, which both led to greater romanticization about U.S. political and racial progress in various parts of the globe. Just as millions of Black Americans had very high expectations for a Black presidency, many Africans were equally hopeful that the United States' election of a Black commander in chief would result in greater gains for the continent. Data from the Pew Research Center shows that foreign perceptions about the U.S. "improved markedly in 2009 in response to Obama's new presidency."[2]

Of course, not everyone wants to be in the U.S., nor sees this country as a model place. Dissatisfaction with the U.S. has long permeated the consciousness. Some of those who had high hopes for Obama were left feeling let down and unmoved by his presidency. As an example, many human rights defenders, in the U.S. and abroad, were deeply disappointed by his unprecedented heavy reliance on drone attacks in countries like Somalia.

Then, for many watching our national politics unfold from afar during Donald Trump's presidency, global confidence in the U.S. diminished and the American image was deeply tainted.[3] Analyzing international perspectives one year after the insurrection at the U.S. Capitol, *Washington Post* correspondent-at-large Anthony Faiola argues that the U.S. displayed that it is "a riven, fact-relative nation still at war with itself."[4] Faiola points to the brokenness in American democracy and "a failure of accountability" as factors that have led U.S. allies to determine "that an erratic United States can no longer be seen as the model democracy."[5] If romanticized conceptions of the United States were not already shattered with Trump's election, then they surely were after COVID-19, as this country's leadership failed to prevent the loss of over one million lives to the pandemic.

The past few years have revealed that countless Americans are living on the edge of poverty. News outlets brought that reality to light in their coverage of people waiting in unbelievably long lines at food banks around the country. The images revealed, as shocking as it may have been for some, that food insecurity ravishes many people in the U.S. An April 2023 PYMNTS and LendingClub survey reported that 60 percent of Americans are living paycheck to paycheck, but that number rises to nearly 75 percent for millennials.[6] Due to living through three recessions and enduring "economic scars" that will have lasting effects "in the form of lower earnings, lower wealth and delayed milestones, such as homeownership," *Washington Post* writer Andrew Van Dam called millennials "the unluckiest generation in U.S. history."[7]

Millennials have also been dubbed the Most Anxious Generation,[8] the Burnout Generation,[9] the Lost Generation,[10] and Generation Broke.[11] The limiting labels are themselves rooted in a problematic socioeconomic framework, seeking to compare generations to determine identifying factors and gauge if one generation stands to surpass or fall behind the others. As an example, while we are classified as materialistic, Gen Z has been dubbed "the most materialistic living generation"[12] and deemed less hardworking.[13] Still, the consensus seems to be that millennials work very hard but have little to show for it. CNN senior writer Tami Luhby wrote in a 2020 article that we, as millennials, will likely not surpass our "parents in terms of job status or income," which would be a new generational precedent.[14] While not all the media coverage has been this dismal, the common thread has been that our generation is struggling to overcome economic challenges.

The painful truth is that there is an ever-widening gap between what life in America professes to be and the reality of what it is. This gap is deeply tied to wages and wealth. In 2020, white households "held 84 percent ($94 trillion) of total household wealth in the U.S." in comparison to Black households, which "held just 4 percent ($4.6 trillion) of total household wealth," according to the Brookings Institution.[15] A 2021 Harvard series on U.S. racial inequality helps give those percentages greater meaning, reporting that "while the median white household has about $100,000–$200,000 net worth, Blacks and Latinos have $10,000–$20,000 net worth."[16] For millions in the U.S., there may not be much thought given to what it means to live in a capitalist society, and how inherently unequal and divisive this system is.

THE LAND OF DREAMS

While capitalism may not be at the forefront of the average person's mind in the U.S., elements of the American Dream might be. For previous generations of working-class Americans, aspirations were often rooted in what are now discussed as necessities or simplicities. This included having a job that paid a living wage, wanting to purchase a home, owning a car, and experiencing some "luxuries" such as family vacationing. With shifts in industries and many manufacturing jobs going overseas, our conceptions of the American Dream have changed through the generations.

The rise of hip-hop as a dominant force within mainstream culture, as an example, led to the creation of more Black millionaires. Similarly, technological advancements and the digital age have led to more income divide and unprecedented levels of wealth. Millennials reflect a higher level of hero worship and now aspire to a degree of excessive wealth that is unattainable for most people. More than ever before, there is an increased obsession with building not only individual wealth but generational wealth.

Capitalism is crafty, offering incentives and rewards to keep us constantly engaged in the system. Similarly, many of us have bought into notions of social mobility and meritocracy—the idea that being educated and/or working hard will afford us tangible advantages and a comfortable, stable middle-class living. Rarely do we comprehensively understand what must be endured for us to actualize that life. What psychological grip does the American Dream have on Black Americans and the African diaspora? How do we cultivate a self-generating love that does not seek America's validation? How can we reimagine freedom and liberate ourselves from ways of being that make us complicit in our own suffering? And is it possible to usher in a renaissance of values that transforms us, our communities, and the United States as we know it?

It's absolutely tiring to constantly be in pursuit of your daily earnings and next meal. We shouldn't have to beat our bodies into the ground until we reach retirement age just to make a livable wage and stay afloat in this country. Deep down inside, we know that we live in a society that judges us based on our productivity. We are only valuable if we are perpetually doing something, ideally as part of the labor force. Our value is determined by how much we have accomplished in the past, what we are currently working toward, how much we have in the bank, and the prospect of greater achievement in our future.

Disposability looms as a threat if any illness, injury, or circumstance renders us unable to work. It's a very dehumanizing measure of worth. This is why it feels like everyone is *always* busy, as if being busy is the only way to prove that our lives have value. It is not uncommon of Americans to have never-ending to-do lists and joke about self-care as a luxury that we do not have. Rather than believing that we have intrinsic value, many of us calculate our self-worth based on capitalism's standards. No wonder there is a mental health crisis in this country. No wonder we hear more and more reports of suicides. How does one ever feel like they are enough when the goalposts keep being moved and the finish line constantly pushed back?

It is psychologically exhausting to always be focused on the next job, destination, achievement, opportunity, etc. The constant striving takes its toll not only on our health, but also on our interpersonal relationships. This all gets in the way of nourishing our ties to loved ones. When most of our time and attention is being put into work, then home will surely suffer. Love and intimacy are diminished when we lack the stillness needed to cultivate life-giving bonds. It takes intentionality to have meaningful connections with people. But we are caught in the never-ending cycle of busyness that is draining us of our joy and contentment.

MILLENNIALS AND TOXIC PRODUCTIVITY

As millennials, we sometimes tend to wear our depletion like a badge of honor, glorifying it on social media. Many of us (not just entrepreneurs) have both internalized and normalized "rise and grind" ways of living and "toxic productivity." Being overworked has become embedded in our cultural framework through terminology like "hustle culture" and "grind culture." What led the U.S. mainstream to embrace and appropriate[17] terminology rooted in Black street culture to inspire and explain the habits of workers?

Journalist Megan Carnegie writes in a 2023 BBC article that the popularization of these mindsets, according to experts, has been driven by start-up narratives that emerged out of Silicon Valley during the meteoric rise of tech companies.[18] According to the article, companies like Google, Facebook, Twitter (X), and Instagram with "intense, all-consuming work cultures" and well-known stories of rapid venture-capital growth helped shift American workaholism from a necessity to an ideology and business model rooted in aspirations. Younger generations, in particular, have become both victims and perpetuators of what *New York Times* journalist Erin Griffith defines as "toil glamour" in a thought-provoking article titled "Why Are Young People Pretending to Love Work?"[19] When we move past all the journalistic analysis, academic jargon, and gimmicky language, what we are left with is how American capitalism and its foremost beneficiaries have seduced, exploited, and reconfigured us as a generation.

In the U.S., the ruling class has fed into our economic insecurities and weaponized our fears over scarcity. As much as former president Trump fed into ignorance, he also fed into these fears. He capitalized on multiple fears: America was changing to the benefit of Black and Brown people, jobs were being taken, neighborhood demographics were shifting, hardworking Americans were being left behind, and America needed to be made great again. Ultimately, this led millions to buy into the lie that there is not enough to go around, the land is full, the doors of opportunity will soon close, and the border walls should be going up.

The majority of Black Americans proved to know better than to believe these lies. But due to poverty and issues of racial inequality, we are still at risk of having a scarcity mindset. According to Amy Novotney in an article for the American Psychology Association, "deprivation can lead to a life absorbed by preoccupations that impose ongoing cognitive deficits and reinforce self-defeating actions."[20] All of this comes at a high cost to our health. Based on CDC data, "stress-related disorders and diseases" as well as "deaths of despair" are taking the lives of many Americans each year.[21] At the same time, the U.S. lacks universal free healthcare and many other medical benefits afforded to citizens of other countries. While our unhealthy work habits are often encouraged, our government is unwilling to put the necessary systems in place to help us prevent and remedy inevitable negative health outcomes.

Too often, we go about our day-to-day without processing what we are experiencing. Busyness numbs us to the reality of the world around us. By being quarantined, we were drawn away from all our sources of distraction and forced to contend with the reality of who we are as individuals and as a nation. Through protest, we sought to be in unison with those who shared our righteous anger. How much closer to a better world might we be if we intentionally and repeatedly sat in the discomfort of our fury over social injustices? Our attention is constantly being taken away from what really matters in life.

BLACK LABOR AND CHATTEL SLAVERY

From *The Kardashians* to *The Real Housewives*, our celebrity-obsessed culture normalizes luxury. We are inundated with images of opulence. From the flashy, flamboyant likes of Floyd Mayweather to the ever-dapper Steve and ever-glamorous Marjorie Harvey to an endless roster of A-list celebrities and mainstream rappers, many within our community know well how to flaunt wealth. We literally wear our success, in the process often making high-end European designers the markers of success. Too often, we have made Black fame and excessive wealth synonymous with Black excellence. If we are focused on the latest Black celebrity to join the billionaire class, then we will likely lack a strong class analysis of the U.S. and overlook the fact that very little progress has been made to tackle U.S. poverty in the past fifty years.[22] The wealth gap in this country is nothing for Black people to celebrate.

Black America is the mecca of hustle and grind culture in part due to how much is required of us to enter, level, and own the playing field. The twenty-first-century demands placed on our bodies operate in a long continuum of inequality, exploitation, and dehumanization. We so easily forget that the foundation of modern-day American capitalism was laid by the institution of slavery, an economic system rooted in human degradation. The United States' economic standing in the world was built on the battered backs of enslaved Africans. Since the days of ships carrying human cargo across the Atlantic Ocean, the worth of Black life has been calculated in terms of its potential to return a profit for white people.

Those who built the system quantified Black humanity and diminished enslaved Africans to their bodily measurements. With no regard for family ties, they removed anything and everything that could instill a sense of love and connection. The goal was to strip enslaved Africans of their human dignity in the hopes that doing so would render them weak and incapable of resistance. For centuries, oppressors cultivated generational wealth while ensuring Black Americans remained a poor, subjugated class.

Today, many mainstream conversations about hustle culture and toxic productivity do not connect these modern-day trends to America's centuries-long preservation of the institution of slavery. Analysis often reduces the conversation to the influence of tech companies on work culture. But it is essential that we, particularly Black women, think critically about what messages American capitalism seeks to send us by telling us (for nearly a decade) that "[we] have the same amount of hours in a day as Beyoncé."[23] These apolitical framings packaged as inspiration have dangerous implications for anyone who might be tempted to judge themselves based on unfair, unrealistic expectations.

It is not always about whether we *can* work harder; sometimes it's a question of whether working harder is in our best, holistic interest. This is an important question for Black women who carry the dual burden of racism and sexism and are still healing from the multigenerational trauma caused by the institution of slavery.

In *Women, Race & Class*, Angela Davis writes about the relationship between work and slavery in the lives of Black women: "The enormous space that work occupies in Black women's lives today follows a pattern established during the very earliest days of slavery. As slaves, compulsory labor overshadowed every other aspect of women's existence."[24]

Debates about hustle culture are often devoid of thoughtful discussion about the psychological, emotional, and spiritual implications of making an idol out of work and success. In an article for *Marie Claire* titled "Hustle Culture Harms Women of Color the Most," Patrice Peck cites the work of behavioral scientist Carey Yazeed, author of *Shut'em Down: Black Women, Racism, and Corporate America*, who argues that hustle culture is often driven by "workplace trauma" and can lead to "trauma bonding" in professional contexts.[25] But there is a light at the end of this tunnel due to intentional and strategic acts of resistance. Peck writes that women of color are recouping holistic health, "pouring their hard-earned lessons back into their communities," and "reimagining new work cultures rooted in wellness, joy, and freedom."[26]

As a people facing so many socioeconomic barriers, it makes sense that individual advancement is praised as much as it is. But why is it that we can criticize capitalism in one moment and then push one another to the brink of mental and physical collapse in the next? The truth is, much of contemporary American popular culture glorifies capitalism. Within the Black community, most mainstream hip-hop artists are unapologetic about their materialism and obsession with wealth. I don't remember the cultural landscape I grew up in being *this* one-dimensional.

I came to love hip-hop as a preteen and teenager, in the era of 1990s rap when lyricism was still a core, defining characteristic of hip-hop. We had A Tribe Called Quest, the Fugees, Arrested Development, Black Star, and countless others. The artists of that era are still celebrated to this day. However, I am reminded that it was that same era that turned songs like Wu-Tang Clan's "C.R.E.A.M." ("Cash Rules Everything Around Me"), Jay-Z's "Dead Presidents," and Bad Boy's "It's All About the Benjamins" into cultural and generational classics.

Materialism has always been a part of the culture, but it has taken on new heights. It defines today's music. Hip-hop is more apolitical than ever before. It's hard to be politically critical of America when you're so busy celebrating your own self-advancement. I am reminded of a profound question asked by Brown University scholar Tricia Rose in her book *The Hip Hop Wars*: "Will market capitalism's enticement to consume and discard continue to be lauded, or will hip hop reconnect more fully with its own legacy of commitment to the nonmarket values of sacrifice and common good?"[27]

In 2005, Bakari Kitwana, author of *The Hip Hop Generation*, founded Rap Sessions to curate spaces that equip millennials with deeper cross-racial, gender, and class analysis. The organization hosts panel discussions and town halls that bring hip-hop artists, intellectuals, and activists together to discuss pressing generational issues. By highlighting the intricacies of market-driven culture and the Black liberation struggle, millennials are better prepared to navigate the political process and avoid the pitfalls of divide-and-conquer politics.

What we may often celebrate as culture (or Black excellence) can in fact be a tool of class division, allowing those who have actualized the American Dream to estrange themselves from those who have not. As an outgrowth of capitalism, the American Dream should not be our conception of freedom. It is a tool used by capitalism to control and manipulate us. Through it, we are given a false sense of equality, fairness, and inclusivity. Watching others advance to the millionaire and billionaire class is reassuring to some people, as it convinces them that this is attainable for others as well.

In the past few years, Jay-Z, LeBron James, Rihanna, and Tyler Perry all reached billionaire status. It's always a social media spectacle when the news breaks. The message is almost always the same: *only in America can a story like this be possible—and if you work just as hard, it's possible for you too.* How often have stories like this served to subconsciously depoliticize masses of working-class people? Why revolt against capitalism when you simply need to work harder to get your own seat at the table? Why resist when you can instead play by the rules of the game? We forget that money and power are not the same thing. White elites are much more willing to share the trappings of success than they are power. It's the power dynamics at play that keep us from advancing.

LIES, TRICKS, AND TRAPS OF CAPITALISM

One of the biggest lies that capitalism tells us is that our economic hardships are all our fault. That our economic conditions are solely a result of personal decisions and actions. We internalize this way of thinking, feeling the shame of what we believe to be our own mediocrity and laziness. Then we apply this same "pull yourself up by your bootstraps" mentality in our assessment of other Black people, judging them as harshly or worse than we judge ourselves. The idea is that, as Americans, we can obtain everything we need to succeed. The underlying message behind this is that if we don't succeed, then there's no one to blame but ourselves.

Within our community, men like Shawn Carter (Jay-Z) are praised for making it "from Marcy to Madison Square." His story is one of many used (by even Barack Obama in a presidential bid) to tell us that the conditions we are born into do not have to be our fate—if we just work hard enough.[28] And while that may be the case for some, we must stop glorifying the anomalies as if they set the standard for the rest of us. We do this at the expense of brothers and sisters who are down and out, trying to survive in a system designed for them to fail.

The cruelty of this country's policies is often understated. The U.S. has historically operated as a racist, sexist, poor-phobic, ableist, and homophobic society that has institutionalized exclusionary practices. White supremacy cleverly masks that fact by cultivating a culture driven by finger-pointing. Still, systemic racism has threatened the value invested in the American Dream by a generation disillusioned by false notions of promised success.

Mass incarceration is one of the most important examples of how white supremacy and capitalism work together to create dangerous societal myths motivated by domination and profit maximization. These myths suggest that we all would be living a better quality of life if we were simply better humans. According to Michelle Alexander in *The New Jim Crow*, "the politics of responsibility" will always fail as a strategy for freedom[29] because it disregards our humanity and the fact that "a seemingly colorblind system has emerged that locks millions of African Americans into a permanent undercaste."[30] Alexander identifies several factors for why there is often greater motivation to expand rather than eliminate the prison-industrial complex: prison privatization, the manufacturing of police weaponry, prison healthcare companies, U.S. military and corporate dependency on prison labor, and the political, legal, and financial matrix of entities that profit off the building of new prisons.[31]

The United States' global record for mass incarceration is not due to unprecedented criminality. It reflects entrenched systemic practices based on race and class, like the War on Drugs, that have devastating implications for Black people. "There is no path to liberation for communities of color that includes this ongoing war," writes Alexander.[32] The U.S. has shown itself to be more committed to advancing capitalism than protecting human rights.

For those of us who have spent our lives chasing after the mirage of the American Dream, accounts of police brutality have also served as haunting reality checks. How does one feel safe in a nation in which property and profit are more fiercely protected than Black life? What is the value of democracy if it doesn't afford all its citizens equal protection under the law? And what does it mean that, in 2020, nearly half of the nation voted to reelect Donald Trump despite all his fascist actions and neo-Nazi propaganda tactics? The time has come for us to reimagine ourselves and the possibilities for this country.

"If a new way of being together is to emerge, we must understand that the imagination is the battlefield," said Princeton University scholar Eddie Glaude in a speech he delivered at the Wellbeing Summit for Social Change in 2022.[33] We do not have the luxury to be held hostage by our limited imaginations of ourselves, our people, our nation, and our world. We must decolonize our understandings of freedom and resistance—and most important, ourselves. We can no longer fight for a romanticized United States that has never truly existed, nor for an American Dream that was never ours to begin with.

First and foremost, remember that we are a communal people.

Individualism is not indigenous to us as African people. We learned it from inside the belly of the beast. It's time that we unlearn the many values and ways of being that are common to life in the U.S. We are villagers who have always had communal ways of doing things. Enslavers always viewed family unity as a threat. By fighting to maintain attachment, the enslaved Africans were also fighting for language, cultural, and religious cohesion. Centuries later, this refusal to be divided is just as important. Today, the prison-industrial complex is one of the greatest threats to the unity of Black families. As the right wing of American politics attempts to ensure voter suppression and implement draconian policies, our survival and strategic resistance are dependent on our solidarity.

Break free from the lie that investing in people is a waste of time and money. Call instead of only texting. Visit instead of only video-chatting. Cultivate a village (a community) that will journey with you through the peaks and valleys of life. And once you have your village, do not be limited by a "no new friends" policy. This isn't to say that we don't need to be self-protective. But leave room for the unexpected yet needed. Never forget the biblical promise that the Spirit of God communes with us when we are a part of a collective. Matthew 18:20 (KJV) states: "For where two or three are gathered together in my name, there I am in the midst of them." Capitalism seeks to breed individualism to ensure that working-class people will not unite against the ruling class. By disintegrating us, capitalism weakens our resistance and capacity to overpower this oppressive system.

We forget that a part of honoring humanity is that we also honor and value ourselves. In resistance to an anti-Black capitalist culture, let us answer the call to radical self and communal affirmation. From the time we wake up in the morning to the time we go to sleep—we are children of God. As hard as it is to accept, we don't have to achieve *anything* to be loved by God. God seeks a relationship with us but has nothing to gain from us. It's important to be intentional about holistic self-care and rest. Whatever replenishment of body, mind, and soul looks like for you, do it to cleanse yourself of the toxicity of this world.

At the same time, be cautious about the self-care industry's promotion of the "cult of wellness"[34] and how it often feeds off our insecurities. There is a major difference between being healthy and spending more money on wellness than any other generation, as millennials have been reported to do.[35] A 2019 Blue Cross Blue Shield Association report shows that "millennials are less healthy than Gen X members were at the same age" with "major depression, hyperactivity and type II diabetes [having] the largest growth in prevalence for millennials."[36]

There are paths to health and wellness that can come by way of a nutritious diet, adequate/quality sleep, outdoor and home-based exercises, nature walks, journaling, breathing practices, free wellness-centered social media applications, and even need-based government-assisted health insurance. There's also healing power in rest, joy, play, and pleasure. Too often, self-care leads us to retail therapy and that's exactly where capitalism wants us to land, insecure and down the rabbit hole of endless consumption. It's a slippery slope, but we can have agency over our well-being without perpetually feeding the pockets of corporations.

WHAT'S ON THE OTHER SIDE OF CAPITALISM?

Many of us can agree that this practice of putting profit above people is hurting us, but we may not agree on or have the capacity to imagine another way. What is most important is that we give our-selves permission to dream outside of this current system. How can we better relate to one another economically and socially? What does your dream for a new, better world look like? What are the dreams for alternative realities that we have suppressed as a community? What are the possibilities birthed through collective dreaming that we have yet to explore? How do we bring those dreams to the surface? When will our collective dream for Black liberation finally prevail over the American Dream as the driving force in our lives?

In many ways, this alarm has already been sounded for my generation. Shifts are taking place. Books like Heather Archer's *The Grind Culture Detox* and Tricia Hersey's *Rest Is Resistance*, both released in 2022, help us guard against grind culture and toxic workaholism. Both authors are Black women. Through her founding of The Nap Ministry, Hersey, a performance artist and theologian, examines "the liberating power of naps" and frames rest as "a form of resistance and reparations."[37] Described as "a rest movement," The Nap Ministry invites people to take time to daydream, listen to rest meditations, and engage in rest practices.[38]

In a 2023 BBC article titled "Hustle Culture: Is This the End of Rise-and-Grind?," Megan Carnegie writes that "new buzzwords including 'quiet quitting,' 'soft life,' and 'Bare Minimum Mondays' have emerged on social media," moving away from phrases like "rise and grind."[39] We are psychologically and spiritually equipped to imagine beyond the confines of capitalism. This requires that we have a redefinition of what is enough—by our own standards, rather than those dictated by social norms. Joy can and should be defined by us rather than corroded by comparison.

I have been fascinated by a show that my husband watches on

cable television called *Building Off the Grid*. In the various episodes, Americans identify locations in remote areas of the country to build a home "off the grid." Often, their budgets are not large, and they build minimalist structures where everything serves a defined purpose. A driving motivation for many of the builders is living mortgage-free. For others, it is a desire to be immersed in nature or to have more intentional time with their loved ones. While I have never seen a Black person on the show, I have wondered what "building off the grid" in the United States means for Black people and Black liberation.

What would it mean for us to strategically buy and share land in collectives? How would our relationship to capitalism change if we lived in self-sufficient communities where we shared resources and knowledge? In times past, Black self-sufficient communities have faced destruction at the hands of angry white mobs and/or law enforcement. This was the case with the flourishing Greenwood District (often referred to as "Black Wall Street") in Tulsa, Oklahoma, and MOVE in Philadelphia, Pennsylvania. But the fear of history repeating itself should not stop us from exploring what self-sufficiency means for us today.

Perhaps this idea is altogether too extreme and unrealistic. Maybe we simply need to turn our energy and focus toward an "off the grid" mindset, a way of understanding and moving through life that stands in defiance to the United States' capitalist culture. For us to truly experience freedom in this country, our individual and collective relationship to capitalism must change. This doesn't mean that we all quit our jobs and sell our homes. It means that we reexamine our values, shift our aspirations, and recalibrate our priorities. This country can't dictate what we value unless we allow it to. For us to have a clear understanding of the way forward, we should first look back to the knowledge of African and Indigenous cultures. What do they have to teach us about ourselves, spirituality, the land, liberation, love, work, life, and death? Many of the answers we seek can be found in the traditions and cultures that were stripped from us. Sometimes freedom means divesting from what's popular and investing in what is divine, ancestral, and countercultural.

There has been a lot of cultural references made to our "ancestors' wildest dreams." The phrase can now be found on shirts, coffee mugs, earrings, journals, and key chains as well as all over social media. But we have not stopped to truly unravel the idea. Materialism can't be it. Capitalism can't be it. Individualism can't be it. I could go down a long list of what I believe were the farthest things from our ancestors' wildest dreams. But surely, we can agree that freedom and all the manifestations of it were likely at the core of their deepest longings.

Our ancestors dreamed of freedom of movement—to have full control over their own bodies. They wanted to travel without fearing brutal attacks. They wanted rest and fair compensation for their daily labor. They dreamed about being free to love and have sexual intimacy without the constant threat of traumatic disintegration. Our African ancestors saw firsthand what capitalism did to the soul of the white enslavers. How could they have wanted that for themselves? Wanting sustenance to build a life upon (forty acres and a mule) is one thing; chasing clout and coveting the finer things in life is another. We have imposed our contemporary American fantasies of wealth and success onto African ancestors, and that calls for repentance. Who gave us permission to appropriate their dreams and, at times, mutilate their desires?

As a minister and liberation theologian, it pains me that capitalism and Christianity so often go hand in hand in the U.S. and throughout the world. I am reminded of the Bible verse in which Jesus said, "Give to Caesar what belongs to Caesar, and give to God what belongs to God" (Mark 12:17, NLT). Living in the U.S., our daily lives center around doing what needs to be done to pay bills, make ends meet, and fulfill our desires. This ranges from necessities like housing and food to luxuries like designer goods, resort experiences, and pampering routines. By polluting our thoughts and actions, capitalism leaves very little room for us to "give to God what belongs to God." Do we make time to live a prayerful life consecrated unto God? Are we truly in service to God and others? How are we honoring God with our resources when capitalism demands so much of us? We forget that we are in danger of idol worship when we put the god of "survival of the fittest" before the one true God.

Sadly, too many pastors (all over the world) have conflated capitalism and Christianity. This explains why so many places of worship are rooted in a theology of scarcity and a gospel of prosperity. They teach false theologies that focus people's attention on economic advancement rather than on God's grace and commitment to the poor and oppressed. It's criminal that they live lavish lives built on the tithes and offerings of their often poor congregants. These prosperity ministries exploit an individual's greatest fear—*I am not enough*. This is also one of the most powerful lies of the enemy.

Prosperity preachers sell congregants a vision of an earthly paradise made of cash, cars, mansions, designer brands, gold, and diamonds. They proclaim wealth and abundance for those seeking prophecy. They never deal with the sense of emptiness and deep voids that people struggle with when the mask comes off at night.

What an injustice they do to Jesus when they worship capitalism and mass distribute it as salvation. The colonial empire can never be the Promised Land!

Thank God that a remnant will always remain to remind the church of its liberation-centered identity. The prophetic Black Church must do a lot of heavy lifting to undo the damage done to our people by prosperity ministries and false teachers. We have been traumatized by capitalism's forceful hands on our most vulnerable spiritual parts. Let's explore what it would mean to adhere to God's economy, spending and saving in accordance with God's priorities for God's people. I imagine it would mirror the Bible's description of the Jubilee Year in Leviticus 25, which describes rest from labor, food security, environmental restoration, community cohesion, and liberation for all people. It would also reflect the Kwanzaa principle of *Ujamaa* (cooperative economics).

Capitalism will never be our pathway to freedom. While economic progress is critical to Black liberation, we cannot buy, invest, pay off, crowdfund, or start up our way out of oppression. We lack nothing. We are born more than enough. That awareness is cemented when we live in a world that better honors our intrinsic self and communal worth. By transforming the media and cultural landscape around us and shifting long-held racial narratives, we better equip ourselves to reclaim all that capitalism and white supremacy have stolen from us.

4

Media

Tale of the Hunt

Until the story of the hunt is told by the lion, the
tale of the hunt will always glorify the hunter.
—African proverb

In May 2015, while I was sitting with four young African American men in the lobby of a Chicago hotel, our group was approached by two uniformed security officers. They asked if we were hotel guests and said our lengthy stay in the lobby had brought about "suspicion." I immediately challenged the hotel staff on what I understood to be stereotyping and Black criminalization. The countless white guests in the lobby weren't being questioned. The hotel management adamantly denied that race played any role, instead pointing out that an ongoing "homeless problem" at the facility had been a factor in our treatment. Nothing about our appearance or behavior suggested that we were homeless. This justification only heightened my anger and confirmed that we had been subject to racial profiling. We were given two options: leave or be removed. And that of course begs the question: What about our presence posed a threat or warranted removal?

My experience was not a unique one; it mirrors the daily reality of countless Black people living in the U.S. That moment was a rude awakening of my own personal vulnerability to racism. Dressed in business casual attire and having degrees from Stanford and Yale, I was still susceptible to being treated like a suspect. There is no shield that we can wear as a protective armor. Pedigree and respectability politics can't and won't save us. Politeness will not suffice when it is assumed that we don't belong. While Civil Rights Movement organizers fought for Black people to have the full rights of citizenship, including freedom of movement, we were quickly reminded that some struggles never cease. As in the days of lunch counter sit-ins, the young men and I felt compelled to maintain our presence despite the threat of violent removal.

While our situation was unfolding, a white male dressed in a tuxedo was becoming visibly angry and violent as he spoke on the hotel's lobby telephone. After slamming the phone down and breaking it, he walked through the lobby shouting. Security guards watched this take place but never stopped or questioned him. Yet, our conversation on the lobby couches warranted two, and then four, uniformed security guards. (It is important to point out that two out of the four guards that approached us in the hotel lobby were themselves Black.) Our mere presence led to a show of force, but the aggressive acts of a white man went unchecked. He had the freedom to move, speak, and *simply be* without any regard for those around him. The benefit of the doubt was accorded him and there were no consequences for his actions. I don't believe the way he was dressed even mattered. The killing of Trayvon Martin revealed how certain clothing (like a hoodie) can signify criminality and evoke suspicion when worn by Black people, whereas whiteness is most often protected from such perceptions. What's really at play is how our society understands belonging, entitlement, protection of property, and who has value.

This is not to suggest that capitalist oppression does not hurt white people, who are also being killed by the police, especially those who are poor. A 2020 People's Policy Project report stated that class is a significant factor in determining the likelihood of a white person being killed by the police.[1] As *Jacobin* associate editor Meagan Day writes, "White people who live in the poorest neighborhoods are at high risk of getting killed by a police officer, but black people are at high risk everywhere."[2] The disproportionality of Black incarceration, brutalization, and killings by police is an undeniable fact. The same People's Policy Project report found that Black people (at a rate of 7.9 per million) are more than twice as likely to be killed by the police than white people (3.3 per million).[3]

Just as it did for the aggressive white man in the Chicago hotel, middle-class to upper-class whiteness often offers a protective bubble when navigating life in this country. Perhaps this is the same bubble that has historically protected so many white men and reinforced feelings of entitlement. An invisible cloak that casts whiteness as permanently safe, trustworthy, and respectable has long been exploited. This protective bubble is not there by happenstance. It is not an accidental byproduct of being white. The machine of white supremacy is always at work and has many arms, one of the most powerful being the media.

MEDIA AS AN ARM OF WHITE SUPREMACY

White, male-dominated media conglomerates have been broadcasting and publishing information for generations. Not only do they oversee mass communication and affect our buying habits, but they also influence our thoughts and movement through the world. This amplifier of white supremacy ensures that we see white people as they want to be seen—be it a blue-eyed, straight-haired Jesus or an all-American superhero like the "Man of Steel." From the news cycle to Hollywood films, the media tells us what white people want us to know (and omits what they want to leave out).

White people have the privilege of waking up in a world that affirms their human dignity, beauty, and intellectual strength. From magazine covers to television correspondents, from award show nominees and leads in films to positions of power, white claims to superiority are perpetually reinforced. As a mother of a Black child, I wage war against these messages in my household daily, recognizing how easy it is for my daughter to unknowingly adopt European standards of beauty and antiquated conceptions of girlhood.

White supremacy is dependent on the media because domination requires submission and assimilation. Systems of oppression (Remember Nazi Germany?) have always understood the power of propaganda. Equally, the second-class citizenship of all non-white groups is also reinforced by the media. It's a white hegemonic culture that dictates not only who is celebrated but also who is deemed inferior and in need of control. These depictions can be subtle or blatantly overt. Through media, white supremacy has built up its own modern Tower of Babel.

Historically, mainstream media has frequently reinforced racial stereotypes in its efforts to appeal to audiences, and commercial companies often do the same to appeal to consumers. In recent years, the international outcry for racial justice has been so strong that it has held many corporations accountable in their depictions of Black people. Long-held branding and marketing strategies have been forced to change.

As Cornell professor Riché Richardson writes in an op-ed, "The Aunt Jemima logo was an outgrowth of Old South plantation nostalgia and romance grounded in an idea about the 'mammy,' a devoted and submissive servant who eagerly nurtured the children of her white master and mistress while neglecting her own."[4] The logo was in place for over 130 years and had six iterations.[5] How were they able to get away with it for as long as they did? It's astounding that it was not until after the murder of George Floyd in 2020 that the brands Aunt Jemima and Uncle Ben's were renamed and their images, steeped in racial stereotypes, removed.

For too long, American culture has exploited racial myths about Blackness, and these myths are often perpetuated in the media. The harsh punishment, criminalization, and disproportionate incarceration of Black people has always run parallel to a media world that fails to reflect the full range of our humanity and often distorts the truth of who we are as a people. Journalist Leigh Donaldson writes in the *Guardian* that there is a media tendency to connect Black men to "drug-related crime, unemployment and poverty."[6] He explains that these associations to "criminality and violence" often lead to "a lack of empathy for black men and boys in trouble, less attention being paid to the bigger picture of social and economic disparity, and increased public support of more rigorous approaches to social ills, such as police aggression and longer jail sentences."[7]

Harmful media messaging often has devastating effects on our life outcomes, as Black individuals, communities, and culture (hip-hop as the most obvious example) are demonized. This starts at a young age, as Black children are equally affected by perceptions of Black criminality. Not surprisingly, data from the Department of Education reveals that Black students in public schools, particularly boys, experience "harsher discipline" and make up (along with Hispanics) "over 70 percent of the students involved in school-related arrests or referred to law enforcement."[8]

In the same way so-called African primitivity was used to justify the institution of slavery, young African Americans today are still treated as deviants in need of taming. With each passing generation, the school-to-prison pipeline remains steadfast, awaiting us from birth. The machine of mass incarceration picks up where zero tolerance policies in schools leave off.[9] The Pew Research Center reports that Black Americans are only 12 percent of this country's population but account for 33 percent of the incarcerated population.[10] The imprisonment rate of Black people is six times that of whites.[11]

LETHAL PERCEPTIONS ABOUT BLACKNESS

Incidents of fatal police violence are tied to many systemic and socioeconomic factors. One of them is the constant dehumanization and criminalization of Black people in the media that creates and perpetuates perceptions about Blackness. While at Stanford in the fall of 1999, my classmates and I protested on campus over the killing of unarmed twenty-three-year-old Guinean immigrant Amadou Diallo in New York City. He had been shot to death by four plain-clothes NYPD officers who said they mistakenly thought his wallet was a gun.

During the trial, the case's lead prosecutor, Eric Warner, said that Diallo "was being looked at in a way that was dooming him right from the start."[12] While the defense cited that the officers were fearful, Warner argued that the cops unjustifiably saw him as "an armed homicidal maniac."[13] The T-shirts we wore to call for justice in his case had a number on the sleeve: 41. That was the number of shots that were fired at Diallo—nearly two for every year of his life. He was wounded nineteen times. In 2006, hours before his wedding, unarmed Sean Bell was met with fifty bullets from undercover officers. In 2012, thirteen Cleveland officers fired 137 bullets at unarmed Timothy Russell and Malissa Williams, killing them both.

Just as unfathomable as the number of bullets used to shoot down Black people is how quickly police kill us. "Less than ninety seconds" passed from the moment a cop encountered Michael Brown Jr. on Canfield Drive in Ferguson, Missouri, in 2014 to the moment an assist car arrived.[14] That same year, twelve-year-old Tamir Rice, who was playing alone with a toy gun in a park, was shot down within less than two seconds of a Cleveland police officer arriving on the scene.[15] In 2022, ABC News reported that "Detroit police said they fired 38 shots in three seconds at Porter Burks, a 20-year-old schizophrenic Black man, as he was in an apparent mental health crisis, killing him."[16]

Whenever I hear or read about the number of bullets or seconds it takes for these officers to kill us, I often imagine bullets being hurled at Superman's chest. A barrage of bullets couldn't do to him what one bullet would do to the average human. Superman, like most superheroes depicted in popular culture, is capable of the seemingly impossible. He is feared by many because he possesses strengths beyond human comprehension and capacity. He is superhuman. It is impossible to use ordinary force against him because his power requires an excessive, debilitating, and even supernatural mechanism of attack (kryptonite) to weaken him.

In white supremacy's calculated use of media, Black people are often dehumanized and depicted as having a high tolerance for pain. It should come as no surprise when these scripts on Black inhumanity are widely circulated. We see this in the narrations of police officers and neighborhood vigilantes on what happened between them and their victims. There is often that same fantasized and exaggerated description of an intimidating and overpowering force.[17] In his grand jury testimony, the St. Louis police officer who killed Michael Brown Jr. in Ferguson described feeling "like a 5-year-old holding onto Hulk Hogan" and referred to the eighteen-year-old as "it" more than once, saying "I just know I shot it" and "it looks like a demon."[18]

Marc Lamont Hill writes in *Nobody: Casualties of America's War on the Vulnerable, from Ferguson to Flint and Beyond* that Brown's killer utilized "phrases that made him sound like he was a game hunter confronting a wildebeest."[19] Hill argues that by portraying Brown as "a Magical Negro with superhuman powers," the testimony "humanizes the officer and dehumanizes the Magical Negro to the jury and the broader public."[20] The testimony of Brown's killer is hauntingly similar to historical depictions of Black men as animalistic, barbaric, beast-like, and savage. One bullet won't do the job because it is simply not enough to stop a Black man; you must instead annihilate him in fear that he will otherwise prevail against death. Only then will he no longer pose a personal and societal threat. In the killing of Brown, the goal was "execution" rather than "mere incapacitation," says Hill.[21]

The media and the white supremacist gaze continue to imagine Blackness as simultaneously lethal and subordinate. We are rendered superhuman *and* subhuman. It is as if Black people are worthy of endless bullets, but unworthy of mouth-to-mouth resuscitation.

We are deemed worthy of on-scene prosecution and death-penalty sentencing, but unworthy of an indictment when police officers who kill us face the courts. Time and time again, Black people are understood to be worthy of demonization and public scrutiny in the media post-death, but unworthy of equal protection under the law.

Before we have time to catch our collective breath after one horrific viral video, countless others begin circulating. We remain in a never-ending loop of witnessing Black demise with little to no police accountability. America treats Black suffering as a commercial commodity. Our pain is their profit. We create the viral hashtags and populate the feeds that fuel America's addiction to Facebook, Twitter (X), Instagram, TikTok, and newer platforms like Threads. In too many instances, the media contributes to white supremacy's stronghold being inescapable, as it keeps us perpetually distracted: focused on "them" and what "they" are doing to us. So much so that we don't have the mental bandwidth to envision, create, produce, invent, and imagine freedom.

We die again and again every time the mainstream media vilifies and crucifies our fallen sons and daughters. Where are the armor bearers for Black trauma? Who sounds the alarm when our pain is treated as anything other than sacred? Our tears are worthy of protection—if by no one else but us. The cycle of death goes far beyond the body counts. We can no longer partake in our own repetitive traumatization. We begin to do this by refusing to watch and listen to media content that feeds our fears and starves our joy. At times, we may even have to fast from media consumption altogether to detoxify from the harmful images and messages.

Mainstream media at times has been grossly negligent in its reporting on police killings of unarmed Black men. By focusing on drug use or the past criminal activity of those killed by police, the media frequently engages in victim-blaming and subliminally suggests that the killings are justified. The U.S. judicial system then reinforces these same messages with little to zero accountability for police brutality and white vigilantism. It is a brutal, inhumane cycle.

In contrast, as we have seen through the years, white killers, including mass shooters who commit acts of domestic terrorism, are often "coddled" by the media and police, says *Salon* senior writer Chauncey DeVega.[22] He writes, "There is no public demand for group accountability or introspective thought about what is 'pathological' about 'white culture'; white men as a group are most certainly not held responsible or stigmatized for mass shootings; there will be no discussions in the corporate news media about 'white crime.'"[23] White masculinity has historically bestowed unmerited media grace. Unmerited when you consider the fact that roughly 64 percent of mass shootings committed in this country in the past four decades have been committed by white men, according to an investigative database created by *Mother Jones*.[24]

While U.S. corporate media often humanizes these mass shooters, it reinforces the racial "othering" of Black victims, an "othering" that can often have misogynistic overtones. As an example, the media is often seemingly silent on Black women and girls who go missing, as to suggest that we are not deserving of the same compassion and protection that is afforded to white women and girls. In a column titled "How the Media Privileges White Victims," *Seattle Times* columnist Naomi Ishisaka reported on a 2015 William & Mary study that revealed that missing Black children only get 7 percent of media coverage on missing children while they make up 35 percent of the cases.[25] Ishisaka explains that many factors play a role in "the empathy and coverage gap," including inadequate racial diversity within media.[26]

In stark contrast to the lack of coverage on our missing, mainstream media frequently replays viral videos depicting adult male police officers violently and brutally handling Black teenage girls. Their aggression is often excessive and unwarranted, with little to no regard for age, gender, and innocence. According to The Marshall Project, Black girls experience a higher amount of police violence directed at teenagers, and the stories are nationwide.[27] These accounts include a fifteen-year-old in Maryland who was pulled "off her bike by her backpack straps," a sixteen-year-old in Texas who was "wrestled to the ground by an officer" at a pool party, and a nine-year-old in New York who was pepper-sprayed while "in handcuffs in the back of a patrol car, crying for her dad."[28]

While it is important to shed light on the forms of violence that Black women and girls suffer at the hands of police, doing so is not without consequences. In a column for *USA Today*, Meredith Clark, a journalism and communication studies professor at Northeastern University, argues that the constant looping of these violent images comes with many (some even research-based) risks—desensitization, anxiety, aggression, decontextualization, and long-term communal effects.[29] Clark writes, "Unless the videos are used with discretion, and paired with [an] ethic of care for the public-health impact of such exposure, user-generated 'content' depicting violence against women adds to the lessening of respect for women overall, not just at the hands of police."[30]

As Clark points out, the saturation of these images in the media matters greatly in a world where many medical professionals believe that Black people biologically have a higher tolerance for pain, according to research from the University of Virginia.[31] It reminds me of reports of Black women complaining about excruciating pain in hospital rooms and their doctors not believing or properly treating them. This well-known issue of racial bias in healthcare regained national attention during the pandemic when Susan Moore, a Black doctor, died in the aftermath of what she believed to be racially biased medical treatment.[32] Prior to her death, Moore shared in a Facebook video that her white doctor's hesitant pain management treatment left her feeling like "a drug addict."[33] This is where the idea of the strong Black woman becomes a dangerous double-edged sword. While we, as a community, can celebrate our collective strength and resilience, we must resist attempts to shrink our humanity and negate our experiences of suffering.

STEEPED IN A RACIST AND SEXIST HISTORY

Black queer feminist Moya Bailey, author of *Misogynoir Transformed*, "coined the term misogynoir which describes the unique anti-Black racist misogyny that Black women experience."[34] Bailey created the term in 2008 in response to stereotypical and narrow portrayals of Black women in media.[35] She was operating within a long history of Black feminist writers who have explored the intersection of racism and sexism, which plays out in society through systems and powerful forces like media.

In an episode of Al Jazeera's *The Listening Post* series on global media, Black women scholars and cultural writers are interviewed about "reductive depictions"[36] of Black women and how they operate on a historical continuum. The episode examines three dominant, well-known racial archetypes: the "submissive" mammy, the "sexy" Jezebel, and the "sassy" Sapphire (or the angry black woman). Black feminist scholars have long argued that these archetypes exist within media and have detrimental effects on the lived experiences of Black women, perpetuating old racial tropes of Black people that date back to the institution of slavery and the Jim Crow era. Bringing viewers to the present, the Al Jazeera episode points to Issa Rae's *The Misadventures of Awkward Black Girl* and *Insecure*, Shonda Rhimes's *Scandal*, and Cecile Emeke's *Ackee & Saltfish* as contemporary examples of Black women taking greater control over our storytelling and media portrayal. There are countless other examples, such as Ava DuVernay, Dee Rees, Gina Prince-Bythewood, Mara Brock Akil, Michaela Coel, and Shola Lynch, to name a few.

It is so easy to internalize racism in a discriminatory country and media world that glorify one group of people and subjugate all others. This has been explored and proven repeatedly through research-based studies, documentaries, and books. Media images imprint both the white *and* Black psyche. Carter G. Woodson perfectly explained the relationship between white dominance and Black internalized self-hatred in *The Mis-Education of the Negro*. Woodson's argument was that by controlling how an individual thinks, you ultimately control the individual—even to the extent that they become an active participant in their own oppression.[37]

Regardless of the perceptions held about Blackness, we too can be agents of the State. (Remember the guards from the hotel in Chicago?) We too can be instruments of State violence and proudly work to maintain the State's monopoly on violence. In 2023, this fact was made crystal clear when five Black police officers in Memphis, Tennessee, unmercifully beat African American Tyre Nichols to death.

Many of us have internalized harmful perceptions about our own community. Unknowingly, we have adopted mentalities and behaviors that lead us to distrust and fear our own people. Representation, content creation, and media ownership by Black people and women matter. Not for the sake of appeasing us or stroking our collective ego. It helps to safeguard us from dehumanizing and criminalizing our own people. It also shows audiences the multi-dimensionality of Blackness.

The totality of Blackness must be given voice. One-dimensional depictions of Blackness are unacceptable. This is why we must be media makers, crafting our own narratives and deciding on the stories that will be told about us and how those stories will be written, produced, and directed. The end goal cannot be limited to more depictions of Black superheroes and extraordinary people. Black people should not have to be supernatural and our experiences sublime in order for us to be worthy of attention. Black normality deserves the same camera time that white normality gets daily. Privileged people so often have the luxury of bringing little to no value to the table and still being seen, heard, and celebrated. Let us be beautifully ordinary in some of our depictions. Let us be angry, timid, hurtful, helpful, greedy, generous, atheist, spiritual, promiscuous, and reserved. This will only begin to scratch the surface; Blackness deserves to take up space. Then and only then will we live in a media world that is worthy of our time and attention.

THE LEGACY OF THE BLACK PRESS

Since the days of Ida B. Wells, the Black press has stood in bold defiance to white supremacist media. It has been a salvific force in our community, equipping us with print and digital tools of resistance. Local Black media has always amplified the untold stories of our people and our struggle, nudging us toward greater healing and helping us envision holistic freedom. Today, many of those outlets are struggling to survive the digital wave that has made it challenging for them to monetize their content. It's important to remember why they were founded. *Ebony, Jet, Essence, Black Enterprise*, and other national publications were created to normalize Black beauty, brilliance, and excellence in the face of a media landscape that would otherwise render Black people invisible, inferior, or pathological. We need those outlets as much today as we did when they were founded. To help sustain them, Black journalism should be granted the same legitimacy that we give white media outlets. It's not just about "buying Black." Black writers should contribute to Black media outlets, and we should be intentional about reading new Black authors. Local and grassroots Black media should be regarded as a legitimate news source. If we do not support these publications and voices, then our communities will suffer a brain drain, with our best and brightest only working for mainstream media outlets.

At twenty-three years old, I was named editor in chief of the *Washington Informer*, a Black-owned weekly newspaper founded in 1964 by publisher and activist Dr. Calvin W. Rolark Sr. to serve the Washington, DC, community. I was the youngest editor in the *Informer*'s history, and I supervised a staff of veteran journalists and photographers. My appointment, made by a Black woman, Denise Rolark Barnes (Rolark's daughter and the heir to his publishing legacy), catapulted my journalism career. A leadership position would have been very unlikely at a mainstream white media outlet, especially without a media-related advanced degree. At the *Informer*, the groundwork was laid for my creation of an online lifestyle magazine and community, *Urban Cusp*, and for a columnist position at the *Washington Post*.

In 2011, I launched *Urban Cusp* with a focus on faith, urban culture, social change, and global awareness. It was created for

Black millennials who love both Jesus and justice, intersect theology and culture, and believe that hip-hop can still speak truth to power. Our content gave voice to those tensions daily. Launched just months prior to the killing of Trayvon Martin, *Urban Cusp* became a tool for mass mobilization in defiance of racial oppression. The platform took off quickly, reaching almost every corner of the globe and amassing half a million social media followers within three years of its launch. At its peak, *Urban Cusp* reached nearly sixteen million people a month on social media. The magazine's rapid success changed my life. It opened the door for many opportunities and, more important, helped to challenge the media landscape to better reflect the multiple layers of who we are as Black millennials. Providing a vision of ourselves as the faith-infused, rhythm-inspired people who have consistently turned pain into purpose and power is what I seek to do through my media work.

I have never stopped serving and working for the Black press in America, because I understand it as a powerful tool of resistance that amplifies our self-generated words, ideas, stories, and images. We need grassroots Black media to combat the media arm of white supremacy today as much as we did in times past. I remain inspired by countless luminaries whose politics have driven their media work and creation of independent publishing. This includes those who are now ancestors like Audre Lorde of Kitchen Table: Women of Color Press, Glen Ford of *Black Agenda Report*, John H. Sengstacke of the National Newspaper Publishers Association (NNPA), and Robert S. Abbott of the *Chicago Defender*. It also includes elders and peers like Haki R. Madhubuti of Third World Press, Jasiri X of 1Hood Media and *Black Pittsburgh*, Jessica Care Moore of Moore Black Press, Kimberly Nicole Foster of *For Harriet*, W. Paul Coates of Black Classic Press, and Roland Martin, who launched Black Star Network after his departure from mainstream cable networks. Black-owned bookstores nationwide also play a key role in amplifying our voices and perspectives.

SUPPRESSING CONSCIOUSNESS AND RESISTANCE

Throughout history, the desire to subjugate Black people has been directly connected to the control and manipulation of Black culture within mainstream multimedia. White supremacy and capitalist forces take the most subversive forms of Black culture and Black political ideology, repackage them for mass consumption, and then disseminate them through their desired channels. Whenever this happens, what once stood as a critique of the establishment is then brought into the fold and celebrated by it. From Malcolm X to Nina Simone, this nation commercializes our most justice-driven heroes to de-radicalize and subvert their legacies. In celebrating what was once feared, you undermine its capacity to challenge the status quo. To this end, mainstream media and culture become pathways to quietly suppressing the political consciousness that has the potential to arise within every generation.

We've seen this play out through the evolution of hip-hop culture. It originated in gritty, low-income neighborhoods in the South Bronx. Rappers back then served as village griots, documenting the conditions of Black poverty and urban inequality. Through the influence of corporate executives pushing for greater album sales, rap music became saturated with violence, materialism, and misogyny. In Lauryn Hill's song "Superstar" on *The Miseducation of Lauryn Hill*, she challenges the notion that artists should simply amass wealth without any awareness of social issues.[38]

What would it mean for hip-hop to reconnect with the heart of

Black people and once again have its finger on the pulse of the Black experience? What would happen if the dichotomy of underground and mainstream hip-hop no longer existed and what remained was lyricism that was constantly propelling the liberation of our people? This is not to advocate for only "conscious hip-hop." This is meant to encourage artists to reimagine Blackness and themselves outside of a capitalist, male-dominated lens in hopes that they will free their art from one-dimensionality.

Rapper Kendrick Lamar's "Alright" on *To Pimp a Butterfly* gave us a glimpse of what can happen when modern movements have protest anthems that echo the vibrancy of a generation's wavelength. In the song's lyrics, Lamar crafts the perfect marriage between Black rage and Black fortitude, describing a personal and communal history of suffering, resilience, faith in God, and unrelenting hope.[39] The song became a millennial freedom chant and spiritual battle cry that enlivened every context it was brought into. I pray that the day comes when hip-hop, as a genre and culture, will once again hold a mirror to the complexity of Black identity, the depths of Black suffering, and the infinite scope of the Black imagination. Black women, specifically, are owed back payments of honor and respect from hip-hop.

The practice of cultural erasure dates to the founding days of this country when Native peoples and enslaved Africans were stripped of their languages, cultural practices, familial ties, spiritual traditions, and identities to ensure their obedience and submission. Deculturalization is one of white supremacy's oldest strategies. Retention of culture and claim to identity make an oppressed people dangerous and difficult to control. Knowing this, white oppressors systematically took power away from Indigenous and African communities. Thus, it's important that we understand that cultural production is part of our modern rebellion. It is part of our armor against erasure and an avenue toward our self-determination.

For both Black and white people, our media and cultural consumption is as important as our dietary habits. By treating it as such, we acknowledge that everything our eyes and ears internalize (our cultural input) affects our worldview, perceptions, biases, and actions (our social output). A commitment to ejecting demoralizing content out of our lives demands that we be very intentional in abstaining from unhealthy and destructive images in our cultural landscape. Put simply, everything that goes into us shapes who we are in the world. If we want to have greater control over how we engage the world, then we must be proactive in keeping white supremacist images, values, and norms out of our media consumption. Again, this applies to both Black and white people.

Radical intentionality will dictate what we watch and who we listen to, where we get our news from, where we shop, what we do, and who we keep company with. The entirety of our existence is made up of little decisions that have very consequential implications. Complicity in white supremacy doesn't begin and end with how one responds to acts of police brutality. It begins with a resistance to intellectual stretching and moral growth. It begins with avoiding articles, books, news networks, television shows, movies, conversations, and interactions that have the potential to transform perceptions and behavior. It is a consistent refusal to being stretched in uncomfortable ways. Complicity is an unwillingness to be humble enough to ask thoughtful questions and to admit that you don't have all the answers.

THE POWER OF SOCIAL MEDIA

This is an information and digital age unlike any other. We have never lived through a media moment like this before. Our smartphone (and watch) can serve as our communication hub, life organizer, news provider, health management system, finance keeper, reading portal, and endless source of distraction. Phones have completely changed how we engage with one another and how we see ourselves in relation to the world. When you consider the evolving popularity of social media platforms, the current generation has a relationship to multimedia unlike any other in human history, arguably rooted in addiction.

Social media is the newest iteration of white supremacy's media arm. Like corporate media, the most used platforms are owned and controlled by the billionaire class. With these historic technological advancements, we must be more self-protective and vigilant than ever before. The obsessive and compulsive yearnings that drive so many to social media are a psychological form of bondage. Our personal data is collected daily by these big tech companies as they study our online habits and determine what kind of consumer we are. Using the information we knowingly and unknowingly provide them, they curate an algorithm-based digital experience intended to keep us online for as long as possible. Scrolling through the feeds of these platforms takes us through endless emotions within seconds, as we read about birth, death, marriage, divorce, victories, and tragedies. We can rapidly alternate from laughter to tears. Intentionally minimizing our screen time is one way to reclaim agency over our mental state.

Tech companies have little to no regard for our physical and psychological well-being or safety. Our usage and consumption are their end goals. This has serious, dangerous implications for young people who are not always able to discern fact from fiction and virtual from reality. I can't imagine navigating the online and offline world of popularity and validation that faces them daily. Maintaining a healthy sense of self-worth was infinitely tough when I was growing up, and I can't wrap my mind around what the future will be like for my daughter.

What is habitual use of social media doing to us? How is social media reconfiguring the essence of who we are individually and collectively? How do we think, see, and feel differently after being on these apps? There are many people who believe that social media is not harmful and that moderation is the key to healthy online engagement. Yet, like other forms of media, there is no question that this medium deeply impacts mental health. It is a part of the matrix of real life versus online, manufactured lives that can lead to comparison, insecurities, depression, and a lack of gratitude.

Social media makes it difficult (nearly impossible for some) to be honest about internal struggles. How do you admit that something is wrong when everyone else has carefully branded their public persona and is posting highlight reels depicting them living their best lives? So often, social media feels like one big talent show. It leaves very little room for openness, transparency, and vulnerability. The perfectionism that is portrayed can be suffocating and contribute to unrealistic expectations of self and others. Inevitably, many individuals end up comparing their lives to the perfectly curated lives they see online. But social media influencers can't (nor should they ever) be our guiding light and measure of greatness.

The ever-changing digital environment entices us to constantly reinvent ourselves, as we inevitably struggle to maintain relevancy in social media's overcrowded space. We feel the need to keep up, which often leads to us being glued to our phones out of compulsion. Both FOMO (fear of missing out) and FOBO (fear of better options) have addictive elements. Social media also pushes us farther down the rabbit hole of individualism. In this attention-seeking world, everyone is seduced into becoming a personal brand. We think obsessively about what is and is not shared, manufacturing images of ourselves based on what we want others to believe about us. Truth be told, social media is designed to turn its most loyal users into attention-seeking narcissists incapable of distinguishing self-love from self-obsession.

We often can't recognize these dangers because we think we're operating in a community when we're on social media. From "Black Twitter" to the comments section of Instagram to private groups on Facebook, we understand these online mediums to be communities. But the reality is that online communities often fall short of helping us do the soul-feeding, healing, and personal development work that happens in real human-to-human connection. Daily, we must cultivate habits that ground our holistic peace and resist technological temptations, tricks, and traps. This demands that we curate an information world where we are politically, spiritually, and prophetically inspired. Who we follow on social media reflects what we value. Let's purge our news feed of sources that do not affirm the world we seek to build.

There are a lot of people inching closer to freedom in virtual spaces, because learning and growth is happening there. Yes, social media can absolutely be a site and tool of resistance. We should not miss out on the opportunity to utilize newly emerging media tools for our communal needs. I am deeply inspired by social media's capacity for bringing about change, as millions have used it in support of humanitarian and social justice causes. There's no denying that social media gives us the capacity to mobilize masses of people in real time at a moment's notice. It allows us to transcend geographical boundaries and unite people along common ground.

In recent years through the Movement for Black Lives, we have seen countless sit-ins, "die-ins," marches, rallies, mall takeovers, and freeway shutdowns take place all over the country. These "on the ground" disruptive protest practices have almost always been coupled with online resistance strategies. While there is always the danger of people engaging solely in "clicktivism" without any protest experiences or tangible connection to community organizing, many young people are using social media in more effective ways. This includes but is not limited to using video platforms for trainings, private chat groups for coordination, electronic newsletters for sharing information, texting for real-time alerts, and social media for mobilization and reflection.[40]

Social media has also democratized journalism, giving underfunded grassroots voices direct, immediate access to millions of people and an international platform that does not rely on corporate media for legitimacy. So much genius, creativity, and momentum have been birthed out of viral hashtags, videos, and images. It has been awe-inspiring to see what my millennial generation and Gen Z have been able to do through acts of resistance to push this country closer toward the democratic ideals it professes.

Media scholar Meredith Clark suggests that it is not essential to create "separate" social media platforms but that we should instead utilize existing platforms to meet the needs of our community.[41] Clark, who is archiving and writing a book on "Black Twitter," highlights people like Genie Lauren as an example. Lauren "created a petition to get a book deal from one of the jurors from the [vigilante killing of Trayvon Martin] trial dropped."[42] No wonder the power of "Black Twitter," defined by Clark as "a network of culturally connected communicators using the platform to draw attention to issues of concern to black communities," has sparked international attention and support.[43] With the growing discontent over Elon Musk's acquisition of Twitter (X) and the changes that followed, a Black-owned alternative, Spill, launched in beta mode in 2023. Its two Black founders were former Twitter employees.

The role of social media platforms in building movements has been debated widely in the past decade—and not only within the U.S. but all over the world. While it can be used as a tool of resistance against white supremacist media, the reality is that it is not a viable tool for many working-class and poor people across the globe. Data usage is a luxury that many do not have. I learned this firsthand when I was recruited to provide media strategy training to organizers in Zambia and South Africa; many individuals could not afford to maintain data on their phones. Some lived in provinces where data was completely inaccessible and others in provinces where it was available but often unreliable and inconsistent. For most of the working-class people I encountered, WhatsApp was much more commonly used than Facebook for organizing purposes, and platforms like Twitter (X) and Instagram had little to no relevance to many of them. In countries where there is no freedom of the press or where organizers face the threat of political persecution by the government, social media usage can lead to arrest, harm, and imprisonment.

Social media has served as one of the most powerful and reliable tools of resistance and organizing for so many within my generation. Research has shown that during the Arab Spring, a series of anti-government uprisings that took place in North Africa and the Middle East in 2010 and 2011, Twitter (X) and Facebook played key roles in some countries.[44] While the role of social media is continually debated, the idea that everyday people have the power to topple authoritarian regimes as a result of the mobilizing they can do online and offline is a profound, controversial notion. And when those governments viciously retaliate against their civilians, citizen journalism allows for their stories to be shared with the rest of the world. This is why various media outlets have claimed that "the revolution will not be televised; it will be tweeted."[45] Now, due to the growing popularity of alternative platforms, it may be Instagrammed, threaded, or spilled.

IMAGINING A NEW WAY FORWARD

We, Black America, make the media landscape a magical space—through our cultural, intellectual, and spiritual contributions. I celebrate us for our genius. What we produce is the fuel that keeps America's cultural engine running. For centuries, our people have been giving cultural breadth and depth to this country and, at times, we have been celebrated for our contributions. But I wonder: Is there anything that we have yet to create due to our imaginations always being patrolled by the white gaze?

White supremacy leads us to believe that imagination is best utilized by the rich and powerful. Our society has historically glorified innovation led by white men. We always hear about the contributions of Steve Jobs, Bill Gates, Jeff Bezos, Mark Zuckerberg, and Elon Musk. However, freedom-loving people must never surrender imagination to a capitalist billionaire class when it is, most often, used to exploit the working masses. We (the everyday people, the poor and the oppressed, the marginalized, and the forgotten) have always known and seized the power of imagination.

We know that cultural assimilation means death to everything that our magic is rooted in. We know that respectability politics (going along to get along) will never guarantee the preservation of our lives. And we know that by policing our appearance and every move to minimize white fear, we will only perpetuate and condone our own subjugation. This is why we continue to wage war on all fronts for a form of liberation that feels tangible, sustainable, and, most important, transformative.

When it comes to the American media landscape, some will argue that the media simply holds a mirror to society, whereas others will argue that it has tremendous power in shaping who we become. I'm asking you to envision a media and cultural world that proudly and unapologetically holds a mirror to the movement. May our films help us see a new way forward and equip us with the inspiration needed to actualize a new world. May we write and publish books that will be our people's blueprint for resistance. May we create art that reflects both the reality and the sublime nature of Blackness. May our song lyrics amplify our deepest yearnings for liberation, which should not be a burden that falls on the shoulders of a few artists. Through jazz, hip-hop, R&B, folk songs, country music, and gospel, may our people cling to new freedom songs. And may a new generation of griots, journalists, bloggers, and photographers reclaim the power of communal storytelling, birthing the narratives and images that transform our time. We can create the cultural conditions for the greatest acts of generational resistance.

5

❖

Uprising

Moments and Movements

Each generation out of relative obscurity must
discover their mission, fulfill it, or betray it.
—Frantz Fanon

I only spent a few nights in the streets of Ferguson, Missouri, but what I experienced there during protests marking the one-year anniversary of the August 9, 2014, police officer–killing of unarmed Michael Brown Jr. was enough to change me forever. Like countless others, Ferguson was where I encountered a militarized police force equipped with armored tanks, machine guns, sniper rifles, flash-bang grenades, tear gas, and rubber bullets. They stood in opposition to legions of protestors—many of them young, Black, and poor. Equally frightening was the presence of unidentified white men in military gear holding assault rifles, who we later learned were part of a far-right white nationalist group. Helicopters hovered above us as we carried protest signs, chanted, and ran in between residential homes for cover. This was the only moment in my life in which I had need for a gas mask and doused a fellow protestor's pepper-sprayed eyes with milk,[1] which was one of many tips shared by Palestinian organizers on social media. Ferguson was where self-professed revolutionaries and gangsters asked me, in a sacred moment away from all the chaos, to pray.

The Ferguson Uprising, which lasted over one year, was comprised of sustained resistance, aggressive direct action, strategic mobilization, and organizational development. While people of all ages were involved in the protests and organizing efforts, millennials were front and center at a crucial time when everything was on the line. During the uprising, Black millennial activists seized the national spotlight and claimed their place on the stage of Black leadership.

The Ferguson moment of unprecedented millennial resistance morphed into a movement by inspiring a ripple effect of urban rebellions throughout the country—drenched in bloodshed, carried out through survival instincts, and driven by marginalized Black youth. In many ways, Ferguson was ground zero for my generation's political awakening. As a site of young Black protestors holding the line for fearless militancy in war zone conditions, Ferguson had become the catalyst for a shift in political tactics. The call was now for radical confrontation and disruption.

The spirit of the uprising was infectious, gripping a frustrated Black millennial generation. It was a spark that ignited nationwide protest action. Many have defined the Ferguson Uprising as short-lived. I understand it as the catalyst to a Black millennial–led movement that inspired working-class and poor Black people within my generation to not only imagine freedom but also to fight for it in the streets of the United States. In Ferguson, the young Black outcasts of American society claimed their space and entered the fold of the movement. They came and made their presence known—not only to the local government and their Black president but to the world. These young people were not only demanding to be seen, heard, valued, and protected; they were also leading an uprising.

Amid the Ferguson Uprising in 2015, I wrote a piece in the *Washington Post* about what was happening in Ferguson and knew from the feedback, reposting, and citing of the op-ed that the reflections resonated with many millennials. "For this generation, there's no need to hide behind a veil of purity or wear a suit to have an authoritative seat at the table. This is a movement that encourages all to 'come as you are.' Natural. Bohemian. Rebellious. Tatted up. Provocative. Ratchet. It seems everything is acceptable—except the constraining rules of our elders' day."[2]

These young people didn't just "throw rocks" at the empire. They occupied urban land that they had been raised on and refused to forfeit their claim over it. Through sustained direct action, they raised the visibility of the poor and oppressed in the media's eye. They also radically altered our conceptions about social justice and possibilities for freedom, shifting our generation's imagining of Black rebellion.

A TWENTY-FIRST-CENTURY LYNCHING

The movement's origin story goes back to Canfield Drive. What unfolded in Ferguson was ignited by Brown's bloodied dead body, pressed against the pavement, being left in the summer heat for four hours. Writer and educator Jelani Cobb described this as "terrorism's theatrical intent."[3] Patricia Bynes, a former Ferguson

Democratic committeewoman, told the *New York Times* that "the delay helped fuel the outrage," describing it as a "message from law enforcement" that "was very disrespectful to the community and the people who live there."[4] Bynes, like so many of us, believed that Brown's body was purposefully left visible, covered only by a white sheet, as a threatening message to the community.

Canfield Drive was eerily reminiscent of the public spectacle made of Black suffering, subjugation, and dehumanization on auction blocks and lynching trees. Author Isabel Wilkerson, in a *Guardian* piece published two weeks after the killing of Brown, compared his death to Jim Crow lynchings and argued that the modern prevalence of viral YouTube videos of police officers killing Black people is "a form of public witness to brutality beyond anything possible in the age of lynching."[5] Wilkerson sounded the alarm that "the rate of police killings of black Americans [one every three or four days] is nearly the same as the rate of lynchings in the early decades of the 20th century."[6]

On November 21, 2014, days before a grand jury decided that Brown's killer would not be indicted, three young protestors staged a mock lynching near Dred Scott Way at St. Louis Old Courthouse. Rapper and activist T-Dubb-O, a cofounder of Hands Up United (an organization that formed in St. Louis amid the protests), was among them. He and two women used white nooses to affix themselves to a tree, chained their wrists, and bound their ankles.[7] T-Dubb-O told the *New York Times* that what happened to Brown was the motivation behind the silent protest: "To us, that was a modern-day lynching; his body left on display as a reminder [of] who's in power."[8] The location was chosen to underscore how little had changed in America's recognition of Black citizenship and dignity in the 167 years that had passed since 1847. That year,

Dred Scott, an enslaved Black man, along with his wife, sued for his freedom at the Old Courthouse. The United States Supreme Court ultimately ruled against Scott in the decade-long case, setting a legal precedent.

While Brown's death was a personal loss for many in the Ferguson community who knew and loved him, it was also a collective defeat for each of us who felt shattered and infuriated by his brutal killing. State violence goes far beyond militarized policing. We are trapped in this intricate, devastating web of systemic oppression that tramples on our human dignity. In his book *Nobody*, scholar Marc Lamont Hill states that Brown was deemed a "Nobody," which is defined in the book's preface as being tethered to vulnerability, physical and systemic State violence, "abandonment by the State," and perceived disposability.[9]

Ferguson protestors demanded that charges be brought against Brown's killer. As history has shown, legal accountability for the killing of a Black person by a police officer is rare in America, especially in predominately Black, working-class, and poor neighborhoods. Cops are protected by the system at every level. Ferguson, as an economically oppressed community that had long endured over-policing, reached a tipping point. A 2015 Department of Justice (DOJ) investigation revealed that the Ferguson police department's goal of generating more revenue for the city affected ticketing, law enforcement practices, and the practices of municipal courts.[10] The DOJ report revealed documented evidence of people's constitutional rights being violated during police encounters with Ferguson police, reflecting a history of racial bias that disproportionately harmed African Americans.[11]

Ferguson became a site of rebellion that illuminated racial disparities and economic inequalities in cities throughout the

U.S. The killing of Brown, including the reckless treatment of his dead body, was a breaking point for a community that decided they had suffered quietly for too long. They were now ready to resist oppressive forces, including the police, head-on. These and countless other factors led to Black rage spilling out into the streets of Ferguson in the days, weeks, and months that followed. A community's day-to-day monotony was disrupted, as young people were enlivened by righteous indignation, many who were protesting for the first time in their lives.

WHOSE STREETS? OUR STREETS!

It quickly became apparent that law enforcement and civilians in Ferguson were engaged in an ongoing "power struggle,"[12] as described by St. Louis rapper and activist Tef Poe, who became a prominent leader and voice in the uprising. Three weeks after Brown's killing, he wrote a *TIME* magazine op-ed piece stating that the young people in St. Louis viewed what happened to Mike Brown and the excessive police force that followed "as a declaration of war."[13] One year later, in a 2015 interview with *Colorlines*, as he reflected on what had unfolded on West Florissant, he said, "We live in a society where they tell you you're free, but if you question the actions of the state, [if] you don't just sit at home watching it on the news or reading a blog about it on Facebook, if you are one of the people that chooses to physically put your body on the line, then you become an enemy of the state."[14]

Day after day and night after night in Ferguson, protestors refused to leave the streets and go home by mandated curfew times. With both arms raised in the air, protestors often chanted: "Hands Up! Don't Shoot!" But the rallying cry that better captured and propelled the energy of the uprising was: "Whose Streets? Our Streets!" Through courageous defiance, they made it known that they sought police accountability and freedom to assemble more than they feared the opposition force awaiting them. In a column for the *Guardian* published days after Brown was killed, author Roxane Gay wrote, "Ferguson is the site of an occupation happening in plain sight, and the police remain undeterred because they can occupy, because they know they have unlimited power, because they know they cannot be stopped."[15]

In October 2014, thousands of supporters from all over the country, including celebrities, civil rights leaders, and clergy, arrived in Ferguson for a "Weekend of Resistance" known as #Ferguson October. By then, two more young Black men, Kajieme Powell and Vonderrit Myers, had been killed by St. Louis police officers. On October 12, at a mass gathering at St. Louis University's Chaifetz Arena, a generational and class divide became undeniable. The audience had heard speeches from several interfaith leaders. Then, as Cornell William Brooks, who was president of the NAACP at the time, was speaking, local protestors began to demand that the voices of young people be heard.

As the scheduled programming was halted and local organizers prepared to take the mic, the audience erupted in cheers, chanting: "This is what democracy looks like!" Tef Poe was one of the voices that the audience demanded to hear. After giving his condolences to the family of Cary Ball, a twenty-five-year-old Black man shot twenty-five times by St. Louis police one year prior but whose case had not been widely covered by the media, Tef Poe passionately shouted the phrase that would name the growing local and national tension: "This ain't your daddy's Civil Rights Movement!"

The audience demand for young people to be heard reflected the reality that millennials, who were a driving force in the Ferguson Uprising, were now asserting their power and their right to a national platform. This moment was symbolic of a generational shift in the control center for an emerging resistance movement. Millennial and youth speakers then left their seats and took center stage, sidelining elder leaders to ensure no one took false claim over the movement they created. Civil rights and interfaith leaders, after being heard for so long (both that day and as far back as the Civil Rights Movement), were told to sit down and listen to the battle cries of a younger generation.

This in no way negates the important role that clergy and public theologians like Traci Blackmon, Renita Lamkin, Michael McBride, Osagyefo Sekou, Cornel West, and Starsky Wilson played in the Ferguson Uprising. "Moral Monday" was brought to Ferguson and countless interfaith leaders repeatedly took physical and legal risks to stand in solidarity with the community. But one of the reasons that they did was because marching orders were now coming from the streets and not the pulpit. Anyone paying attention to how Ferguson protestors engaged in resistance and what they had to say was forced to acknowledge the secular dimensions of the uprising. They had no interest in political correctness or "playing nice in the sandbox" for the sake of the media.

By constantly sharing information released to them by the police department and focusing so heavily on property destruction, the media played a major role in presenting dangerous Black criminality narratives to the public. Debate followed nightly protests in Ferguson about the difference between protestors, rioters, and looters. The young people protesting in Ferguson were often classified as "thugs," a charged term historically rooted in racism and classism that is often used to criminalize Black men. Meanwhile, faith leaders were regarded as respectable, disciplined, and orderly.

Civil Rights leaders have always ranged in class status, differed in political ideology, and encouraged divergent strategies for liberation. Martin Luther King Jr. was calling for nonviolent civil disobedience while Stokely Carmichael was chanting "Black power" and Malcolm X was declaring "by any means necessary." These tensions have always existed in our movements, undergirding the good protestor versus bad protestor dichotomy that drove national discussion during the Ferguson Uprising. "Good" protestors are understood to march, chant slogans, maintain a political ethos of nonviolence, and work within the system to reform it. "Bad" protestors are perceived as hyperaggressive, violent, unruly, and having complete disregard for social order, property, rules, laws, and respectability. "Good" freedom fighters hold protest signs and petition for change. "Bad" freedom fighters carry weaponry and call for revolution. Empires have always tried to set the terms for how oppressed people imagine and fight for freedom.

During the Ferguson Uprising, the distinctions were glaring and voiced repeatedly: brothers and sisters draped in (at times gang-affiliated) bandannas were in the streets daily fighting for Black liberation and protecting one another (not "respectable" Black folks). The face of frontline freedom fighters had shifted, drastically, in Ferguson. It now reflected a millennial and largely poor post-hip-hop generation. Some of the voices coming from Ferguson were young, hardworking men and women who wanted a better quality of life for themselves and their children. Others reflected the full range of our complicated, divergent experiences as humans. The protestors, some of them unapologetically queer, had no intentions of quietly fading into the background or taking a back seat as the freedom train accelerated. The uprising brought in a refreshing new tide of radical inclusivity.

BUILDING ORGANIZATIONS AND BRIDGES

In addition to the already mentioned Hands Up United, newly formed collectives like Millennial Activists United (MAU) and Lost Voices were strategically pushing back in the streets and collectively envisioning the way forward. They all had different points of entry into the movement, and they took different paths in carrying out their vision. But the interconnectedness of these organizations was undeniable to anyone in close contact. MAU, for example, focused on providing care to protestors by way of meals and "survival supplies"[16] as well as helping those who had been tear-gassed. Lost Voices, a group that was organically formed out of the protests, camped out and collectively slept in tents, promoting nonviolent civil disobedience. Veteran groups like Organization for Black Struggle (OBS), founded in 1980 with a focus on addressing the holistic needs of the Black working class, were already in operation in St. Louis and were instrumental in the resistance efforts. Many of the emerging leaders in Ferguson were also being mentored by movement elders like Anthony Shahid, a longtime St. Louis activist, who stayed engaged during the uprising.

Over a period of months from 2015 to 2016, I traveled to St. Louis to support organizational development and maintained strong ties to the community and its young leaders. I was organizing alongside Michael McBride (known as "Pastor Mike"), who leads Live Free, a national organization focused on addressing gun violence, criminalization, and mass incarceration. On various projects, we worked in collaboration with Hands Up United, which modeled the Black Panther Party's "survival programs." The organization's five cofounders developed several community programs, including Books and Breakfast, People's Pantry, and a tech institute.

In July 2015, four of the Hands Up United cofounders, Pastor Mike, and I traveled to Paris, France. After having built strong ties to racial justice activists in Paris, I envisioned a delegation in which the two communities could learn from one another's resistance to police brutality. The trip marked the ten-year anniversary of mass rebellions that erupted in France over the deaths of two teenagers, Zyed Benna and Bouna Traoré, who were electrocuted while running from the police. We met with organizational leaders, visited the housing developments where the teenagers died in the outskirts of Paris, hosted a panel discussion, and had cultural exchange experiences.

The delegation is only one example of countless ways in which internationalism was a critical component of the Ferguson Uprising. Protest chants spoke to the intersections that protestors saw in global struggles: "From Ferguson to Palestine, killing people is a crime!" Several Ferguson organizers even traveled to occupied Palestine as part of a Dream Defenders–led delegation. The connections dated back to the days of Black Panther Party and Student Nonviolent Coordinating Committee (SNCC) leaders demonstrating support for occupied Palestine. Resistance in Ferguson was not detached from history, as many of the local organizers understood that they were operating in a continuum of Black freedom fighters who resisted imperialism. When these rebellions begin to be understood as human rights movements, then the internationalist scope of the Ferguson Uprising will be better understood.

It was obvious that Ferguson offered inspiration to people from all walks of life. During an interfaith-led act of civil disobedience on August 10, 2015, one day after the one-year anniversary of Brown being killed, I was arrested for blocking the entrance to the St. Louis federal courthouse with nearly sixty other demonstrators. In a small jail cell full of women protestors of all ethnicities, ages, and faith traditions, we spent hours in conversation discussing the movement, faith, our lives, and the experiences of that day. As the last person to be released from detention, I stepped out to find Pastor Mike and Cornel West waiting for me. We left to break bread and discuss next steps now that every protestor had been accounted for. That moment reflected a truth of many resistance efforts: the collective call for accountability is what often propels movements forward.

RIPPLE EFFECTS

While writing this chapter, I interviewed Pastor Mike about the Ferguson Uprising and his role in it. He spoke about the parallels to the ongoing and at times violent protests that broke out in Oakland, California, in the aftermath of Oscar Grant being killed by a Bay Area Rapid Transit (BART) police officer on New Year's Day in 2009. The inauguration of President Barack Obama three weeks after the killing of Grant was "a kairos moment," Pastor Mike said. While the officer who killed Grant was charged with manslaughter, he was released after only two years. *Fruitvale Station*, a film directed by Oakland-born Ryan Coogler and starring Michael B. Jordan, brought Oscar Grant's story and the issue of police brutality to national attention in 2013, one year prior to the killing of Mike Brown Jr. In highlighting what made the Ferguson Uprising unique, Pastor Mike told me: "Ferguson was a turning point in our generation's fight—a culmination of all the energies, wisdom, and experiences that happened before then."

Many felt the spirit of Ferguson was best memorialized through an iconic photo of Ferguson protestor Edward Crawford Jr. Wearing a T-shirt with the American flag on it, he can be seen "clutching a bag of chips in one hand as he cocks his arm back to throw a burning tear gas canister that riot police had fired to disperse protesters," according to CNN.[17] While Crawford told the news outlet that his purpose was to get the canister away from himself and nearby children rather than to hurl it back at police,[18] the image came to represent the revolutionary zeal in Ferguson.

The protestors, unwavering and aggressive in their pursuit of justice, were seemingly not shackled down by the fears and respectability politics that keep millions of us from being free. They rightfully understood that demeanor, language use, social etiquette, political niceties, and attire cannot shield Black people from racial bias, injustice, and all forms of State violence. Fears of uncertainty, consequence, and public opinion did not appear to deter the Ferguson protestors the way they so often inhibit the rest of us. For those in my generation who came of age in the aftermath of the Civil Rights and Black Power movements, the Ferguson Uprising materialized what had always been in our political imagination. These were *our* millennial, women, poor, and queer heroes.

Yet, every act of rejecting Black humanity will inevitably inspire new forms of radical Black self-love and resistance, as it should. When Baltimore erupted in a Black-youth-led rebellion in April 2015, many of us felt that we were seeing something new in U.S. cities. The Baltimore Uprising was born in response to Freddie Gray Jr.'s death while in police custody. Many believed Gray's fatal spinal cord injury was brought about by the actions and negligence of the officers. In 2016, riots broke out in Milwaukee in response to a police officer killing Sylville K. Smith.

There's no denying that something rare was happening in U.S. cities in the rise of the Movement for Black Lives, self-described as a "post-Ferguson Black liberation movement" with an "ecosystem of over 170 Black-led organizations."[19] In the aftermath of police killings of Black people, protestors left their homes and went out into the streets to engage in civil disobedience. Legal consequences and rolling media cameras were not enough to subdue what was happening. Protestors blocked roads and traffic on interstate highways in cities like Chicago, Cleveland, Minneapolis, Oakland, and San Francisco. The Brooklyn Bridge was flooded by masses of people in New York. Other iconic photos of fearless protestors began to circulate widely, including one from Baton Rouge of a young Black woman in a dress standing steadfast in front of police. Nationwide, protestors disregarded curfew mandates, disrupted the programming of public events, and occupied spaces where protestors were not permitted to be. These courageous actions helped us to collectively imagine and experience freedom even if for just those brief, bittersweet moments.

Media coverage and political commentary primarily focused on police brutality. Connections were rarely, if ever, made to the predominately white-led, class-focused 2011 Occupy Wall Street protest movement, which sought to draw attention to wealth inequality in the U.S. The class dimensions of the rising tide of Black discontent were underemphasized, to say the least. How could underemployed millennials not be infuriated? How could they not see State violence as an extension of the failures they had experienced in the housing, education, and healthcare systems in their communities?

Hands Up United cofounder Tara Thompson spoke about our societal misconceptions about freedom in a docuseries titled *The Mike Brown Rebellion* produced by Rebel Diaz for teleSUR English. She said, "The freedoms that you think you have (like your car, your house, your all of that), you don't have those freedoms. You have the right to get up, to go to work, to pay your taxes, and to keep functioning in this system. And if you not trying to do that, then [the State is] trying to shut it down."[20]

THE COST OF FREEDOM

In the time I spent with countless Ferguson and Baltimore organizers, job security, sleep deprivation, and PTSD were common threads uniting their personal struggles as protestors. Many talked about how all-consuming and draining their respective uprisings were. Rarely do we explore the psychological dimensions of straddling survival and rebellion. Ashley Yates, who cofounded Millennial Activists United with Brittany Ferrell and Alexis Templeton, touched on this in a *Huffington Post* interview, saying, "Lots of different [psychological] and physical tactics were used by the police to try to suppress our efforts to stand for justice. But each and every day we learned from their actions and their lies on TV, and we grew more resilient and more determined. And each day we went back out to show them that fear no longer works as a weapon against us."[21]

Political risk-taking often comes at a cost. One of the most tragic examples of this is Joshua Williams, described as "the only remaining political prisoner from the Ferguson/St. Louis uprisings" on the site FreeJoshWilliams.com.[22] Williams, who was then eighteen years old, is in prison serving an eight-year sentence for his role at a December 2014 protest over the police killing of Antonio Martin. While Williams was charged with burglary and arson, the crime amounted to "stealing a bag of chips and lighting a QuikTrip trash can on fire," according to *GQ* senior staff writer Zach Baron.[23] Williams told *GQ*, which interviewed him shortly after George Floyd was killed, that he wrestles with being made "an example out of" while "the [officer] that killed Michael Brown didn't do a day in jail."[24]

Williams is not the only example of Ferguson protestors facing tragic consequences. Several local activists died mysteriously or through self-inflicted means within the five years following the Ferguson Uprising. Deandre Joshua, twenty, and Darren Seals, twenty-nine, were found dead in torched cars with bullet wounds.[25] Palestinian American Bassem Masri, thirty-one, died from a fentanyl overdose.[26] The deaths of three men were ruled a suicide: Edward Crawford Jr., twenty-seven; Danye Jones, twenty-four; and MarShawn McCarrel, twenty-three.[27] Crawford was the protestor in the famous Ferguson photo mentioned earlier in this chapter. He died due to a self-included gunshot wound to the head, but his relatives have said they believe it was accidental and not suicide.[28] The deaths of these men deserve more national attention. Their stories should never be forgotten.

BEYOND PROTEST

In *Class Notes: Posing as Politics and Other Thoughts on the American Scene*, scholar Adolph Reed Jr. defines a political movement as "a force that has shown a capability, over time, of mobilizing popular support for programs that expressly seek to alter the patterns of public policy or economic relations."[29] When his book was published at the turn of the twenty-first century, in 2000, he argued, "There simply is no such entity in black American life at this point."[30] Reed's argument that contemporary national organizations focused on Black liberation did not constitute a political movement are reminiscent of debates that have unfolded over the past decade about whether we have been witnessing moments or movements.

The reality is that we don't all share the same definitions of a movement, nor do we all understand success in the same terms. In our social media– and celebrity-obsessed times, movement-building has often been analyzed with the same criteria that we judge Hollywood productions: Who is in the leading role, how successful was their latest project, is their work gaining traction, can they appeal to the youth, who do they remind us of, and will they have a lasting impact? Too often, mainstream media and culture have recklessly equated sustained social media virality with the making of movements. The word is used to describe almost anything these days; I have even heard high-profiled individuals who are a one-man or one-woman operation described as a "movement." When and how did the word become so commercially defined? "Moment versus movement" debates suggest that success is measured by communities and organizations keeping themselves at the epicenter of America's focus. Legitimacy is sadly often gauged by visibility, followers, titles, and proximity to elder statesmen or celebrities. However, liberation work continues long after microphones have been turned off and news cameras have left.

The media's desire to fit the Black liberation struggle into neat, convenient framings has meant that a large majority of local organizing efforts are overshadowed by a hyperobsession with "national leaders." The distractions are endless. While the organizing efforts of Black Lives Matter chapters throughout the U.S. cannot be ignored, it's upsetting to think about how much time and intellectual effort has gone into debating and defending the phrase and hashtag itself. The "All Lives Matter" counterargument is a prime example of how white supremacy weaponizes distraction.

If the history of the Ferguson Uprising is to be properly remembered, it should include that the battle was fought on multiple fronts. After President Obama met with Ferguson protestors at the White House, he then established the Task Force on 21st Century Policing in December 2014. The Ferguson Commission, also established in 2014 by then Missouri governor Jay Nixon, studied racial equality in the region and released a report identifying priorities. The community then institutionalized accountability for implementation through the organization Forward Through Ferguson. Several entities collaborated to create the St. Louis Regional Racial Healing + Justice Fund, which provides grants to organizations led by Black and Brown people doing racial equality work in the region. Recognizing that police reform was a limiting strategy, countless collaborating St. Louis organizations released The People's Plan, which focuses on "re-envisioning public safety," in 2021.[31]

Part of the Ferguson history should also include greater emphasis being placed on electoral politics to build Black political power. Action St. Louis, cofounded by organizer Kayla Reed, was born out of the uprising and has reached "almost 5,000 young people" through voter registration and election efforts.[32] The organization's grassroots work and innovative approaches to attracting millennials have been instrumental in shifting local politics, playing a key role in the election of St. Louis's first Black woman mayor and St. Louis County's first Black prosecutor, as well as "flipping the Board of Aldermen."[33]

Voters also claimed several victories in electoral politics by sending Ferguson activists to seats of power. Ferguson activists Bruce Franks Jr. and Rasheen Aldridge went to the Missouri House of Representatives, Fran Griffin won a seat in the Ferguson City Council, and Cori Bush claimed victory over a twenty-year incumbent in Congress.[34] The history of the Ferguson Uprising must also account for what the *New York Times* called "the most tangible legacy of Ferguson," body cameras on police officers, as nearly half of the police departments in the country purchased cameras by 2016.[35] This was a core recommendation of the Obama task force on policing.

THE STRUGGLE CONTINUES

The Ferguson Uprising was not born nor was it sustained in isolation. National millennial-led organizations like Black Lives Matter and Black Youth Project 100 had come into existence in the aftermath of the killing of Trayvon Martin. Area-focused organizations like the Dream Defenders (Florida), Justice League (NYC), and Leaders of a Beautiful Struggle (Baltimore) were already engaged in the ongoing work of addressing systemic racism. Organizations exist all over the U.S. that address socioeconomic injustices in our communities. A few examples are Africatown Community Land Trust in Seattle, the Chicago Anti-Eviction Campaign, FAAN (Fostering Activism and Alternatives Now), and the Florida Rights Restoration Coalition. Some, like the Poor People's Campaign, build on the vision of our forebearers. Then there are many, led by LGBTQIA+, Afro-Indigenous, and Afro-Latinx individuals, that reflect the identity intersections within our community, our shared commitment to human dignity, and the spirit of resistance that unifies us all. Grassroots organizing (in unison with the Black Church, mosques, and nonprofit organizations) has always strengthened our communities amid unspeakable trauma.

In the aftermath of the murder of George Floyd on May 25, 2020, by a police officer, the country, already grieving daily loss of life due to a pandemic, was forced to reckon with the epidemic of State violence. Less than a year prior, in August 2019, Equal Justice Initiative had published an article titled "Five Years After Ferguson, Policing Reform Is Abandoned."[36] Floyd's murder led to a multigenerational awakening with unprecedented national and global protests. What was also unique to that time was the "more than 1,100 companies and philanthropic institutions" that committed $200 billion to racial justice work, with financial institutions accounting for nearly 90 percent of the funding, according to the McKinsey Institute for Black Economic Mobility.[37]

While worthy of celebration in that organizations and initiatives got commitments for needed and long overdue support, this shocking promised influx of capital from corporations should not go uncritiqued. One reason is that many companies shaped their contributions in profit-driven models of (primarily mortgage) loans and investments; many grants had long-term disbursements that spanned, in some cases, over a decade.[38] There were also countless corporate pledges and Diversity, Equity, and Inclusion (DEI) promises made that were not kept.[39]

Capitalism, through countless systems within society, cleverly imprints our psyche and reframes how we think, operate, engage others, and view the world around us. None of us, as individuals, organizations, and movements, are immune to being seduced by fame and fortune. History has taught us that capitalist trappings can be used as a Trojan horse to destabilize movements and rebel groups. How do we ensure that our struggle is not turned into a commercial product for American mass consumption? What are the sacred, ancestral dimensions of our freedom journey that capitalism should never have? And how do we guarantee institutional, individual, ideological, and fiscal accountability to the communities we profess to represent and serve?

Many community organizations have rightfully understood that we must not only rebel against systems but must also resist our hunger for instant gratification. Through their monthlong occupation of the Florida State Capitol in 2013 in response to Trayvon Martin's killer being acquitted, the Dream Defenders demonstrated a generational courage that inspired youth to take action nationwide. They were just getting started. In the last decade, their organizing efforts have focused on the political education of young people, getting laws changed and student debt canceled, registering voters, creating a community-based public safety program, and imprinting youth culture. What I have found to be most inspiring about the group is their commitment to global solidarity. By leading several delegations of organizers, faith leaders, and artists to occupied Palestine, the Dream Defenders have helped rebuild international and generational bridges that organizations like the Black Panther Party knew were important.

Our struggle is not only a global one; it is also economic. The organizers of the Montgomery bus boycott understood that. Their yearlong refusal to ride the buses in protest of segregated seating was a pioneering act of economic resistance. Our contemporary movement has rightfully understood that we too should organize boycotts to combat the ways in which economic injustice traumatizes our communities. In November 2014, filmmaker Ryan Coogler, mentioned earlier as director of *Fruitvale Station* but best known for the *Black Panther* series, founded Blackout for Human Rights. The collective sheds light on racial oppression, raises funds, hosts special events, and mobilizes boycotts like #BlackOutBlackFriday. Filmmaker Ava DuVernay, who is part of Blackout, told *IndieWire* shortly after the group launched that she hoped "Blackout and its allied organizations can instigate elongated pressure on power structures and systems that neglect the sanctity of life and human rights."[40]

On November 24, 2014, the night it was announced that the officer who killed Michael Brown Jr. would not be indicted, I (like millions of other people throughout the country) felt an immense sense of helplessness, hurt, and anger. Sitting on my couch in my Harlem apartment, I knew that the greatest power I could exert was through *Urban Cusp,* an online magazine I launched three years prior that had amassed four hundred thousand followers. Realizing that the country was days away from Black Friday, I created a black-and-white meme calling for #NotOneDime to be spent over the Thanksgiving holiday. After posting the meme on my various social media platforms, I left my apartment to join the protests taking place in Times Square. When I woke up the next morning, I had several emails from various media outlets, including *Forbes*. During that night, the meme had been shared by several celebrities, causing it to go viral, and reporters had traced its origin back to me. Without knowing it, I had created a viral sensation, calling on Black America to channel our collective community rage toward an economic boycott and weaponize our spending power in response to police brutality and systemic oppression.

In the coming days, I created a series of memes to offer direction and guidance for the boycott. #NotOneDime was to be a national day of action, service, and economic resistance. People were encouraged to also boycott Cyber Monday. The memes were an online organizing strategy, but the real power of #NotOneDime and #BlackOutBlackFriday came by way of nationwide grassroots organizations mobilizing acts of resistance in their local communities. Acts of disruption were planned to prevent shoppers from being able to enter stores, block highway exits leading to malls, and prevent public transportation users from boarding trains headed to shopping districts. Were we successful? Although several media outlets reported an 11 percent ($6.5 billion) drop in online and in-store shopping during Black Friday weekend in 2014 as compared to 2013,[41] media outlets, as expected, did not credit the online and offline boycott efforts as being factors in the drop. In partnership with Hands Up United in Ferguson and Pastor Mike of Live Free, I coordinated the #NotOneDime boycott again the following year, in 2015, working alongside Coogler and the Blackout for Human Rights team. Economic resistance was also the challenge put forth by the Nation of Islam's Justice or Else mass gathering in Washington, DC, on October 10, 2015, in honor of the twentieth anniversary of the Million Man March.

As the world learned from the anti-apartheid movement in South Africa, divestment and sanctions pose the greatest threats to oppressive governments. In imagining freedom, how can we boycott and divest from what stands in opposition to our liberation? This must be an individual, institutional, and communal pursuit. We cannot continue to pour resources into companies and entities that do not serve the interests of our people. Like those who were part of the Montgomery bus boycott, we should be willing to make individual and collective sacrifices for the greater good.

While capitalism is pervasive and difficult to break free from, it is possible to weaken its control over us. We can live within this capitalistic system without surrendering full control to it. This will require us to make tough decisions about our consumer habits and, at times, to sacrifice convenience. One example of this is the choice that many have made to boycott e-commerce and franchise giants and shop locally at businesses owned by minorities and women. When workers organize strikes to resist low wages and unfair working conditions, we can stand in solidarity with them by taking our dollars elsewhere. Making these decisions may not always be comfortable in the process, but it will strengthen movements focused on economic justice.

When I reflect on my organizing experiences with the Florida-based Coalition of Immokalee Workers and the Student/Farmworker Alliance, I am reminded of how integral political education was to our work. Space was held for working-class organizers to learn and teach across racial, class, and generational lines. The point was not to train a coalition of youth that could regurgitate information; the point was for organizers to seize the intellectual and cultural tools needed to propel the people's movement. Political education undoubtedly unifies us and undergirds our intersectionality. It teaches us why the protection and liberation of various groups (Indigenous, LGBTQIA+, people with disabilities, imprisoned people, etc.) cannot be ignored as it has been in movements of the past. Our struggle requires *everyone* on deck. At the same time, grounding our work in identity politics makes us an easy target for division and conquest. It's incapable of unifying all oppressed people and ushering in freedom for all.

Some of our organizations have been born out of knowing where more work has to be done. The role of Black male leadership has often been a controversial and divisive issue in the Movement for Black Lives. Many organizers advocated for a movement led by women and queers; Black men were often asked (or at times, told) to "fall back" to ensure that the movement would not succumb to patriarchal and misogynistic leadership. Black Men Build (BMB) evolved out of the belief that Black men equally need safe space to heal, learn, and organize. In June 2020, Phillip Agnew, a cofounder of the Dream Defenders who now codirects BMB, asked me to write a poem for their launch meeting. On the few occasions that I participated in or watched BMB's mass meetings, I was deeply moved by their passion and authenticity. The conveners weren't afraid to shed tears in one instant and talk about dismantling the prison-industrial complex in another. Today, BMB has hubs in several cities and is contributing to the political awakening of masses of Black men.

I name these organizations to highlight the significance of building communities and platforms that propel our people to new heights. So often in the U.S., we are told that entrepreneurship and the willingness to lose one's financial security are the epitome of fearlessness. We often equate entrepreneurship with liberation as if they are one and the same. But Black holistic liberation will not be born out of individual success and wealth. Purpose will always be tied to community.

Ours is a collective struggle that stands in bold defiance to all enemy forces. With that in mind, what safe spaces can we join or create for our people to grieve, release rage, and assert power? What is required of us to usher in the world we want to live in? And how do our individual dreams connect to and build on Black America's dreams for itself? The Ferguson Uprising was a clarion call to all who are on the margins of society. It was the site of a Black millennial reframing of the Statue of Liberty's (often misappropriated) invitation: "Give me your tired, your poor, / Your huddled masses yearning to breathe free."[42] Come as you are, and let us cocreate the conditions, tools, languages, and ideas that will materialize the freedoms we seek. Together, we possess the power to birth the dawn of a new day.

6

Pan-Africanism

Diasporic Solidarity

I've been searching for Africa all over the
world but forgot to look within me.
—Thabiso Daniel Monkoe

It was April Fools' Day in 2019 and the warmth of the morning sun was piercing through the bay windows in the bedroom of my home in Johannesburg, South Africa. Images of thirty-three-year-old Ermias Joseph Asghedom, a rapper and activist best known as Nipsey Hussle, filled my Instagram feed. In the nine hours that separated Central Africa Time from Pacific Daylight Time, countless individuals and media outlets had been posting about him. As the captions shifted from "prayers up" to "rest in peace," my eyes widened. I gasped out of utter disbelief. An African American male alleged to be an aspiring rapper and longtime acquaintance of Asghedom had murdered him in broad daylight. He was violently killed outside the Marathon Clothing store he had spent years pouring time, talent, and resources into.

I spent the day excavating old online interviews in which Asghedom, an Eritrean American, spoke passionately about economic empowerment and the evils of colonialism, and wanting to amplify the story of Eritrea's freedom struggle. He had credited a trip he took to Eritrea with his father and brother when he was nineteen years old as having grounded his sense of identity and inspired his community efforts.[1] Over the next two weeks, I watched in awe as members of the hip-hop and global community, in remembrance of him, honored my small homeland in the Horn of Africa. They joined millions of others, particularly in the Eritrean diaspora, in communal mourning for our fallen brother. As a bridge builder (even in death), he briefly linked together two worlds that historically have not been in conversation with one another. During that time, in which our language, history, and flag were on the world stage, not a single day passed without tears flooding my eyes. Like countless other young Eritreans worldwide, I felt seen and honored by the African American culture that had so often felt at odds with my African identity.

In mainstream media's coverage of Asghedom, there has been little to no focus placed on his radical millennial understanding, full of Pan-African overtones, of the plight of African Americans and Africans. Often drawing parallels between the exploitation and resistance of both, Asghedom's interviews suggest that he understood the Black American freedom struggle was deeply tied to the anti-colonial struggle of Africa.

In a 2013 interview with *XXL* magazine, Asghedom explained his breakaway from mainstream record companies and the reasoning behind him being an independent artist.[2] The interview took place one week after Nipsey's infamous $100 apiece price tag for a limited one thousand copies of his *Crenshaw* mixtapes. Many of us know that Jay-Z, through Roc-A-Fella Records, purchased one hundred of those mixtapes, helping Asghedom quickly rack up a self-made $100,000. Some might even know that Asghedom's #Proud2Pay campaign idea was inspired by him reading *Contagious: Why Things Catch On* by Jonah Berger, who writes about a $100 cheesesteak in Philadelphia.[3] However, few of us know his underlying political ideology about culture and economics that led him to make these calculated moves.

Asghedom was heavily invested in capitalist ideals rooted in enterprise and ownership. Yet, he was also keenly aware of how Black artists like him are often threatened, intimidated, and discouraged by "arrogant" mainstream record companies.[4] Using militaristic language to describe "the war that we're fighting" and evoking the "David and Goliath" metaphor, Asghedom argued that hip-hop, as a culture, was being colonized.[5] In the *XXL* interview, he said, "Hip-hop is like Africa right now; our natural resources, we're watching them get taken from us. The people that control and own the lion's share of the assets aren't indigenous to the culture at all."[6] Asghedom spoke of hip-hop's "indigenous" having greater control over "the natural resource—the pain, the struggle, the story" that makes hip-hop so powerful throughout the world.[7] Arguably, he was more committed to artists having greater independence and control over the means of production than he was in forging a Pan-African pathway for hip-hop. That does not negate his powerful act of imagining "[a] new generation of artists," like him, decolonizing hip-hop.[8]

Asghedom would use that same "David and Goliath" metaphor later in his life to describe Eritrea's independence struggle.[9]

In a 2018 interview he did while visiting his father's birthplace, he spoke about the inspiration he found in an "outnumbered" nation defeating "superpowers," comparing that to his own struggle as an artist to maintain self-sufficiency and avoid the crippling effect of "taking handouts."[10] Asghedom's reflections on his Eritrean identity and him boasting about the country's legacy of resistance echo the sentiments of many Africans who are deeply shaped by their cultural heritage.

A PAN-AFRICAN DOUBLE CONSCIOUSNESS

As an Eritrean, home will always be hot *injera, shiro, boon,* spiced tea, homemade popcorn, and Tigrinya songs like Yemane Barya's "Kemey Aleki" blasting in the background. As an African, home is African people with their African ways of seeing the world and their African ways of doing things. Culture is the glue that binds us together. It is often unspoken (yet heavily enforced) traditions of communalism embedded in everything and everyone African. Home is an amalgamation of rituals that unite us as a people. In this home, we feed the village with "five loaves of bread and two fish"[11] every single day and then humbly go on about our business.

But home is also the South Bronx community I have been attached to my entire life. It's Afro-Indigenous city women like Brenda (traced to the bloodline of Southern women like Bessie and Lillie May) who miraculously make something out of nothing. It's the hallway of Christopher Court, a low-income housing project on the Bronx's Grand Concourse, drenched in the smell of Auntie Eleanor's candied yams, mac and cheese, and turkey wings. Styrofoam cups filled with red or blue Kool-Aid. A turquoise outfit, white tights, and matching barrettes on Easter. It's the feeling we get when The Gap Band's "Outstanding" comes on at the cookout. African Americans, Puerto Ricans, and Dominicans sharing in the joys of arroz con pollo[12] at Family Day. And it's also the imprint of hip-hop and "thug life" on a young Black girl growing up in Marion "Mayor for Life" Barry's DC. Tastemakers, artists, and freedom fighters having Sunday brunch on Lenox Avenue in Harlem or on U Street in DC. Home is Blackness standing on the foundations of Black love and Black joy. It is the superpower of creating daily magic out of the mere essence of who we are as a people.

I have lived at the intersection of those two dichotomous worlds nearly my entire life. Growing up, the front door of our family's apartment in downtown DC represented the entry into and exit out of cultures. Today, we know it as code-switching. But I wasn't just alternating between languages. I was alternating daily between personhoods—the African one that I had to adorn when I was at home and the Black American one I needed to navigate public schools in "Chocolate City," as DC was affectionately known until gentrification drastically shifted its demographics. The two personas often felt very binary, as if life was constantly forcing me to pick a side. And the more I leaned into one identity, the greater the tension I felt with the other. I've heard this same struggle echoed in the sentiments of countless other Africans trying to make peace with their existence in the United States. I have also heard it in the yearning that so many African Americans have to better connect with their African ancestry. As children of Africa, we so often travel on opposite lanes of a two-way street, wondering where the other is coming from and headed to.

While my birth in Africa constitutes my understanding of it as my homeland, African Americans have always, throughout every generation, sought to reconnect to the home of their ancestral origins. This has not been limited to reasons of identity formation; many thought leaders and freedom fighters, both in Africa and the U.S., have long understood that a unified, class-based anti-imperialistic approach to liberation is a critical strategy in building a sustained, effective global movement. In the diaspora, we have two homes and therefore two battlegrounds. Africa's struggle is our struggle. Africa's future is our future. Our destinies are forever intertwined.

Too often, the modern-day link between Africans and Afro-descendants is reduced to cultural commonality and ingenuity. We collectively laugh at the wide range of "you know you're Black if" jokes on social media. We have dissected our Blackness down to a science and use all forms of multimedia to celebrate what it means to be Black. Yes, we are an awe-inspiring people. Whether you find us in the streets of Kingston, Houston, Lagos, or London, our beauty and brilliance remain intact. All subjugated people have always been and will always be fire personified. Our survival has necessitated this.

We must never forget, however, that Africans and Afro-descendants share much more in common than just culture. We have more in common than just blood ties and history. Nothing binds us together more than our shared dream of freedom. Our quest for liberation is intricately woven together—from the housing projects of Queensbridge, New York, to the comunidades of Brazil and townships of Soweto. Until all our people have broken free from the chains of neocolonialism, until oppressors no longer have their knees on our necks and their hands in our pockets, and until capitalism ceases to exploit our natural resources and corrupt our humanity, our freedom quest continues. The struggle extends from the U.S.-Mexico border to Gaza because white supremacy has caused terror and destruction in every corner of the globe.

AFRICA AS A SOURCE OF DREAMS

For three years in my late thirties, I traveled back and forth between Johannesburg, South Africa, and the U.S., living and working throughout the continent. I always knew I would return to live in the United States. But I was wrong about how long it would take me to return. I also didn't realize how blurry my conception of home would become during that period and how fiercely I would come to love Africa and want to fight for her. Two weeks into my arrival in Johannesburg, I met a middle-aged Zimbabwean man who was questioning my decision to come and live on the continent. He said to me, "I thought dreams were on *that* side, not on this one." He was an artist, a painter, yet he couldn't understand how I (and the millions of African Americans I spoke of) perceive Africa as a source of dreams. He voiced the cringeworthy sentiments that I would hear repeatedly during my travels throughout Africa: What could Africa possibly have to offer you? What could be better than life in America? And why would you leave the place that so many of us are trying to get to?

His statement about the U.S. as the source of dreams always reminds me of a journalistic delegation to Darfur, Sudan, that I was part of in 2004. I met a young, orphaned boy living in a camp for internally displaced persons (IDPs) and asked the boy what he wished to become when he grew up. He smiled but didn't seem to know how to answer the question. One of the elder members of my delegation attributed the question to my age (I was twenty-three at the time), saying I was too young to recognize that my question was rooted in an American conception of "dreams." The argument was that there was no equivalent of the American Dream in Africa because the real-life hardships that people endure in Africa are too vast for Africans to "waste" their time dreaming of what the future holds for them.

"An estimated 5,444,900 persons were under the supervision of adult correctional systems in the United States" in 2021, according to a Department of Justice report published in 2023.[13] We have an endless cycle of no accountability for police officers and vigilantes. We know how close the U.S. can get to the edge of democratic collapse and that our government remains unapologetic about mass atrocities. The U.S. houses all these realities while professing perfection and marketing self-advancement, which is why it remains a source of dreams for so many people throughout the world. These are not head-in-the-clouds visions of excess and lavish lifestyles, but rather a longing for survival and economic stability. For many African migrants and asylum seekers fleeing their countries, other African countries are often the first point of refuge, but Europe, Asia, and North America are often desired final destinations.[14]

While my travels throughout the continent introduced me to many who had romanticized ideas about life in the United States, I also met countless working-class individuals, students, scholars, organizers, artists, and techies who had no interest whatsoever in exploring life in the U.S. They described Africa as their "inheritance" and spoke confidently about a united Azania[15] reclaiming her power from European domination. It's vitally important that we know this type of geographical and political commitment to Africa exists within a generation of African millennials and elders who take great pride in knowing they are the rightful heirs to Africa's vast economic and cultural riches. They don't see Europe and the U.S. as ideals—Africa is the promised land.

IDEOLOGICAL BONDS ROOTED IN FREEDOM

In the twentieth century, there were countless prominent Pan-Africanist thinkers and practitioners in and outside the U.S. who were making connections between the African, African American, and diasporic freedom struggles. They saw Black liberation as a global fight and understood the need for all people of African descent to reclaim their stolen history and identity. In *How Europe Underdeveloped Africa*, Walter Rodney describes how some of these ideological bonds emerged and powerfully supported Africa in defining her own destiny:

> It is not in the least surprising that Pan-African ideas should have been most forcefully expressed by West Indians like Garvey and Padmore and North Americans like W. E. B. Du Bois and Alphaeus Hunton. Those individuals had all been educated within the international capitalist structure of exploitation on the basis of class and race. Having realized that their inferior status in the societies of America was conditioned by the fact of being black and the weakness of Africa, the Pan-Africanists were forced to deal with the central problem of Europe's exploitation and oppression of the African continent. Needless to say, the metropolitan powers could never have foreseen that their humiliation of millions of Africans in the New World would ultimately rebound and help Africa to emancipate itself.[16]

Rodney identifies "an interplay of forces and calculations" and historical, political events within and outside of Africa that all contributed to Africa's reclamation of independence, but he emphasizes that self-determination was "*initiated* by the African people" and actualized by their "motor force."[17]

There were many (some less recognized) contributing factors to how Pan-Africanism undergirded Africa's liberation movements. As an example, some of Africa's leading anti-colonial leaders lived, studied, and taught in the United States, learning about the plight and resistance of African Americans firsthand. Nigeria's first president, Nnamdi Azikiwe, and Ghana's first president, Kwame Nkrumah, are both graduates of Lincoln University, a historically Black college or university (HBCU) in Pennsylvania.[18] Azikiwe, who also studied at Howard University in Washington, DC, was a mentor to Nkrumah.[19]

Nkrumah's politics were heavily influenced by Marcus Garvey, a pioneering Jamaican-born Black nationalist and Pan-Africanist in the United States. According to an article titled "The Impact of Marcus Garvey" by historian John Henrik Clarke, the 5th Pan-African Congress, which took place in England in 1945, had Garvey's teachings as its "main ideological basis."[20] Both Nkrumah and Azikiwe attended, along with Pan-African thought leaders George Padmore and W. E. B. Du Bois of the U.S.[21] Clarke argues, "The Pan-African Congress in Manchester was radically different from all of the other congresses. For the first time Africans from Africa, Africans from the Caribbean and Africans from the United States had come together and designed a program for the future independence of Africa."[22]

Over a decade later, in 1957, several African American Civil

Rights Movement leaders traveled to what was then known as the Gold Coast, a British colony in West Africa, to attend a ceremony cementing it as the newly independent country of Ghana. Martin Luther King Jr. and his wife, Coretta Scott King, were in attendance per invitation of Nkrumah, then the new prime minister of Ghana.[23] One month after his return, King preached a sermon titled "The Birth of a New Nation" at Dexter Avenue Baptist Church in Montgomery, Alabama. While drawing parallels between the European colonization of Africa and the subjugation of Black Americans in North America, King spoke at length to his congregation about African geography, Nkrumah's experiences of poverty in the U.S., and all the sacrifices that led to Ghana gaining independence from Britain.[24] Describing nation-building as a "wilderness" experience similar to the biblical Exodus story, King challenged African Americans to offer their skills and strengths to the building of Ghana, closing out his sermon with a prayer that began by asking God to "help us to see the insights that come from this new nation."[25]

In 1974, the 6th Pan-African Congress became the first congress to be held on the continent, in Dar es Salaam, Tanzania. It also marked a shift away from the patriarchy of past congresses with an intergenerational group of African American women playing a major role in coordination, logistics, programming, and resolution-building.[26] Activists like "Queen Mother" Audley Moore, "mother of the reparations movement"[27] and one of the founders of the Republic of New Afrika, and Mae Mallory, a militant Black nationalist and proponent of armed self-defense, were in attendance.[28] Many felt the 6th Pan-African Congress is when Pan-Africanism opened its eyes to all the contributions of Black women within the liberation struggle and made a commitment to combatting gender oppression.[29]

IMMERSION: THE POWER OF AFRICAN SOIL

The Civil Rights and Black Power movements were full of these intercontinental convergences, in which freedom fighters were learning from their experiences abroad and supporting one another's struggles. For some, like Malcolm X, this resulted in several trips to Africa where he traveled to various African countries and met with many dignitaries, intellectuals, and students. While in Nigeria in 1964, he was given the Yoruba name Omowale, which means "the son who has come home."[30]

In a review of Manning Marable's *Malcolm X: A Life of Reinvention* published in a 2011 issue of the *New Left Review*, writer and activist Tariq Ali highlights how Malcolm's multiple trips to Africa shifted his politics further away from separatism and toward Pan-Africanism and socialism.[31] Ali writes about the trip, "Soon after his return, he gave a speech drawing parallels between European colonial rule and institutionalized racism in the U.S.: the police in Harlem were like the French in Algeria, 'like an occupying army.' As Marable notes, 'For the first time he publicly made the connection between racial oppression and capitalism.'"[32] Envisioning an institution that would unify African Americans with Africans on the continent, Malcolm established the Organization of Afro-American Unity (OAAU) after his return from Africa. His inspiration was the Organization of African Unity (OAU), which later morphed into the modern-day African Union.

During my three years of organizing with various movements

on the continent, I heard often that the independence of African countries would have never been possible without internationalists who were driven by Pan-African ideals. Cuba's role in the various independence struggles of Africa by way of military and medical support was frequently referenced and praised. While guiding me on how internationalists have stood in solidarity with Africans living on the continent, an elder Zambian freedom fighter would always draw lessons from Che Guevara being engaged in guerilla warfare alongside Congolese[33] rebels and the tens of thousands of Cubans who served, fought, and died in countries such as Angola.

The focus of his advice was not a call to arms. His belief was that nothing better reflects a commitment to Africa than leaving one's own home, physically coming to the continent, experiencing the joys and pains of daily life, and being intimately engaged in the ongoing liberation struggle. It's reminiscent of the Christian call to "offer your bodies as a living sacrifice" (Romans 12:1, NIV). This is Pan-Africanist immersion—an unwavering commitment to the liberation of African people as demonstrated by socioeconomic self-sacrifice (what some understand as "class suicide"), solidarity, and oneness with the continent.

The majority of Black Americans will never travel to or live in Africa, and that is fine. However, it is important that with the growing commercial appeal of Africa via Hollywood and social media, we not engage in "poverty tourism" and mistake it for truly seeing and serving Africa. When the Student Nonviolent Coordinating Committee (SNCC) went on a delegation to Africa, they coupled that experience with political education, "hungrily devouring" the works of African revolutionaries, writes Barbara Ransby in *Ella Baker and the Black Freedom Movement*.[34] Fannie Lou Hamer, John Lewis, and Julian Bond were among the 1964 delegation of eleven, sponsored by Harry Belafonte, that traveled to Guinea.[35] The delegation strengthened the organization's commitment to Pan-Africanism, with SNCC even using "'One Man, One Vote,' a rallying cry in African anti-colonial struggles" for its voter registration campaign.[36]

In 1969, Stokely Carmichael, former SNCC chairman and Black Panther Party prime minister, relocated to Guinea and spent the last three decades of his life there. Carmichael, who had popularized the concept of "Black power" in the U.S., renamed himself Kwame Ture in honor of his Pan-African mentors Kwame Nkrumah and Sékou Touré, and tirelessly advocated for Pan-Africanism through his work with the All-African People's Revolutionary Party. It's important to note that there were also leaders in the movement who never stepped foot on African soil but viewed themselves as internationalists and Pan-Africanists nonetheless. Ella Baker is a primary example of a Civil Rights leader who grounded her international solidarity in interpersonal relationships and support of Pan-African causes on the U.S. front.[37]

U.S. institutions have continued to draw our attention toward the contemporary relevance of Pan-Africanism. Organizations, like TransAfrica Forum, founded by Randall Robinson in 1977, have sought to influence U.S. foreign policy toward Africa and the diaspora. TransAfrica was instrumental in the formation of the Free South Africa Movement. During the 1980s, Black student unions and campus organizers politicized a generation via their participation in the South African anti-apartheid movement. Student leaders organized support to get their campuses to divest from corporations that were doing business in South Africa. Countless hip-hop-generation activists have pointed to this, along with Jesse

Jackson's 1984 and 1988 campaigns for presidency, as formative to their political evolution.

In 1993, Malcolm X Grassroots Movement (MXGM), a Black nationalist Pan-Africanist formation, was founded. One of the organization's core principles is "Free the Land," which it adopted from the Black activist organization the Republic of New Afrika, founded in 1968. The slogan is shorthand to proclaim "South Carolina, Georgia, Alabama, Mississippi, and Louisiana, as well as other areas of what is now called the Black-Belt South" as an "independent Black Nation."[38]

THE TIES THAT BIND

There are countless U.S.- and Africa-based organizers developing interpersonal relationships and supporting one another's organizations. This became apparent to me during my years of living on the continent, as I would often break bread with organizers within the Movement for Black Lives who were visiting African countries (oftentimes South Africa) on delegations or fellowships that sought to align U.S. racial justice and human rights organizations with African ones.

In an ideal world, Pan-African voices would be just as prominent today as they were in times past. Many in my generation were not familiar with Nigerian writer and MacArthur Genius Grant–winner Chimamanda Ngozi Adichie's work until Beyoncé sampled her TEDx Talk, "We Should All Be Feminists." While Adichie was already an award-winning writer and in the national literary discourse, she remained relatively unknown to most Black American millennials until the sample in "Flawless" made her increasingly popular in the mainstream. Yet still, her popularized work was always placed within a U.S. feminist framework, without substantive parallels made between the struggles of African American and African women. Media was all too eager to market Adichie as a beauty, style, and fashion icon, with little attention given to her decision to primarily wear Nigerian designers due to what she called the "disastrous economic policies"[39] of the Nigerian government.

In our modern media climate with vast information sharing, it can be even harder to be in consistent, meaningful conversation with African thought leaders because so much of U.S. mainstream coverage is American-focused. In contrast, social media platforms like Facebook, Instagram, Twitter (X), and TikTok have drawn a generation of young Africans down the rabbit hole of American cultural trends. They know our artists, dance trends, and latest crazes. U.S. entertainers and organizations have taken notice of this and are now making efforts to reach young African audiences. Examples of this are the Afropunk Festival and Global Citizen Festival: Mandela 100 (headlined by Beyoncé and Jay-Z) that was hosted in Johannesburg, South Africa.

Nigerian musical artists like Burna Boy, Davido, Rema, Tiwa Savage, and Wizkid have now gained immense popularity in the U.S. with a generational adoration for Afrobeats. We have also seen a growing interest in South African house music, particularly amapiano, and dance trends like the gwara gwara. It's hard to forget Bose Ogulu, mother of Nigerian singer Burna Boy, accepting a BET award on her son's behalf in 2019 and saying, "Every Black person should please remember that you were Africans before you were anything else."[40]

As much as I would caution us against the pitfalls of social media, I must admit that it has simultaneously become a tool of transcontinental unity and "virtual pan-Africanism," as Yannick

Giovanni Marshall wrote about in a May 2020 article in Al Jazeera.[41] Black Americans are not the only ones utilizing social media to voice outrage over injustice. Africans who share the same dreams of freedom are also using social media as a tool of social activism. During the COVID-19 pandemic in April 2020, reports arose accusing China of profiling and mistreating Africans, which Marshall defined as "Chinese Jim Crow."[42] He went on to describe the power that social media has in unifying the African diaspora against "pandemic anti-Blackness."[43] Marshall writes, "While we wait for the red, black, and green jets to take to the air, pan-Africanism is already here. Black and African social media reflects a pan-Africanism of the everyday. [Mobilizing] seemingly out of nowhere, community forms to rage against racist evictions in China, to rally against police killings in France or to discuss the latest Solange album."[44]

Virtual Pan-Africanism was at play in 2015 when South African students led the Rhodes Must Fall protest movement, calling for the University of Cape Town to stop honoring the legacy of Cecil Rhodes by removing his statue and stirring a larger, global conversation about decolonizing education. These protests garnered international support, especially among Black college students all over the world who saw Rhodes as a symbol of the disparities at their own institutions of learning. For example, Wabantu Hlophe, a freshman at Yale at the time, wrote an article titled "Rhodes Must Fall Everywhere," rightfully connecting the struggles faced by students in South Africa to white supremacist practices within higher education globally.[45]

Two years later, in 2017, protesting Yale students celebrated a victory when Calhoun College, one of the university's residential colleges, was renamed in honor of computer scientist and naval officer Grace Murray Hopper. The students argued that John C. Calhoun was a known white supremacist who advocated for the institution of slavery. While initially refusing to make the name change, the university later conceded. According to the *New York Times*, "Addressing a related concern, the school also decided then that the leaders of the residential colleges would no longer use the title 'master,' and would instead be called 'heads of college.'"[46]

THE CASE FOR CONTEMPORARY PAN-AFRICANISM

For communities enduring constant marginalization and imperialistic oppression, self-isolating and being insular is not an option. Internationalism becomes a matter of survival and a strategy for progression that understands that successful movements have often had a global dimension. Black Americans and Africans must find common ground in our shared pursuit of liberation. Commonalities should be recognized in our assertions that we have a right to self-determination, sustenance, and safety. This struggle, rooted in human rights, justice, dignity, and land ownership, has played out throughout history across the globe. And the struggle continues (or "a luta continua").

Common threads in our plight are easily identifiable, but long-term solutions to our problems are harder to pin down. When you look back to the fall of apartheid in South Africa, you can see the power of economics in the struggle for freedom when consumer boycotts, economic sanctions, and corporate divestments come into play. Unfortunately, the modern-day African American buying power has never been fully weaponized to the extent that it should be in the U.S. What would happen if Africans and Afro-descendants unified in global boycott campaigns against brands that don't serve our Pan-African interests? Why don't we collectively divest from North American and European corporations implicated in racial and economic injustice? What would it mean to wield the Black dollar in the name of resistance and liberation? How much more powerful would we be if we viewed our consumption as a key factor in gaining liberation for all?

Tragically, so many Americans do not have a healthy curiosity about other countries and their people's plights. It's not merely intellectual laziness and the myth of American exceptionalism. By American socioeconomic conditioning, we are engineered toward individualism. From our academic institutions to our daily media coverage, this country is committed to navel-gazing at every level of society. Just compare CNN's news coverage to that of Al Jazeera. Even BBC World News has a "Focus on Africa" segment, whereas many U.S. news networks would lead you to believe that we live in a one-continent world. Anyone wanting to learn more about what's happening in Africa and the diaspora would have to curate their own information portals and experiences to ensure they are not limiting themselves to the North American bubble.

Complex tensions arise when African Americans seek to connect with Africa in meaningful ways. There will always be the threat of anti-American sentiments. Good intentions and racial solidarity can so easily be overshadowed by the negative perceptions widely held about Americans in various parts of the world. The most common accusations will be ignorance, romanticization, and poverty tourism. There is often a social price for Black Americans to pay when dreaming about Africa.

In contrast, the American Dream (despite all its failings) is given a global pass and celebrated by so many nations. This is why African Americans, whenever engaging Africa, must be fully aware of their dual identity as descendants of enslaved Africans *and* citizens of the most privileged country on earth. For this reason, Black Americans would ideally be humble and knowledge-seeking in the desire to reconnect with Africa and, in turn, Africans would ideally be gracious and compassionate in their responses to those efforts. As mainstream media has fed both of us endless lies about one another, we have a lot to unlearn and learn.

DECOLONIZING OUR MINDS AND HABITS

For me, learning about Africa meant I had to interrogate my own privilege. I also had to center Africa in my understanding of the world and decentralize the U.S. Centering Africa meant allowing Africa to teach me about herself rather than leaning on what I had previously learned about her through elite Western education and mainstream media. I had to do this because although I was born in Africa, I am now American in citizenship and assimilation. My years living on the continent revealed how Americanized my worldview and day-to-day practices are.

When I think back on the lessons learned, I most often remember all the men, women, and even children I met on the continent who were anything but aid-seeking, unlike how Africa is stereotypically depicted. For those who didn't know where their next meal would come from, it was clear that they had been socialized to never speak the truth of their hunger. In fact, it is customary in many African cultures to reject food offerings repeatedly, accepting only when you are "forced" to eat out of respect. And when you do eat, you should ensure that those around you can as well.

I learned this lesson early on when my Zambian husband and I were dating in Johannesburg. He often worked long days at the clothing store his family owned and rarely took time out to sit and eat. I would try to surprise him with a meal every now and then. One day, I went there with a sandwich, fries, and a can of soda. He kindly handed the food back to me and said, "I can't eat this." Knowing that he wasn't allergic to anything, this puzzled me. I asked, "Why? What's wrong?" His response was one I would have never expected: "I can't eat it because there's not enough for everyone." I had never noticed that he and his brothers always ensured they had enough food for every individual present in the room. From that day onward, I always bought enough food for the collective that often gathered at their clothing store. Instead of buying food for one person, I would order family-size options. Through rationing and sharing, we always made it work and no one was ever left out. What a never-forgotten lesson about the power of communalism and economic interconnectedness that was for me. It speaks to the small but transformative ways that we can continue to build Pan-African ideological bridges from anywhere in the world.

A MILLENNIAL'S PAN-AFRICAN AWAKENING

For so many of the poor and working-class Africans I met on the continent, sustenance was a day-to-day burden. I was among a people whose daily bread and labor were so deeply connected to the temperament of the land that reverence for God was not optional but a means of survival. During the three years I was there, southern Africa (like much of Africa) was in a perpetual state of drought. The people were looking to the sky for rain and the farmers were looking to the ground for vegetation. The situation was particularly dire in Cape Town, as the dried-up dams led to water supplies being cut off in homes. No one was permitted to use water on their lawns or cars. And news reports showed video footage of people lined up for miles at designated water suppliers, holding empty containers. Similarly, an energy crisis in South Africa often led to load-shedding, in which scheduled power blackouts would take place in various regions and neighborhoods, halting activities and shutting down all businesses.

It was around this same time, in May 2019, that TIME magazine's cover story on "The World's Most Unequal Country" depicted South Africa as divided between impoverished townships and affluent suburbs.[47] Aryn Baker, a TIME senior correspondent, writes in the article, "The World Bank last year deemed South Africa the world's most unequal society, estimating that the top 10% owned 70% of the nation's assets in 2015. And the split is still largely along racial lines; the bottom 60%, largely comprising blacks . . . controls 7% of the country's net wealth. Half the population lives on less than $5 a day."[48]

It was because of these very reasons that South Africa became the site of my own Pan-African awakening. It has been nearly thirty years since the fall of apartheid, and everything about the land still preserves white supremacy and white monopoly capital. The policing of Black people is a very profitable industry in the country. Private security companies are hired to do what privileged people don't trust the South African Police Service to do: prevent Johannesburg's notoriously dangerous organized crime network from reaching the white suburban neighborhoods. This is similar to the U.S. use of militarized policing to dominate communities of color.

Make no mistake, there are Black South Africans who have come into previously unimaginable power and concentrated wealth. Some are living lives of excess and opulence, while the majority is barely surviving. Still, Mother Nature herself has been woven into the fabric of de facto segregation in the country. Proximity to abundant greenery (and lack thereof) seems to directly correlate with economics and race. It became impossible for me to see trees hovering over segregated housing without thinking of a fortress that shields the wealthy and conspires with oppressive forces. Even the positioning of branches and bushes is manipulated in favor of the rich and their obsessive desire for protection from the "locals."

This obsession with containment reminded me of my ministry in prisons. Through security screenings, every effort was made to ensure nothing entered that could free the imprisoned people—always disproportionately Black. Beyond the Bible, that is. In the U.S. context, these practices of occupation originate with our government's genocidal acts and ongoing atrocities against Indigenous peoples. More than any other place, occupied Palestine made me personally aware of freedom of movement, as well as the link between liberation and land. As I witnessed in the West Bank, Palestinians are dominated through border walls, checkpoints, and the presence of the Israel Defense Forces. Gaza, which is facing the threat of genocide and ethnic cleansing (a 2023 Nakba) as I write this, is widely known as "the world's largest open-air prison." Palestinians, like South Africans, have continuously resisted settler colonialism and apartheid—a crime against humanity. In post-apartheid South Africa, the privatized, residential replication of prisons prevails to keep the oppressed "where they belong."

I wondered how South Africa, with its Black presidential and parliamentary leadership, could still be living through what looks to the human eye like modern-day apartheid. This led me to think back to the efforts of Nelson Mandela and the African National Congress (ANC) to negotiate a new way of life for free South Africans. In the *TIME* article, Aryn Baker argues that "Mandela's rainbow nation was supposed to show the world how a new, equitable society could be built out of the ashes of repression and racism. But by some measures, inequality in the country today is worse than it was under apartheid."[49] We, especially us outsiders, weren't there in their moments of sacrifice, we didn't face death like they did, we didn't have to bury hate to go on living, and we will never know what led them to make the concessions they made.

The ANC inherited political power from the apartheid regime, but Black South Africans did not collectively gain economic power. In May 2023, South Africa's unemployment rate stands at 32.9 percent, according to Reuters.[50] As a point of comparison, the U.S. unemployment rate is 3.7 percent.[51] The unemployment and housing crisis faced by Black South Africans has led many prominent anti-apartheid leaders, including Winnie Mandela herself, to be very outspoken about their critiques of the ANC. According to *USA Today*, "Mandela's ex-wife, Winnie Madikizela-Mandela, told [journalist] Nadira Naipaul in 2010 that, 'Mandela let us down. He agreed to a bad deal for the blacks,' she said. 'Economically, we are still on the outside. The economy is very much "white." It has a few token blacks, but so many who gave their life in the struggle have died unrewarded.'"[52] Opposition parties like the Economic Freedom Fighters (EFF) continually voice these same sentiments. Unlike other newly independent African countries, South Africans were left to share a vast amount of their land with their oppressors.

I wonder how history may have unfolded differently if martyred South Africans Steve Biko and militant Chris Hani had lived to manifest their visions of a liberated South Africa. The Black Consciousness Movement, led by Biko and others, understood that a mandate for liberation was that oppressed and exploited Black people had to reclaim their sense of collective pride and intrinsic worth. Considering so much anti-colonial and anti-apartheid resistance has been rooted in Marxism, I always wrestled with how critics of "identity politics" reconcile the role that race and identity have always played in African and U.S. liberation movements. In 2016, historian Vijay Prashad explained to me the importance of "dignity politics," which affirms the particularities of who we are as we seek collective freedom from oppressive forces. This crystalized an understanding of how important human dignity is in having a Pan-African framework.

AN AFRICAN PILGRIMAGE COMES TO AN END

The natural beauty of South Africa will forever be etched in my mind as one of the reasons that the apartheid regime fought so hard to hold on to its claim to the land. But it was always about the country's mineral resources. According to the South African government, "South Africa holds the world's largest reported reserves of gold, platinum group metals, chrome ore and manganese ore, and the second-largest reserves of zirconium, vanadium and titanium."[53] That's why Dutch and British settlers sought to occupy and Europeanize Cape Town, with their homes perched alongside its mountains and waterfronts. That's why they bore generations of children raised to believe they are all parts African and that the land belongs to them and their descendants—they had no intention of ever leaving. Africa had become home and no longer a mining or colonial endeavor.

I knew that there's no corner of the globe we can go to escape white supremacy, certainly not South Africa of all places. Still, I had come in search of freedom, believing that history had proven the land to be equally devoted to this quest. I wanted so much to believe that freedom would be found there, as the struggle was so hard-fought in the country. But the systemic greed of the elite class was too powerful, creating masses of people so economically disenfranchised that they believed they had nothing to lose or live for. South Africa, like many other so-called developing nations, teaches us that poverty should not evoke our pity but instead our sense of urgency.

As #BlackLivesMatter grew to be an international phenomenon, many in South Africa said that the sentiment didn't apply in a country where xenophobic attacks against foreigners are so common.[54] In 2019, the severity of attacks was haunting, with dozens reported dead and hundreds arrested for looting. Storefronts owned by foreign nationals were being burned down, and many believed the South African government was doing very little to curtail the violence. Opportunistic politicians spewed dangerous rhetoric that blamed African foreigners for mass unemployment among South Africans. The situation became so volatile that Nigerian nationals began to board airplanes to leave Johannesburg and repatriate to Nigeria by invitation of the Nigerian government.

This doesn't change the fact that during my time in southern Africa, I experienced a sense of peace and wholeness unlike anything I had ever known before. I ceased obsessing over productivity and gave myself, daily, the gift of stillness. My pace of life in various countries of Africa gave me permission, for the first time, to live fully in the present and not be imprisoned by my regrets over the past and fears of the future. I was transformed by the spirit of South Africans who, in declaring *"Amandla Awethu!"* ("power to the people"), taught me to never lose faith in people's capacity to change the world around them. I was equally transformed, however, by seeing the socioeconomic disparities between Black and white South Africans. The divide made me more committed to reclaiming Africa back to Africans.

Learning of Nipsey's murder months before my return to the U.S. was a painful reminder of the world I was stepping back into and the world I was leaving behind. His death symbolized, for me at the time, the dying of a cutting-edge, community-driven ideology. Those bullets put an end to a young life that had beautifully housed two freedom-driven worlds. Similarly, I was terrified that a return to the United States would mean death to the new Pan-African identity and values I had cultivated. I knew Africa had changed me, and I was terrified that I would quickly slip back into old ways of being.

As I found myself grieving the end of my time on the continent, Gregory C. Ellison II, a professor and author, shared the words that led to a breakthrough: "Africa was a pilgrimage for you. You've taken many in your life, but South Africa was different. It reminds me of Malcolm's journey to Mecca and how it transformed him. You've now taken your hajj. This hajj has renamed you and given you a new identity. You will never be the same again."

Today, I am comforted in my knowing that the freedom struggle lives on, despite the soil that may hold it up. I look out from this American wilderness wondering: What is the pathway for twenty-first-century Pan-Africanism? What does the millennial Pan-Africanism landscape look like? What are intercontinental examples of Pan-Africanist activism and efforts among millennials? Where can we find inspiration and hope for the future? Who are some of the emerging intellectuals and practitioners? What should millennial activists be doing to build out the next generational phase of Pan-Africanism? How can we continue to build in small ways? And what new languages of intimacy can we create?

Ellison's words gave me hope that the sense of death I was experiencing was rooted in a rebirth. His words released me from the fear that my freedom was fixed in a particular place, in Africa, or a particular time, the past. By leaving Africa, her people, and culture, I was not losing my access to liberation or ending my journey of self-determination. Freedom is reclaimed when it is embodied—housed and carried within our minds, bodies, and souls. Present regardless of geographical or socioeconomic circumstances. In the words of Kwame Nkrumah: "I am not African because I was born in Africa but because Africa was born in me."[55] Similarly, freedom must be (re)born in us.

PART THREE

◆

REDEMPTION

The Promised Land: A Site of Divine Fulfillment

This final part turns to what we can do to find generational resolution and healing. These chapters focus on
crafting the new earth and "beloved community"—with
Black liberation, love, and spirituality as the bedrock.
As this section seeks to paint a vision of wholeness, it
weaves together empowerment, social transformation,
and liberating theology. We are guided toward contemporary framings of self-determination and a vision of
revolutionary love. This part speaks to the manifestation
of God's promises to God's people, both individually and
collectively. I approach God as a source of hope, vessel
for healing, and pathway to freedom. Be encouraged to
take full ownership of the promise that "God has not
given us a spirit of fear, but of power and of love and of a
sound mind" (2 Timothy 1:7, KJV).

7

❖

Self-Determination

The Real Black Excellence

*If you have come here to help me, you
are wasting your time. But if you have
come because your liberation is bound up
with mine, then let us work together.*
—Aboriginal activist group from Queensland

While I was a student at Yale working toward my Master of Divinity degree, feminist icon Gloria Steinem was a guest speaker. Someone in the audience asked her, "When will we know that women have arrived in terms of freedom and justice?" Steinem responded, "When women can birth themselves before they birth their babies." This answer has now been etched in my mind for nearly two decades. I reflect on it often, asking myself what I have left to "birth" within myself and how to balance that with motherhood. Without saying it explicitly, Steinem was making a statement about self-determination—the capacity to craft our lives on our own terms. She rightfully understood that freedom and self-determination must go hand in hand.

As Black people living within the American empire, our human rights continue to be violated and our efforts at self-determination are systematically undermined and sabotaged. We have seen this through redlining, loan discrimination, the FBI's targeting of Black freedom fighters and organizations, educational and housing inequalities, and racist hiring and promotion practices. Some of our leaders have endeavored to build a self-governed Black nation. Others have called on the U.S. to remove legal, political, and socioeconomic obstacles that prevent us from obtaining justice and living lives of dignity. This would require implementing policies and institutional groundwork so that Black Americans are no longer treated as second-class citizens. In an era that is hyperobsessed with defining "Black excellence" as individual self-advancement and exceptionalism,[1] self-determination is the real Black excellence.

A FUNDAMENTAL HUMAN RIGHT AND FREEDOM

According to the United Nations charter, self-determination can be understood as a part of what it means to be human, is foundational to human rights, and is a "fundamental [freedom] for all without distinction as to race, sex, language, or religion."[2] The complex postcolonial realities faced by young, independent African countries have shown that freedom is very difficult to actualize in any quest for self-determination. We can aspire to it, imagine it, take up arms for it, and work to build a free, sovereign nation. But nothing guarantees that we will ever truly experience *freedom*, because it's one thing for nations to declare themselves liberated and something categorically different for civilians on the ground to be living freely. History has shown that liberation movements can come at a huge cost to human rights, as victors morph into dictators. So many African countries have yet to fully reap the holistic fruits of their independence struggles.

At the same time, Pan-Africanists are called to abhor and resist the imperialistic hand of superpowers that seek to obstruct the self-determination of nations. As it did with Cuba, the United States can make indefinite enemies out of countries asserting their sovereignty, punishing innocent civilians through blockades, embargoes, and sanctions. While forcibly shoving democracy down the throats of others, the U.S. maintains a "democratic" process that is polluted by voter suppression, monied interests, the electoral college, and a combative two-party political system that often ties the hands of the sitting president. As U.S. politicians critique the leadership of "Third World" leaders, their own constituents are reduced to awaiting rhetorical crumbs falling from legislative tables paid for by lobbyists.

It is important to pay attention to how the self-determination of various groups is being undermined. While this nation was founded in the aftermath of the American Revolution, it has always struggled to honor the rights of all. One of the reasons is that, at times, politicians selectively ignore the line that demarcates Church and State. Like millions of other Americans, I never imagined *Roe v. Wade* would be overturned in my lifetime. Among all the atrocities of Donald Trump's legacy, we must factor in the appointment of three conservative Supreme Court justices who will shape U.S. policies that will affect generations to come. We are collectively living under the power of the most conservative Supreme Court to exist in the past ninety years.[3]

The near half-century precedent of the constitutional right to abortion came to an end seemingly overnight. This vicious attack on bodily autonomy was a haunting reminder that conservatives want full control over our lives, and they have no intentions of stopping until they get what they want. While conservatives claim to be pro-life, many do not support the social policies that improve the quality of life for children such as access to free and universal healthcare, quality public education, and living wages for the working class. Rather than fighting for policies rooted in the will of the people, they are committed to their own utopian ideals—regardless of what the consequences are for people's everyday lives. And Democrats have not done enough to stop them.[4]

The political arena has every aspect of our privacy under siege. Conservatives want to dictate who we are intimate with, what does and does not happen in the bedrooms of consenting adults, and the decisions we make thereafter. This is truly an extension of a heteropatriarchy that uses laws to police our bodies. But the State has no right to control who we love, what consenting adults do sexually in the privacy of their homes, or reproductive decisions that have lifelong implications. The emerging anti-abortion laws in various Republican states reflect archaic conceptions of womanhood. Women are viewed primarily as homemakers and child bearers whose function in life is to tend to the needs of husbands and children. The individuality of women is completely disregarded. There is no concern for our health challenges, personal circumstances, desires, and fears. According to conservatives, what matters most is the woman's role in society as a conduit of life.

At the same time, government investment in the socioeconomic advancement of marginalized groups continues to be critiqued, resisted, or altogether blocked. As an example, there has been no cross-class, culturally enshrined investment in adequate paid maternity leave, equalizing wages with men, or affordable childcare. If there was a commitment to quality of life for all citizens, then everything would be done to equip women and families with what is needed to flourish in and out of the home. If conservatives were truly committed to reducing abortion rates, they would more widely support policies that protect women and girls, provide working families the holistic support needed, and ensure better health outcomes for all Americans.

UNDERMINING POLITICAL AUTONOMY

Another enduring targeted attack on self-determination is on Black political power. The United States would benefit from having more political parties at the forefront of American politics, particularly more that speak honestly about exploitation and oppression with no desire to maintain political correctness. How do we even begin to speak of self-determination without political autonomy? The Democratic Party has taken us for granted for generations. Most recently, millions of people worldwide have demanded a cease-fire in besieged Gaza. After years of being associated with empathy, President Joe Biden maintained unwavering support for Israel's bombardments and invasion, as did almost all of Congress. Despite around-the-clock killings of civilians, mostly children and women. Only by continuously raising up our own political leaders and pushing forward our own agenda will this country take us seriously. Despite all the social mobilization and uprisings that have taken place in the U.S. over the past sixty years, this country's two-party system strategically consolidates power to keep new parties from emerging and having viability.

By contrast, in South Africa, a country where the Black population fought fiercely for the right to self-determination, the political terrain is slightly different and offers us nuances for consideration. The African National Congress (ANC) has maintained political power since the end of apartheid and the formation of a democratic government in 1994. They win every presidential election, essentially making South Africa a one-party democratic system. However, the people of South Africa benefit from having several registered political parties that can hold the ANC accountable.

The Economic Freedom Fighters (EFF), which describes itself as "a radical, leftist, anti-capitalist and anti-imperialist movement"[5] fighting for "economic emancipation,"[6] is the most outspoken and visible opposition party. Julius Malema, a member of parliament and former ANC Youth League president who was ousted in 2011,[7] cofounded EFF in 2013 and serves as its leader. EFF prioritizes remedying a mass housing and unemployment crisis. In its "2021 Elections Manifesto," EFF lists "seven non-negotiable cardinal pillars" that include government ownership of land in South Africa; land redistribution without compensation; "[nationalization] of mines, banks, and other strategic sectors of the economy, without compensation"; and "free quality education, healthcare, houses, and sanitation."[8] While the EFF is not without its faults, like any other political party, it reflects an unapologetic commitment to imagining and building the socialist Africa that so many Pan-African leaders envisioned. Political victories should not only be measured by votes; every generation needs a political arm that reflects and speaks to the deepest needs of the people.

In the U.S., the political process continues to work against our self-determination through unfulfilled promises, frustrating many

Black voters, particularly millennials.[9] The election of Barack Obama as president showed that Superman is not coming to save us. While charismatic, inspiring leadership may invigorate us and offer hope, the U.S. political system is not designed to bring about radical social change. Time and time again, we have learned that the transformative policies we desperately need will not be enacted by a single political leader.

Yet, we continue to place our faith in the Democratic Party, believing that we will not endure the same harm under their leadership as we would under Republican rule. There is absolute truth in this when you consider the reversal of *Roe v. Wade* and countless other conservative policies. But it is tragic that we must *always* succumb to a default "lesser of two evils" vote, viewing Green Party or independent candidates as a "wasted vote" that divides liberals and empowers conservatives. And even that vote is not fully protected. Will it always be like this? We deserve so much better.

To disenfranchise Black voters they fear will support Democrats, some conservatives are complicating and frustrating the voting experience in Black communities, which is yet another attack on our self-determination. If we believe our vote won't count, we will remove ourselves from the political process. And that's exactly what many want us to do—surrender electoral politics over without a fight.

BUILDING BLACK POLITICAL POWER

This is why the work of Georgia politician Stacey Abrams is so critical. Through the New Georgia Project and Fair Fight, she has helped put election reform at the forefront of the American news cycle. Similarly, Black Voters Matter, founded by Cliff Albright and LaTosha Brown in 2016, and When We All Vote, launched by Michelle Obama in 2018, have been working toward voter education, registration, protection, and engagement.[10] Black Voters Matter also focuses on policy advocacy and organization development and training.[11] These are a few national organizations, but countless local grassroots entities are also driving this work.

In a long history of Black conventions that dates to the nineteenth century, our people have always known the importance of building Black political power. The 2004 National Hip-Hop Political Convention, which met in Newark, New Jersey, used the 1972 National Black Political Convention in Gary, Indiana, as a model. The 2004 convention sought to create a national political agenda for Black people via an inclusive, from the ground up, participatory process. Both were built on the successes of the Mississippi Freedom Democratic Party of 1964, in which Fannie Lou Hamer was an original member, and the Lowndes County Freedom Party, which was originally formed as the Lowndes County Freedom Organization in 1965.

In recent years, the Movement for Black Lives, which held its own national convening of young Black activists in 2015, has laid out a robust policy platform called the "Vision for Black Lives." Within it, there is a higher calling toward abolition of all forms of State violence that demands this country "end the war on Black people."[12] The policy calls for the U.S. to divest from "exploitative forces" and "exploitative corporations"[13] and instead invest in Black communities. It demands reparations and economic justice. In relation to public safety, the policy calls on the U.S. government to enact and finance community control. Another demand is the respect and protection of protestors' rights. Perhaps one of the most important policy demands is for "independent Black political power and Black self-determination in all areas of society."[14] As we navigate our way through a militarized society, we are challenged and inspired to imagine a world where all systems of oppression and exploitation have been abolished. This creates the conditions for political autonomy and power.

REVOLUTIONARY INTERCOMMUNALISM

The Black Panther Party gave us a model of what revolutionary intercommunalism could look like. More important, through their "survival programs," the Panthers presented a road map to self-determination. They offered over sixty community-based programs, including child development support, educational classes, free breakfast programs for children, free health clinics, employment referral services, and legal clinics.[15] By meeting the holistic needs of Black communities, they debunked the idea that the government had to be the sole provider of a community's needs. According to PBS, the Panthers' programs reflected "Black people getting themselves organized together so that they could survive outside the municipal, state or federal systems, which were already under-servicing the Black community. It was not a new idea: minority communities across America had done this in previous decades to support new immigrants through communal associations and political machines."[16] How can the Panthers' commitment to "revolutionary intercommunalism"[17] inspire and guide us today?

Human Rights Watch rightfully states that we must "reimagine public safety through the lens of community health" because "neighborhoods with adequate housing, economic opportunity, supportive health services, and quality education best ensure safety."[18] In U.S. communities, organizations have sought to define public safety on their own terms. In East Pittsburgh, for example, Jasiri X (1Hood Media) and Brandi Fisher (Alliance for Police Accountability) worked together with other organizations in the aftermath of the local George Floyd protests in 2020 to convene a coalition that would create a community-led vision for public safety.[19]

They were in conversation with people in other cities that were pioneering the work and then built on that. According to *Black Pittsburgh*, "They'd seen things like cuts to the police budget in Seattle; ending qualified immunity for officers in New York City and getting healthcare professionals instead of police to show up for mental health calls in Denver."[20] Community organizing efforts in Pittsburgh have contributed to many public safety and political victories, including the removal of police officers from schools in Woodland Hills School District, the police force in East Pittsburgh being dissolved, and the election of the first Black mayor in Pittsburgh.[21]

Too often, the focus is placed on solutions to police brutality when what is really at stake is Black self-determination. There is no way that we can have autonomy over our lives and our communities when we are under constant threat of violence at the hands of police officers. Our people are incapable of living free, self-actualized lives while under the threat of incarceration for the simplest of infractions. Self-determination and abolition are two sides of the same coin. One side envisions the liberation we seek and the other puts an end to systems that hold us in bondage.

The legacy of the Panthers serves to remind us that our self-determination is dependent on our eradication of *all* forms of State violence, including attacks on our well-being through environmental racism. How do we put an end to "food apartheid"[22] and ensure that Black people have access to quality, nutritious food? How do we protect our communities from the pollution, infestation, waste, lead, and asbestos that contribute to countless long-term illnesses? How do we work to prevent and address toxic water systems? What needs to be done to ensure millennials and Gen Z are equipped for green-collar jobs?

Cutting-edge work has been and continues to be done in the realm of environmental justice. Pioneering and contemporary models include but are not limited to: WE ACT, Alternatives for Community & Environment (ACE), Sustainable South Bronx, Soul Fire Farm, Black Dirt Farm Collective, the Center for Rural Enterprise and Environmental Justice, BLK + GRN, and the Black Church Food Security Network (BCFSN). Founded in response to the 2015 killing of Freddie Gray Jr. and the Baltimore Uprising, BCFSN seeks to "help Black churches use their assets to establish gardens on their land, host miniature farmer's markets, and buy wholesale from Black farmers."[23] Strategies for self-determination have always existed within our communities. Too often, finances and infrastructure have prevented us from actualizing them. The Baltimore Children & Youth Fund (BCYF), which funds community-based organizations servicing Baltimore youth through "3 percent of the city's property taxes," offers a model for funding that isn't dependent on the "nonprofit industrial complex."[24]

SELF-TRANSFORMATION: WHOLENESS AS REFUGE

Challenges to self-determination are systemic and, of course, individual. We should not ignore and neglect the personal dimension. Many of us have seen too much and lived through too much. So many of us walk through life in defense mode, constantly ready to "fight or [take] flight." This type of existence can make us a hindrance to our own self-determination. In reading Glennon Doyle's *Untamed*, I was deeply moved by her assertion that stillness is the pathway to a knowing that helps free us from fear, indoctrination, and the need to constantly seek other people's approval.[25] She writes, "The more consistently, bravely, and precisely I follow the inner Knowing, the more precise and beautiful my outer life becomes. The more I live by my own Knowing, the more my life becomes my own and the less afraid I become. I trust that the Knowing will go with me wherever I go, nudging me toward the next thing, one thing at a time, guiding me all the way home."[26]

There's a voice within us that intuitively knows more than what meets the eye. In my Christian framework, it's the assurance we have of the Holy Spirit's indwelling that guides us and protects us. Regardless of where you are in your spiritual journey, you too have an inner knowing that dwells deep within your gut. It offers a supernatural perspective on earthly matters. There's also a knowing that we cultivate through the trials and tribulations of life that programs fear into our hearts. One brings us closer to freedom; the other prevents us from ever being truly free.

Self-determination is a quest toward wholeness, and wholeness is refuge. It is the dream that God has for our lives. It is the ability to hear one's own inner voice and to allow God's whisperings to speak louder than anything else in our lives. God's dream for us is so much greater than any dream we could ever envision for ourselves. We all deserve wholeness and the internal certainty that we are a part of God's grand creation—no matter how chaotic or dismal the world around us may be. And no matter how far we may stray from a life of freedom.

As a guerilla fighter in Eritrea's war for independence, my eldest brother carried tactics of annihilation within his psyche all the way to the South Bronx and Washington, DC. During the crack epidemic, he made a name for himself in the streets of the nation's capital as a drug dealer. He went from fighting for the self-determination of an African nation to contributing to the drug proliferation that ravaged Black communities. The devil had a tight grip on him for decades, and it hurt everyone in his path, especially our family. Then, one day, it all finally caught up with him when he was sentenced to spend years in federal prison. Ironically, my brother believes it was while he was incarcerated that he found redemption and broke the chains that held him captive. His former self died in that prison, and he reemerged in society as a repentant, self-sacrificial man. He had become a new creation.

This became most apparent to me when he traveled all the way to Johannesburg to walk me down the aisle and flew to London during the pandemic to attend the funeral of an uncle who we lost to COVID. When our mother and sister died in the span of two months, he humbly assumed the role of an elder. As my mother's remains were in the cargo section of an airplane headed to Eritrea, he was on that flight, having laid the groundwork for her to have a dignified burial in her homeland. A man all too familiar with burial, who as a teenager had heaped mounds of soil on the bodies of his slain fellow comrades. Throughout my life, his animated, detailed stories normalized being a freedom fighter, political prisoner, and refugee. He gave me glimpses of revolution that I will hold on to my entire life. But now, his stories also speak of the responsibility of being a son, husband, and father. Out of my parents' eight children, it was he who built a home for our family in our grandfather's village in Eritrea and turned it into the final resting place of our mother and father.

My brother relates to young Black youth with the same intensity that he embodies African identity. Although he speaks with an immigrant's accent, you can always hear an intimacy with the streets and its rules of survival in his voice. From him, I learned that one's socioeconomic hardships and environmental conditioning can steer them toward a life of criminality and self-inflicted harm.

He taught me that unfreedom is the dehumanization and exploitation of poor people. Unfreedom is coveting what your enemy has and lacking gratitude for what God has given you. Unfreedom is loving money more than yourself, your family, and your community. Unfreedom is a soul surrendered to and imprisoned by the materialistic idols of this world. Unfreedom is a human being incapable of fully experiencing the joys of life because the lies of the enemy are constantly being whispered into their ears. But through the transformative and merciful power of God, as well as his own personal commitment to being a better human, my brother metamorphosed into a vessel of newfound, glorious self-determination. The spiritual awakening and holistic transformation of people who are determined to be liberated helps us imagine freedom as a finish line we can collectively reach.

When I had my own spiritual conversion experience at the age of twenty-one, I was finally freed of habits and ways of being I once thought were inescapable. The social norms of my culture and the behavioral trends of my generation no longer defined me. I truly felt that I had become "a new creation" and that "the old [had] passed away and the new [had] come" (2 Corinthians 5:17, LSV). My faith opened a gateway to self-determination. It was how I found the courage to not conform to who my family said I was supposed to be and who my peers expected me to be. Now the question was: Who did *God* create me to be? Trying to make sense of that question compelled me to turn inward and rediscover what my life experiences were trying to teach me. Self-determination is soul-searching and soul-excavating work. It takes a lot of courage and self-discipline to quiet the noises of this world and listen to the voice of an Eternal God.

PEOPLE POWER AND PROPHETIC DESTINY

On September 23, 1960, Ghana's first president, Kwame Nkrumah, stood before the United Nations General Assembly and spoke about "the dawn of a new era" for Africa.[27] He said, "The United Nations must therefore face up to its responsibilities, and ask those who would bury their heads like the proverbial ostrich in their imperialist sands, to pull their heads out and look at the blazing African sun now travelling across the sky of Africa's redemption."[28] Nkrumah was calling for a collective imagining of a self-governed, self-reliant Africa—one that had defiantly risen out of the ashes of colonialism. He didn't speak of a return to an Africa of the past; he was focused on the birth of an Africa that had never been.

The word that comes to mind when reading Nkrumah's statement is *destiny*. In one dictionary definition, *destiny* is defined as "the predetermined, usually inevitable or irresistible, course of events."[29] In this definition, the focus is on the outcome—the change itself. But in the Oxford Pocket American Dictionary, *destiny* is defined as "the hidden power believed to control what will happen in the future; fate."[30] The focus is on the *source* that will bring about change. In revolutionary struggle, that source that has the capacity to alter our collective destiny is the power of the people. The inexplicable strength and will that are cultivated when the masses unite against a common enemy. But what if we gave equal attention to the "hidden power" that equips the people to be steadfast and victorious?

As we try to grasp twenty-first-century self-determination, how much more strength would we derive from knowing a "hidden power" is propelling us toward the future we seek?

Within this framework, we are challenged to think beyond the natural world and consider the supernatural realm's hand in shaping our individual and collective destinies. A power greater than us is at work in our lives to guide us toward a future that now only lives in our imaginations but has a place in the world. Wouldn't we all want to think that God is a coconspirator in our struggle for freedom? If we believe we are *destined* for liberation, then it shifts our mindset from mere activism to prophetically ushering in the divine will of God.

Think about Harriet Tubman and Nat Turner to better understand what I mean. Both believed they were being supernaturally led. In *Scenes in the Life of Harriet Tubman*, she spoke about "dreams and visions" that showed her what was waiting for her "on the other side of that line" between terror and freedom.[31] Many believe that Tubman understood her dreams and visions as communication with God and used the North Star as her liberation compass. Similarly, Turner is believed to have looked for signs from God and been inspired by the Bible to lead a bloody revolt by enslaved people. Rex Ellis, a museum curator at the National Museum of African American History and Culture, where Turner's Bible is now housed, suggests that Turner was liberated by deciding to act: "From that point on, he had broken the chains, the chains that bound him mentally—he had broken them. That's a fabulously difficult thing to do."[32]

Historically, Americans have celebrated and paid homage to Tubman for her audacity, but vilified Turner because his vision included violence and a direct assault on white oppressors as a pathway to freedom. Through revisionist history, this country waters down our remembrance of their suffering and, in the case of Tubman, commodifies her legacy. What is our generation's North Star and what is it leading us toward? What in our own lives and communities serves as a guiding light that brings us closer to our individual and collective destinies?

Centuries later, it is rare to hear of the marriage between Black resistance and the Holy. God often seems distant and detached from our modern struggle. We are depicted as an earthly, divided army equipped with digital weapons and foundation funding. Rarely do we speak of the fight against white supremacy as a form of spiritual warfare. We do not consider the demonic realm's use of human evil to perpetuate traumatization. Our perception of battle is too narrow, too worldly. If we rely solely on our own capabilities, then we will surely be defeated and disappointed. However, if we lean on a power greater than ourselves, then self-determination can be reframed as Spirit-determination. The Spirit has a plan for our lives and is available to us as it was to our ancestors. Let us lift our eyes on high to derive supernatural, liberating power for ourselves and future generations.

IN THE AGE OF "SELF-MADE"

In the United States, individualism is normalized. People are celebrated for being successful even if that means they were unjust and unkind along the way. Our culture glorifies stories of how people overcame all the odds stacked against them and went on to achieve the American Dream. TV stars and their lavish lifestyles are idolized without consideration for the generational imprint they are making. Billionaires become thought leaders and political influencers simply because they have inherited or amassed limitless wealth. In our context, self-determination has morphed into "self-made" with the likes of the Kardashians being celebrated for building up media, beauty, and fashion empires.

Let the day come when the legacy of America's "heroes" is evaluated by our community-driven standards. On that day, we will separate the narcissists from the truth-tellers. We will glorify our martyrs rather than those who perfected the use of the enslavers' tools. Success will be based on communal principles rather than individual profit. No longer will we center "the table" as our benchmark for progress. Instead, we will celebrate the visionaries and griots of our time who can envision Afrofuturistic freedoms that have yet to be actualized. The American empire's desire to identify our heroes for us is a tool of domination that has multigenerational implications. The media cherry-picks the names it wants to immortalize.

Deep within us rests the knowing that we can define our best and brightest for ourselves. I am not calling for denunciation of celebrities. Instead, what I'm envisioning is that we prioritize liberation and self-determination over celebrity and hero worship. We owe our abolitionists so much more. We owe them our refusal to name contemporary figures as legends and icons simply because they meet capitalistic standards of achievement. I pray that we would redefine Black excellence so that it honors the sacrifices of our freedom fighters who were committed to self-determination.

AFRICA'S REDEMPTION AND OURS TOO

This begs the question: How has American imperialism deterred and even halted the African diaspora's search for freedom? The

U.S. has had many covert operations in Africa that have helped destabilize African countries and dethrone some of Africa's most beloved postcolonial leaders, particularly through coups backed by the Central Intelligence Agency (CIA).[33] Angola, Chad, the Congo, Ghana, Libya, Somalia, and Sudan are some of the countries that have been politically affected and/or wounded by the United States "meddling in Africa."[34]

A lot of history is distorted and censored by corporate media. In the meantime, hardworking Americans are so overwhelmed and defeated by the rat race that they do not have the bandwidth or time to compensate for the information deprivation. Our deepest concern is often the well-being of our own nuclear family, particularly our children, and that is more than enough to keep us occupied. Being American is an all-consuming reality that wreaks havoc on our physical and mental health. Daily, most of us are simply trying to survive and keep up with all the demands being hurled at us.

Yet, due to how our tax dollars are being used overseas, we should care more about U.S. foreign policies and practices. Yes, some of Americans' lack of knowledge of foreign affairs is due to disinterest and the myth of "American exceptionalism," but that does not always apply when it comes to working-class people who are trying to keep their heads above water. No matter the reasons, collective compromise happens. It is so easy to become a noncritical mass of people who are indifferent to the brutality inflicted on us and others by our government.

As anti-apartheid activist Winnie Madikizela-Mandela once said, "If you are to free yourselves, you must break the chains of oppression yourselves. Only then can we express our dignity. Only when we have liberated ourselves can we cooperate with other groups. Any acceptance of humiliation, indignity or insult is acceptance of inferiority."[35] Self-determination is not only about what we alter, cocreate, and control. There is more to it than just personal, economic, and political autonomy. Self-determination begins when we have individually and collectively shifted in consciousness, understanding how we have been oppressed, by whom and what, and to what end as well as how our oppression is part of a larger global history that connects us to other oppressed people we have never seen, met, or perhaps even heard of.

We experience an awakening from learning the "people's history,"[36] as Howard Zinn popularized, equipping us to contemplate and strategize pathways to liberation. All along this process (because it truly is a process), we are unlearning the propaganda perpetuated by white supremacy. The journey commences when we commit ourselves to seeking knowledge, listening deeply, and decolonizing our minds. In *Assata: An Autobiography*, former Black Panther Party and Black Liberation Army member Assata Shakur writes, "Nobody is going to give you the education you need to overthrow them. Nobody is going to teach you your true history, teach you your true heroes, if they know that that knowledge will help set you free."[37]

REVOLUTIONARY DISCIPLINE

When old ways of thinking and being are no longer serving us or our families, we must shift our focus and attention to becoming who our communities and the movement need us to be. As I researched Eritrea's protracted struggle for self-determination, I learned how important "revolutionary discipline"[38] was to the liberation movement. While some rules like forbidding alcohol use, profanity, and sex were considered rigid and harsh, the discipline of soldiers led to what became respected as "an intensely serious movement," according to historian and journalist Dan Connell in his book *Against All Odds*.[39]

Revolutionary discipline is a powerful oppositional stance for individuals and communities in defiance to oppressive forces. It has not always been the mode of operation in our movements, as some leaders become motivated by self-interests and personal gain. In contrast, the Panthers resisted the trappings of the status quo and the establishment at every turn. Their implementation of "survival programs" was intended not only to meet the basic needs of our people but also to start building a militant cadre of Black people ideologically committed to the principles of self-determination. They put their own lives at risk to create a better world. The significance of the concept of revolutionary discipline is that it gives us a blueprint for a self-sacrificial, transformative mindset. How should freedom seekers understand the world and in turn shift how they operate in it?

Self-determination is the heartbeat that keeps our freedom search alive. Today, we continue to be driven by a sublime vision of what we and the unborn generations deserve. Our minds, hearts, and souls yearn constantly for autonomy, longing for the day when we will live up to the promises and possibilities of Black power. We are fully equipped to be self-reliant—no longer suffocating under the unbearable weight of America's white elite greed, brutality, and narcissism. We are fully equipped to honor our sacred history, name our own leaders, draw the road map to our future political victories, and carve out the path for our own holistic liberation.

The oppressor has always lied and told us that freedom is unattainable and that the finish line is far from our reach. Yet, we know that we are the heirs to a predestined, glorious victory. As descendants of resilient and transcendent warriors, we must never forget that liberation is our birthright and self-determination is our destiny.

8

◈

Love

The Forgotten Revolution

Love is contraband in Hell, cause love
is an acid that eats away bars.
—Assata Shakur

Our present-day minds cannot grasp the full scope of the institution of slavery. One of the worst facets of the barbaric
system was that it ripped families apart from one another. Imagine
how traumatic it was for African husbands and wives to be disconnected not only from each other but also from their children,
parents, and siblings. The family unit has always been at the center
of African life. When Europeans seized Africans as their property
and labor force, they disrupted the communalism that is at the
heart of African identity.

Today, the U.S. prison-industrial complex and War on Drugs
are modern examples of the systemic disintegration of Black
families. These racist, institutionalized practices include unjust

sentencing laws and welfare stipulations that deter African American men from living at home with their partners and children.[1] As we imagine freedom, let's imagine a world in which we are healed of our division and are adamant about loving one another fiercely. How do we liberate ourselves from a love-obstructing country that we do not plan to leave? There's power in us reclaiming love as the forgotten revolution.

MARKET-DRIVEN CONCEPTIONS OF LOVE

Throughout the centuries, the message has been sent loud and clear that Black people are disposable. We are still combatting that lie today. We do so with every new incident of police brutality that shows this country's unwillingness to hold officers accountable for senselessly killing Black people. We also combat the lie when urban, drug-ridden communities are terrorized by homicide and gang violence. It is not easy to love what you have been told has no value and is unworthy of protection. Unlearning this lie about Black disposability puts us on the path to finding a love that transcends the stronghold of white supremacy.

We live in a dehumanizing era in which online dating applications allow you to "swipe" people away when they are not of interest to you. And in today's marketplace, workers are instructed to work as hard as humanly possible with the least number of benefits and protections. Our value in this country is determined by our capacity to earn "passive income" for others. While we may like to think that we check this mindset at the door when it comes to romantic love, that is not always the case.

The late YouTube star Kevin Samuels, who started his career as an image consultant, made it his business to (crudely) advise Black women on relationships and speak on the pitfalls of the "modern woman."[2] His legacy is a controversial one, having once called middle-aged unwed Black women "leftovers."[3] Samuels glorified men who are in control of their finances and have social status. In a *Guardian* op-ed, writer Andrew Lawrence says, "Casually drawing on relationship and income statistics, Samuels delighted in playing the role of market adjuster and scolding 'average' Black women for pursuing Black men in the Talented Tenth—good-looking men with minimum six-figure incomes, no kids, no priors, and no hang-ups in bed."[4] Samuels, like so many others who claim to be relationship experts, treated love as transactional. In this business-inspired framework, love is to be perpetually earned and reciprocated (rather than unconditionally bestowed). Yes, of course, love can be given as well as taken based on whether the person's expectations are being met, but at what point does love transcend the rules of market economy?

In a capitalist society, transactional love often comes as second nature due to our socialization in American culture. We even have holidays to reward people with gifts when they have met our standards for love. The commercial holiday of Christmas, for example, has little to do with the Messiah's arrival and has instead been branded as a gift-giving holiday. Valentine's Day commercializes love and reduces it to dinners, getaways, and gifts. Anniversaries and birthdays are equally capitalistic celebrations of couples and individuals. Additionally, a couple's engagement revolves around the size and cost of a ring, and their wedding planning fixates on the size and cost of the wedding day. Can we be more critical of these American "traditions"? How has capitalism corrupted our understanding of love? How do we reclaim love from profit-driven corporations?

Capitalism has even defined who our models of love should be. Due to the prominence of entertainment culture, our generation glorifies celebrity couples much more than we should. The concept of the "power couple" has been used to root our romantic aspirations in money and fame. The reality is that these couples tend to market their love story to the masses and turn it into a profitable product for public consumption. We may start out as spectators of their relationships, but they transform us into consumers. This has taken the form of contemporary Black celebrity couples launching joint business ventures, signing unprecedented deals, creating products targeted to children, and cultivating celebrity for their own children. Through social media, interviews, documentaries, and song lyrics, celebrity couples have often brought audiences into their intimate family experiences.

It's no secret that celebrities have long been racking up endorsement deals and releasing consumer products with their popularity driving sales. White celebrities were pimping out their lifestyles for public consumption long before Black people ever did so, but we cannot ignore how our societal obsession with celebrities is being used for market appeal and profit gain. While we don't expect entertainers to be selfless, some of us are conflating a commitment to capitalism with a love for Black people. The cultural landscape has not given us fertile ground for revolutionary love. Mainstream media has been reluctant to uplift the role models needed in music, television, film, social media, art, and so on. We are living in the most commercially driven era in human history. The market has nearly wiped out all traces of genuine love. Sex devoid of attachment is popularized everywhere you turn.

A PATHWAY FOR REVOLUTIONARY LOVE

Past generations had models of revolutionary love like Martin and Coretta, Malcolm and Betty, Nelson and Winnie, and Ossie and Ruby, who all gained prominence in the community through a shared commitment to Black liberation. Wealth was never the basis for the respect our community held for such well-known couples. Our leaders were revered based on their commitment to justice.

While there may have been moments or even seasons of glamour in their lives, they experienced hardships that many of us could not imagine today. They paid the price for freedom throughout their lives—to the point of imprisonment, death, and widowhood. Couples of the movement taught us that a life devoted to liberation means that you belong not only to yourself, your partner, and your family, but also to the people. You are part of a larger collective. Your life is your own, but it is also your love offering to your community and greater humanity. While we should not be criticized for trying to build generational wealth, there is a need to be very thoughtful about our individual and communal benchmarks for success. In recent decades, we have allowed capitalism to dictate our heroes and sheroes.

Actor Jesse Williams, whose passion for social justice has been evident from Ferguson to Gaza, is a gem. He walks in the footsteps of Harry Belafonte, who supported the civil rights struggle and mentored a new generation of freedom fighters, and Danny Glover, whose racial and labor justice work dates back to 1968.[5] Viola Davis, who once told *Vanity Fair* that "[her] entire life has been a protest,"[6] has spoken boldly about European standards of beauty in the media and the racism that Black women face in white, male-dominated Hollywood. A consistent truth-teller, Davis admitted to regretting her role in the 2011 film *The Help*, saying: "I betrayed myself, and my people, because I was in a movie that wasn't ready to [tell the whole truth]."[7] Kid Cudi, Jamie Foxx, Michael B. Jordan, Kehlani, John Legend, rap duo Black Star, Amandla Stenberg, and Kerry Washington also come to mind as celebrities who have amplified social justice and human rights issues. There are many more—too many to name—impacting change.

This is not to say that our role models today must all undergo what Joel Payne, a Democratic strategist, calls a "woke litmus test."[8] But as Union Theological Seminary professor Cornel West has said, "Justice is what love looks like in public, just like tenderness is what love feels like in private."[9] We should more often gauge the love that public figures have for our communities by their visible and tangible resistance to injustices. In religious, political, and entertainment circles, love is often reduced to charity. But sporadic acts of benevolence are not a sustainable means of social transformation. Charity and philanthropy are incapable of dismantling oppressive systems. The altruistic actions of well-meaning people will never be able to mend multigenerational racialized trauma. Whereas charity and philanthropy may be optional, justice is mandatory.

What is needed today more than ever before is revolutionary love that manifests itself in radical ways in every facet of society. This love, which is centered in justice and vows commitment to the holistic betterment of self and humanity, has the capacity to transform everything and everyone in its path. What would it look like to hold politicians without a capacity for revolutionary love accountable? How can we redesign the political fabric of our nation?

When we are personally and communally driven by revolutionary love, we become powerful agents of individual and social transformation. We possess the capacity to reconfigure the world around us through minute-to-minute and day-to-day acts of boldness and self-sacrifice. It takes unwavering compassion to declare that the poor are deserving of safety, housing, food, water, education, and employment. It takes fierceness to advocate for and strategize toward wealth redistribution and land reclamation and to call out the absence of universal health coverage in the United States as a human rights failure. It takes courage to demand the immediate release of all political prisoners and call for the abolishment of this country's prison-industrial complex. And it takes audacity to not accept things as they are but instead have a vision of what they could and should be.

MENDING THE BROKENNESS

My mind so often returns to 1 John 4:18 (ESV): "There is no fear in love; but perfect love casts out fear, because fear involves punishment, and the one who fears is not perfected in love." Being perfected in love does not mean that we possess a magic wand that miraculously erases all harm done. Intentionality (on all sides) and mediation are often needed to mend brokenness. When suitable and consensual, restorative justice brings victim and offender together for dialogue and to explore pathways for repair. Obviously, the victim's needs should drive this process. In a love-centered world, people would not only be held accountable for their actions but also given an opportunity to take responsibility, repent, receive unmerited grace, and be reintegrated. Our society has a lot to gain from investing in community-based models of care, healing, and restoration.

Popular culture has normalized infidelity and divorce but has not equally normalized forgiveness and reconciliation. As Americans, we often have a "what have you done for me lately" mentality, as popularized by Janet Jackson's iconic song on her 1986 *Control* album. Reciprocity often becomes a measuring stick rather than a way of life. Loving freely requires us to accept the full complexity of human nature. There are those times in life when only grace can restore peace between individuals or groups.

Too often, the burden is laid on women to "forgive and forget" for the sake of family cohesion. This is not meant to suggest that women do not cause harm, but society often places superhuman expectations on women, especially Black women, to absorb deep pain and keep coming back for more, as if a badge of honor is earned every time we return to our source of trauma. This is akin to the media's tendency to expect Black families to publicly forgive white perpetrators who killed their loved ones.

As a society, we rarely speak about restoration and how it is not an immediate act but instead an enduring process. Forgiveness doesn't always feel good and is unnatural and unsettling at times, but often beneficial. Repair requires repentance—a genuine regret over one's actions and a once-and-for-all turning away from the destructive behavior. You cannot love what continues to wound you without experiencing anger, resentment, and bitterness. When that happens in a relationship, the communication, intimacy, trust, and respect between two individuals may undergo irreparable damage. What parts of your own life need holistic repair? What tools do you have at your disposal to bring about greater healing in your home and community?

DREAMING UP WAYS TO LOVE BLACK WOMEN

When thinking about the repair that needs to happen within our community, it is important to collectively process how Black women have not always experienced the intimate, communal, and societal love and protection we deserve. As Malcolm X famously said, "The most disrespected person in America is the black woman. The most unprotected person in America is the black woman. The most neglected person in America is the black woman."[10] This still holds true today.

As an example, expressing justified anger without judgment is a luxury that Black women have not historically had in intimate and professional relations. We saw this play out in a 2022 Father's Day sermon by pastor and author T. D. Jakes, in which he said, "We are raising up women to be men."[11] He went on to say that women are not applauded for their femininity but instead "are applauded in the contemporary society by how tough, rough, nasty, mean, aggressive, hateful, possessive you are [while] you're climbing the corporate ladder, but we're losing our families."[12] He argued that women are bragging about their self-sufficiency but fail to see the impact that has on the men in their lives.[13]

While likely unintentional, Jakes was evoking the Sapphire caricature (also known as the Angry Black Woman trope) often depicted in mainstream media. According to the Jim Crow Museum at Ferris State University, the "tart-tongued and emasculating" Sapphire caricature is "a social control mechanism that is employed to punish black women who violate the societal norms that encourage them to be passive, servile, non-threatening, and unseen."[14] While Jakes's ministry has been a steadfast source of healing and deliverance for millions of women and men across generations, he was not the first preacher to make these types of comments—and he will not be the last.

Stereotypical conceptions of Black womanhood are deeply embedded within American culture. Sadly, those who seek to tell us "hard truths" about ourselves often fail to account for the systemic factors that render so many Black women single heads of households. Michelle Alexander points out that, at the time of her writing *The New Jim Crow,* "The public discourse regarding 'missing black fathers' closely [paralleled] the debate about the lack of eligible black men for marriage" in that there was little "public acknowledgment of the role of the criminal justice system in 'disappearing' black men."[15] Countless African American women were left to raise children on their own with only one income earner in the home. Alexander reminds us that the nearly one million "missing" Black men "did not walk out on their families voluntarily; they were taken away in handcuffs."[16] This inevitably required many Black women to be burden bearers. We are not only the "backbone of [American] democracy,"[17] as Kamala Harris said in her victory speech as vice president–elect, but we have often had to be the backbone of our families. You can't speak about the psyche of the Black woman without holding in balance the heavy loads we carry. Anger is the birthright of subjugated people, and Black women are entitled to our share.

Too many stereotypes rooted in racism and misogyny are perpetually used to describe us, and it is psychologically exhausting to have to repeatedly defend one's humanity. If a Black woman has become hardened, as is often depicted in popular culture, then it is rarely without reason. Of course we want a break from having to constantly be in survival mode. Of course we want to share responsibilities and lean on someone else for support. Of course we want to let our guard down and be emotionally vulnerable. Yet, Black women have too often had to be self-sufficient and not simply as a matter of preference.

Has this country forgotten the ways in which enslaved African women were ravaged during the institution of slavery? Their breasts were often the feeding machines of white babies. Their bodies were treated as the enslaver's property. And amid all the sexual exploitation, they were not spared the backbreaking work in the fields. They "had no legal means to resist or protect themselves from sexual assault by white slaveowners" and "white men refused to relinquish their freedom to violate Black women with impunity" after the institution of slavery was abolished, according to a report from the Equal Justice Initiative.[18]

How could anything other than self-preservation become the enduring modus operandi of Black women? Are Black women who harbor an inner, unexpressed anger about being unprotected by society not justified in how they feel? Instead of accounting for all the ways in which we are harmed by systems, this country absolves itself of responsibility by dehumanizing us and exploiting our resilience. But Black women are not only deserving of protection; we are also deserving of intimate and communal love. We not only deserve to lay our burdens down, but we also deserve to know that someone will be there to help us carry life's heaviness. The American empire has latched onto the figurative and literal bosom of the Black woman for centuries, feeding off our ingenuity, wit, and capacity to enliven anything we touch. We've seen this on Twitter (X) when Black women create viral trends and spark national debates, through the appropriation of Black women's beauty aesthetics, and all the ways in which Black women prove to be powerhouses in every facet of society.

At times, discourse about Black liberation focuses on the preservation of Black men's lives. But we need to equally think about the preservation of Black women's livelihood, joy, and sanity. It is not our duty to "play nice." When I think about all the dynamic sisters in my life who are single and seeking healthy love and intimacy, they have not (despite social myths) made it their life mission to resist love and emasculate Black men. In contrast, they often blame themselves for loving too easily and too often. Black women have been historically loyal to Black men. Many of the Black women I know (myself included) wish that we had been more discerning about the brothers we allowed to have access to us. Some of us have allowed parts of our heart, mind, and body to be neglected to keep breathing life into Black love. Black men have not always been as loyal to us. There are those who reach the pinnacle of success and marry a white or "ethnically ambiguous" woman, uplifting her as the greatest marker of Black male achievement.

IN DEFENSE OF BLACK WOMEN

This is why discussions about Black love so often touch on the protection (or lack thereof) of Black women. When actor Will Smith slapped comedian Chris Rock during the live airing of the 2022 Oscars award presentation, Black America broke out into a heated debate about whether Smith's action was an inexcusable act of violence or an understandable effort to protect his wife, Jada Pinkett Smith. While I and others deemed it patriarchal and excessive, there were many sisters who celebrated the "lesson" that was taught to Rock about not denigrating Black women in public.

Many viewed Rock's "joke" to be an act of violence itself and supported Smith retaliating in violence. This should sound an alarm to society about how sick and tired Black women are of not being publicly defended.

Many people forget that the #SayHerName campaign was created to specifically raise awareness about police killings of African American women.[19] While some use "His" and "Her" interchangeably in the hashtag, we should all remember that the hashtag was created to be gender-specific. #SayHerName is a clarion call to protect Black *women* at all costs and to resist how heteropatriarchy dominates our conversations about the value of Black life. Whether it is critiques about Black women's physical appearance or acts of physical violence against us, we are ready for Black men to step up, speak out, and help us combat misogynoir.

This is why "cancel culture," collectively detaching from problematic/predatory public figures and entities, is such a controversial topic within our community. We are a people of cohesion, not destruction. At the same time, some men and women are more committed to glorifying our cultural icons than they are to protecting the lives of Black women, children, and queer and trans people. Part of this is due to the miseducation in our community when it comes to gender politics and class issues.

It's not only men who fiercely defend patriarchy. Some Black women have knowingly or unknowingly embraced patriarchal values (just as many white women have embraced white supremacist ideology). I think back to when I was operating my online magazine *Urban Cusp* and there were countless Black women on social media who adamantly defended Bill Cosby and R. Kelly, ignoring the dozens of women who made allegations against them. They accused the victims of being "out for money" or "groupies who knew what they were doing." Sympathizing with the rich, famous men, they bought into conspiracy theories about "bringing the Black man down" as a punishment for the money and power the men had attained. These women will defend Black men at the expense of women who they describe as liars, sexual temptresses, gold diggers, and vixens.

Loving and protecting Black men should not require that we hate, put down, and distrust ourselves or our babies. Preserving the Black family does not mean that we must defend Black men who engage in abusive behavior. Black liberation requires not only systemic accountability but also individual and communal accountability, shielding one another from all homegrown and foreign predators. The call to #ProtectBlackWomen is being made wide—sometimes left unanswered. In 2020, Congresswoman Robin L. Kelly (D-IL) introduced a bipartisan Protect Black Women and Girls Act that has yet to be passed.[20]

Nonetheless, there have been hopeful moments of progress. It is important to remember that, as *Variety* senior correspondent Elizabeth Wagmeister wrote in a 2023 article, "Kelly's circumvention of the justice system damaged his career as an artist but didn't end it. It wasn't until *Surviving R. Kelly* premiered in early 2019 that public opinion began to change."[21] Kelly is now in prison, serving a thirty-year sentence. In a 2020 *New York Times* op-ed, rapper Megan Thee Stallion wrote about the public criticism and shaming she experienced in the aftermath of holding rapper Tory Lanez legally accountable for shooting her twice in the foot "as [she] walked away from him."[22] As Megan points out, male hyper-aggression and violence happen both within and outside of intimate relationships.

RADICAL GENTLENESS

Toxic masculinity is a disease eating away at the souls of men who are not yet (and may never be) a healthy romantic partner. Diagnosis may rarely be accepted, as the individual may be incapable of seeing how their mindset and behavior are destructive. Like any other path to healing, acknowledging there is a problem is the first step. But we live in a dichotomous society that either tells Black men they are worthless or exalts them for doing the most basic of things. At times, the most loving thing we can do is to tell a man that he may benefit from therapy and accountability partners. A masculinity that defines itself based on domination and/or exploitation, as well as hatred and violence toward queer men and trans women, is not worthy or deserving of our love. Dismantling patriarchy liberates all of us, including men.

I am reminded of a time when a man threw a glass beer bottle at my feet because I did not respond to his catcalling. The bottle shattered all over the concrete sidewalk and I had to jump to avoid being injured. Experiences of violations like this are so common but not often discussed. If building a man up means leaving ourselves open to woundedness or tearing others down, then the price of his self-esteem is too high for any of us to pay. As Nina Simone said in her song "You've Got to Learn," we have to know how to walk away when love is not what's being dished out and be unapologetic and resolute about our departure.[23]

I express eternal gratitude to every Black man who is helping us collectively reimagine masculinity. One prime example is Karega Bailey, a prolific artist and educator, who is promoting the concept of "radical gentleness."[24] In 2019, he and his wife, Felicia, tragically lost their firstborn daughter, Kamaui, when she died shortly after birth. While describing this unimaginable loss on an episode of the *Dear Future Wifey* podcast, Bailey spoke about what it looks like to be a loving husband during traumatic experiences. He describes a new type of man code[25] rooted in praising God and "praying to keep the enemy out of my home, out of my psyche, out of God's territory."[26]

Bailey's words embody revolutionary love, as he tells of the quick decisions he made (while still at the hospital) to not allow Satan to stop him from serving and uplifting his wife in a time of tremendous pain.[27] The following words spoken by Bailey on the podcast read like a spiritual declaration that should be passed down through the generations: "[Satan,] you get nothing because I know how you show up in these moments of loss, this feeling of despair, and this feeling of being alone. I know the deception you create. I know the tricks you play. I know the anger you make one feel so righteous for having. And though I still learned how to have my anger, I learned how to keep [you] out of my experience."[28] Bailey shares that his navigation of grief looked very different five years prior when his brother Kareem Johnson was shot and killed in 2014. He says that experience was "complicated by Black masculinity" and "intercepted by so many values that you learn growing up and what retaliation look like, and what respect look like and what not being a victim again look like."[29]

One Black man's capacity to house these varying realities suggests that spiritual, emotional, and psychological internal work really can make a life-altering difference. This is not limited to what is uncovered in therapy, but includes a deep dive into learning about gender liberation and Black feminist thought. Love Black women enough to explore the ideologies and schools of thought that will help us all be free. In *The Hip Hop Generation: Young*

Blacks and the Crisis in African American Culture, Bakari Kitwana writes about the unwillingness of young Black men within the hip-hop generation to understand feminism: "Despite our coming of age in an era of feminist awareness, too many hip-hop generation men—blinded by their own egos and culturally entrenched sexist beliefs—fail to grasp the critical issues, and they see little value in becoming educated in feminist issues."[30] Men would ideally detach their conceptions of manhood from reckless hypersexuality and dangerous bravado. It is easy to craft yourself into the man that popular culture says you should be, but it is much harder to "die unto self" to become the servant leader that God created you to be and your family/community needs you to be.

Revolutionary love begins with self-awareness and self-education. If we do not have a healthy curiosity for learning and a willingness to be taught, then we are not serious about transformation. We are instead dangerous. As Dr. Martin Luther King Jr. writes in *Strength to Love*, "The soft-minded man always fears change. He feels security in the status quo, and he has an almost morbid fear of the new. For him, the greatest pain is the pain of a new idea."[31] Revolutionary love goes hand in hand with deep listening. Lovers must be great listeners who can hear what the ego has a hard time digesting. It may not be easy for us to acknowledge where we fall short, but our love should transcend the desire to be right and protect our pride. Love must overpower unrealistic ideals.

LOVE AMID STRUGGLE

In any quest for love, we will have to discern if the emotional baggage we are carrying has made our hearts impenetrable. While society may celebrate those of us with a "type A" personality, we may need to check our perfectionism at the door. Love and freedom can only intersect when we bring our most liberated selves to the relationship. This doesn't just happen by accident. This is day-to-day cleansing work, purifying our mind, heart, and spirit of the toxicity within and around us. We are not free in this country, which is why we struggle so much to be free in our own bodies, relationships, and homes.

We must learn how to help one another replenish all that life takes from us daily. When I come home to you, I am a Black woman returning from a site of dehumanization and exploitation. My body has been crudely dissected in the media, and I have been sent endless subliminal messages that my beauty is not the desired standard. I have had to work ten times harder yet do not receive equal pay. My value has been equated with the size of my butt, and my complexion determines my status in society. I have endured a day's worth of catcalling and a lifetime of carrying the weight of the world on my back.

I know that you, as a Black man, are returning to me from a world that criminalizes you. You are exhausted from constantly having to self-monitor to not be deemed a threat. Code-switching is taking a toll on your mental health, but you never feel free to cry or vent. The fear of law enforcement haunts you daily, as you are bombarded by viral videos of Black men being executed by the police. And you are sick and tired of having to guard yourself from the potential harm that other Black men can inflict upon you. You would do anything to experience the freedom of being fully vulnerable. Gratitude to a new generation of men who are redefining manhood, bringing us all closer to a safer, more peaceful future.

As Black men and women, we breathlessly crawl back to one another, desperately seeking to be resurrected after what has felt like social crucifixion. We are lovers living and struggling in modern-day Babylon, which is why home must always be a place of refuge. Our love is imperative for our liberation. Let us come together to break free from these chains weighing each of us down. Future generations are depending on us to defy the odds and prevail against the enemy's ongoing attacks on unity and marriage.

If I look closely enough, I can begin to identify the sources of your bondage and hope that you can do the same for me. Help me name and give voice to the ineffable. Together, we can gather up the courage to speak truth to power. Much of what surrounds us has been constructed to bring about the demise of our love. Our solidarity is our resistance. We can defy division. The closer we draw to one another, the weaker the hold that the oppressor will have on us. We can be unapologetically unified. For centuries, every tactic was used to break us apart. But here we are—four hundred years later—still loving one another, infinitely.

THE ROLE OF HIP-HOP AND THE BLACK CHURCH

While the generational tensions between Black men and women are already present and undeniable, they are exacerbated by a cultural lifestyle that glorifies misogynistic, money-hungry men and reduces women to pleasure-providing sexual objects. For many young people, culture shapes conceptions of identity, love, and intimacy. As a teenager, I was influenced heavily by Lil' Kim. Her sexualized lyrics and female bravado resonated with me in a 1990s generational moment that popularized Black gangster culture and "thug life," particularly in my hometown of Washington, DC. However, I gravitated to Lauryn Hill more than any other female artist of that time. I was inspired by her intellect and vast array of talents. Hill modeled a femininity and beauty that was not dictated by racist societal standards. Her popularity in hip-hop culture helped reframe my understanding of Black womanhood and inspired me to use my writing and oratory for activist purposes.

Today, as in generations past, female rappers who have prominence in the mainstream hip-hop landscape have commodified their sexuality. While I realize that many women find their artistry to be sexually liberating and even empowering, I personally join the chorus of hip-hop lovers who find the hypersexualization and glorification of stripper culture boringly redundant. Artists like Jean Grae, Rapsody, Maimouna Youssef (aka Mumu Fresh), Sa-Roc, and Akua Naru are few and far between. There is so much more to us than what profit-driven artistry glorifies.

The voices of our community griots have been muffled. We are in desperate need of a new sound/soundtrack—artistry with the same medicinal powers as the "balm in Gilead to make the wounded whole."[32] Our generation is deserving of music that has restorative powers, repairing our broken relationships and divided homes. Let us, as a people, write the melodies and lyrics that will liberate us from lovelessness and disunity. We have untold love stories awaiting the big screen. There are images of Black love that have yet to grace the pages of our favorite magazines. How can we ensure that our cultural consumption reflects the breadth and depth of Black love? How can we hold musicians, writers, filmmakers, content creators, and ourselves accountable to being more honest about Black intimacy?

Black love deserves a sacred space in the cultural climate of our time. Black children deserve to see love center stage. We cannot continue to internalize images and messages that are eating away at our capacity for love. As we clean house, let us not forget the role of the Black Church in shaping our views about love and unity. Too often, sermons of condemnation and chastisement are used to guilt-trip people into a certain way of life. But God-loving people do not need to be drenched in shame; we need to be held tight in love. Pastors that obsess over sexual purity are ignoring the experiences of this generation. Millennials are approaching marriage and family life differently than previous generations. According to a 2020 Pew Research Center report, "A majority of Millennials are not currently married, marking a significant change from past generations. Only 44% of Millennials were married in 2019, compared with 53% of Gen Xers, 61% of Boomers and 81% of Silents at a comparable age."[33]

I pray the day will come when millennials and Gen Z will unquestionably view the Black Church as a reservoir of love, a place they can go to for replenishment and strength when the challenges of life have become overwhelming. The Church has always been called to be a source of healing, but that begins with the Church itself no longer being a site of trauma. I pray that church leaders would do their internal, self-improvement work at home to ensure that they do not perpetuate trauma in the sanctuary. Ideally, clergy would model love at its best, mirroring for us the sacrificial, unconditional love of Christ. All over this country and throughout the world, these pastors already exist. They hold in balance the individual needs of hurting people and the communal needs of a disenfranchised, oppressed group. Let us celebrate these men and women as beacons of light and love.

There are infinite possibilities for how we can deepen the bonds between our people. Love is the forgotten revolution that can bring our communities closer to the world we seek to create.

But revolutionary love does not claim victory in solitude. There is much that we can learn from African values that are rooted in interdependence. In the South African languages of Zulu and Xhosa, the word *ubuntu* is used to describe an ethos of humanity's connectedness. The concept is present in many parts of Africa and speaks to how Africans understand their existence and social responsibility in connection to those around them. In the U.S., the most common translation of ubuntu is "I am because we are." In this paradigm, love is not limited to romance or family ties but is instead a knitting together of one's humanity with others. When embodied by individuals and communities, ubuntu is a powerful force that can bring about social transformation.

We must imagine love beyond borders. Bridges must be built, and they must cross lands and bodies of water. This country has historically failed to love all human beings, especially Indigenous, Black, Brown, LGBTQIA+, Muslims, people with disabilities, and those living in impoverished communities. American lovelessness is killing and harming us each day. When it comes to love, this nation has demonstrated that, for now, it cannot be our North Star. Thankfully, the answers already abide deep within us.

9

Faith

Decolonizing God

Any theology that is indifferent to the theme
of liberation is not Christian theology.
—James H. Cone

There was a two-year period in my childhood in which I lived with an African American woman and her son in the South Bronx. Her immediate family became the village that nurtured and loved me as I transitioned into life in the U.S. During that time, I lost my ability to speak and understand my native language, Tigrinya. When I was once again living with my Eritrean relatives, many cultural challenges presented themselves due to my previous immersion in Black American culture. One of those challenges was rooted in spirituality.

There was a huge difference in how the two cultures engaged their faith lives. The Bibles in our Eritrean household were written in Tigrinya, which I could no longer understand. Because of this, the Word of God was foreign and inaccessible to me. The orthodox churches we would occasionally attend were equally alienating. The male priests would burn incense as they recited incomprehensible chants. If anything was ingrained in my mind growing up, it was gender inequality. The divide was glaring. Men and women sat on different sides of the church. Only male voices could be heard, and women held no visible leadership roles in the church. Undoubtedly, these childhood experiences of religious life shaped my faith walk for decades to come.

In 2005, while on my first return trip to Eritrea, I saw firsthand how deeply embedded Christianity is in our culture. My mother and other female family members attended church numerous times throughout the week. They prayed daily and spoke often about the power of "Yesus Christos." In our home in the capital city of Asmara, a wall rug hung in the living room that depicted a white Jesus, sheep by his side, knocking on a door. Wanting to know how she would react, I asked my mother whether she knew that Jesus was Black. While my mother and I were sadly disconnected by language limitations, she jokingly suggested that I not bring my "American talk" to our homeland.

While Eritrea (like many African countries) has a powerful history of resisting colonial powers and imperialistic intervention, the culture still bears many wounds of European domination. Colorism is so deeply embedded in Eritrean (and Ethiopian, as well as African and African American, for that matter) standards of beauty that it's no surprise it imprints perceptions of God. In many cultural, individual, and systemic conceptions, whiteness is attached to goodness, beauty, and purity, whereas darkness is often linked to evil, suffering, and subordination. This dichotomy was first introduced to me, at age eleven, through Spike Lee's 1992 film

Malcolm X, in a scene in which an incarcerated Malcolm X (played by Denzel Washington) is guided to read dictionary definitions of the words *black* and *white*, the inherently racist and demeaning connotations of the definitions crystallized.[1]

THE POWER OF LIBERATION THEOLOGY

Today, many of us continue to struggle with the racialized history of Christianity that rendered white men enslavers and Black people enslaved. So often, I have been asked how I reconcile my commitment to Black liberation with my self-identification as a Christian. There is no denying that the relationship between Christianity and Africa has been a traumatic one. Jomo Kenyatta, the first president of Kenya post-independence, said it best in his description about the arrival of British missionaries in Kenya: "When the missionaries arrived, the Africans had the land and the missionaries had the Bible. They taught us how to pray with our eyes closed. When we opened them, they had the land and we had the Bible."[2]

Christianity has been a centuries-long tool of subjugation in the hands of white supremacy. White oppressors manufactured a Jesus in their own European image, altering his identity from the working-class Jewish man born to an unwed teenage mother in modern-day occupied Palestine. How much more empowering would it be if Jesus's marginalization and minority status were uplifted for the poor and oppressed masses to connect with? For society's rejected class, it would be spiritually (and perhaps politically) transformative to know that God incarnate embodied their conditions and took on their suffering. But instead, white oppressors gave us a self-designed savior who would further their imperialistic agenda in the world. If we are honest, we can admit that Christ has long been used for domination rather than liberation. This is why the Church's call to "find Christ" should not be the final destination of anyone's spiritual journey. Freedom-seeking people of faith must decolonize the Jesus found in mainstream culture.

I began the work of decolonizing my faith in seminary at Yale Divinity School (YDS). While Yale was the most elitist and Eurocentric place I had ever been, it also was where I befriended and organized with justice-centered white Christians for the first time. Together, in New Haven, we marched, were trained by elders, led social justice committees, and amplified issues of racial inequality at the seminary. In one instance, I joined the family of my white, Catholic classmate in traveling to Haiti on a humanitarian trip to provide free dental services. Her father, who had his own dental practice in an affluent neighborhood in Connecticut, viewed the annual journey to Port-au-Prince (during which he personally treated hundreds of Haitians on every trip) as a form of ministry. No proselytizing of any kind took place. The only words exchanged were about people's pain and how to effectively heal it. And the only teaching that took place was on how to self-treat wounds and implement a long-term regimen of cleansing and care. By operating within the context of poor, oppressed people's lived experiences and meeting their most immediate needs, this experience helped me to reimagine what ministry means and can look like. Beyond what I was learning in the classroom, this trip confirmed that what unified us was a shared passion for liberation theology.

It was then that I learned the teachings of Catholic theologian Gustavo Gutiérrez and how peasants in Latin America were mobilizing around the theology he helped found. Liberation theology compels us to reimagine how we understand Christ's origins, life experiences, ministry, and death through a lens of poverty and oppression. Christ's social and economic standing was not a coincidence; it was by divine and intentional design. As God came incarnate in the person of Christ, God sent a message to the world about who God is, what God values the most, and how God imagines the world should be. God came as a poor person within an oppressed community living under a repressive empire and declared: "Blessed are you who are poor, for yours is the kingdom of God. Blessed are you who hunger now, for you will be satisfied" (Luke 6:20–21, NIV).

Liberation theology, in its purist form, is an anti-imperialistic way of understanding and talking about God. Gutiérrez wrote in *A Theology of Liberation* that "there can be authentic development for Latin America only if there is liberation from the domination exercised by the great capitalist countries, especially by the most powerful, the United States of America."[3] In liberation theology classes, I read books by James Cone and Howard Thurman that gave me a theological framework to understand the Black freedom struggle and Black Power movement. Womanist Delores S. Williams (among so many others) and feminist Letty Russell helped me reconcile my gender identity in the context of a male-centered religion. I read African, Asian, Latino, and queer theologians all working to make sense of Christ through their own identity, experiences, and positioning in society. While I lost fluency in my native language as a child, I learned a new spiritual language of liberation as a seminarian that united me with all oppressed people.

"MY YOKE IS EASY AND MY BURDEN IS LIGHT"

The theologians we were reading weren't the only ones wrestling to make sense of Christ. Describing her own seminary training at Yale, Bonita Grubbs, executive director of Christian Community Action in New Haven, Connecticut, would always say to me: "They took my Jesus from me and it was my job to figure out what they did to him." For liberation-centered Christians, following the way of Jesus is reclamation work, requiring us to repair the distortions to his image and ministry to understand him in his most organic form.

White supremacy is not the only barrier standing between believers of Christ and our God. Very often, parental figures and other people we know intimately are the ones who interfere with our relationship to God. We make the mistake of attaching human characteristics to God, molding God into a reflection of those who have influenced and/or harmed us the most. If our parents were punitive, then we expect punishment and judgment from God. If the lovers in our lives rejected or abused us, then we struggle to feel loved unconditionally by God. If some church leaders or members we know lack integrity and stay involved in messiness, then we have a hard time trusting the nature of God and come to expect betrayal. Maybe this isn't your reality, but it has been a part of my journey. I have spent my entire adult life trying to mute the voices of people who were the source of my life's trauma to be able to hear the voice of God. It has taken twenty years of consistent and intermittent therapy to draw a line of distinction between how I perceive God and what life has taught me about human evil.

Many of us grew up in homes where we were trained to fear our guardians. That fear likely transferred over to God when we became a Christian, as we feared God's judgment and punishment. Anticipating consequences for "disobedient" actions, our world may be limited to black and white, right and wrong, cause and effect. In this context, God is like Santa Claus, checking a list to see whether we have been "naughty or nice." It is difficult for many of us to embrace God's unconditional love, because we were not loved unconditionally as a child. Adults who use fear as a tool of control end up corrupting young people's relationship to God. They develop a fear-centered rather than love-centered understanding of their Maker. In a religious order driven by condemnation and perfectionism, nothing we do is ever good enough.

Spiritual decolonization often requires us to detach our childhood experiences from our perception of the Holy. We can't blame God for what *they* did to us and must stop making our spirituality an extension of the pain life has dealt us. This is the power of Matthew 11:28–30 (NIV), which says, "Come to me, all you who are weary and burdened, and I will give you rest. Take my yoke upon you and learn from me, for I am gentle and humble in heart, and you will find rest for your souls. For my yoke is easy and my burden is light."

Seminary challenged me to grapple with my faith assumptions. For the first time in my life, I was asked to stop thinking of God as a man and father. What would it mean for me to picture God as a woman and mother (or grandmother)? What changes once I understand God as simply Spirit with no gender attributes? No one struggled more with these spiritual reconfigurations than the African American male students I went to school with. Some of them were very invested in a male God, using biblical inerrancy as their justification. They couldn't see how they were personally benefiting from the male renderings of a Christian God. They easily pushed back on how the Bible was used to justify the enslavement of Africans but did not equally resist the ways women are subjugated in the Bible. Their arguments, often rooted in patriarchy, were infuriating and led to very intense debates. They didn't recognize that they were fighting to preserve their own power.

From my first readings of the Bible as a new Christian, I struggled with the Old Testament's violent treatment of women and Paul's New Testament assertions that women should remain silent in the church. The latter was especially challenging for me, as I felt called to ministry and went to seminary to pursue that calling. It upset me that most of the churches I attended or followed online were led by male pastors—even though the pews were filled with women. How could God both call me to ministry *and* want women to maintain silence in the church, as some claim?

While I've always pushed past this tension and asserted my theological voice, I now understand the discomfort I have always felt on the pulpit as a form of spiritual impostor syndrome. Stages have always been my sweet spot, but pulpits have often evoked self-doubt. Partly because of my feelings of disconnect from not having grown up in the Black Church, but also because I (sadly) didn't think my past and identity aligned with the making of a preacher. I've greatly evolved on this, now understanding that my intimacy with suffering undoubtedly qualifies me for ministry and preaching. Anointing must always prevail over patriarchy.

Similarly, I continue to wrestle with biblical passages that are incongruent with my liberation-centered theology and lived experiences. We must never forget that the Bible reflects the social, economic, and cultural norms of its day, as seen through the eyes of the men who authored it. While I absolutely believe Scripture is divinely inspired and has supernatural capacities for real-time revelation and healing, I cannot deny that it is also male-centered and often painful to read as a woman. The Bible has been both a source of divine inspiration *and* a tool of mass oppression.

WOMEN PRAYER WARRIORS

African women of the older generation, like my mother, often did not have extensive formal education nor many socioeconomic opportunities for self-actualization. They were often constrained by narrow perceptions about womanhood. Particularly in the teachings of Eritrean households I knew growing up, women and girls were called to maintain sexual purity prior to marriage, submit themselves to the men in their lives, prioritize household upkeep, and do their best to honor (arguably rigid) cultural traditions. Some of them tended to carry rosaries in their purses and have images depicting white biblical figures as saints hanging on the walls of their home. The splashing and drinking of "holy water" played an integral, ritualistic role in spiritual cleansing and blessing. The African women of my mother's generation rarely wore pants, their heads were often covered in public, and much of their lives were spent birthing and raising children.

The sexual pleasure and contentment of women was a nonexistent notion in my African cultural framework. In many parts of Africa, women are subjected to female genital mutilation (FGM) for a variety of reasons, including religious ones. Money, jewelry, livestock, and other goods are often presented to African brides and their families depending on her perceived "value," often based on family affiliation, age, virginity, social status, education, etc. I was a teenager when I first learned that, in some cultures, wedding-night bloodstained sheets are celebrated as proof of the bride's virginity.

While these matters vary greatly depending on regions, ethnic affiliations, religions, and cultural traditions, the underlying issue of gender oppression cannot be ignored. Growing up, I rarely saw women in church leadership roles, but when the doors of the church opened, they were often the first present. Thinking back to the Black American and African women-led households I grew up in and around, I remember how utterly dependent the women were on God for their every need. Praying, tithing, and attending church regularly, the women around me replaced the absent lovers in their lives with the presence of Jesus.

As the epitome of an African woman, my mother devoted her entire life to her husband, children, country, and Savior. Her legacy, like so many other Eritrean women, was one of self-sacrifice and soft-spoken prayers. And it was through those prayers that I bore witness to the ways that African and Black American women powerfully use their faith to combat various forms of oppression. Through prayer, she drowned out the sound of military forces outside her door. Through prayer, she overpowered the fear that her people and children would perish at the hands of enemies. Through prayer, she found the courage to carry on when left widowed with no resources. My spiritual inheritance from my mother is invaluable.

She was in her early twenties when Eritrea's armed struggle for independence began. Through the decades, she lived to see that victory actualized. My mother's story is one of millions of heroic women who may have never taken up arms like other African women but symbolically and literally carried generations of Africa's children on their hunched-over backs. They compensated for the pillaging of Africa with their prayers, bare bosoms, calloused hands, and swollen feet.

A generation later, daughters are wondering, as theologian Kwok Pui-lan asks in *Postcolonial Imagination and Feminist Theology*, "But how do we track the scent of women who were [deeply] marginalized, shuttled between tradition and modernity, and mostly illiterate, and who therefore left no trail that could be easily detected?"[4] For me, my mother's lingering "scent" is found in the individual and collective miracles her prayers made possible. Like millions of other women of African descent, I am the heir to a postcolonial legacy rooted in wielding spirituality as a weapon against political *and* spiritual oppression. As descendants of Africa, we owe the mothers of African nations our commitment to what scholar and pastor Vincent Harding called "a liberating spirituality," which he said could in turn become a pathway to an "emancipatory way of being, moving toward a fundamentally unchained life."[5]

WHY HAGAR'S STORY RESONATES

During my childhood years, the African and Black American women in my life had more in common with the Bible's Hagar, an enslaved pregnant Egyptian girl who encountered God in the wilderness while fleeing abuse, than Sarah, the Jewish enslaver who was abusing her. Many of their male partners (who had often been physically and emotionally abusive) were long gone, and they were left to raise their children alone. They were poor or working-class women from all walks of life. Struggling to make ends meet, they often worked multiple jobs and had very little to no time to care for themselves. Their day-to-day lives centered around survival—not only in financial matters but also in their fight to maintain good health amid hazardous environmental and work conditions. These women had been beaten down by the hardships of life and wore invisible (and in some cases visible) scars of resilience. At the time, I did not fully know how much of an inspiration they were to me, because society teaches us to glorify Sarah—a married woman who has power, social status, and resources.

In my own theological decolonization, I wrestled with God's treatment of Hagar. I found reassurance in the fact that God met her in the wilderness in her moment of despair and desperation. But I struggled with God telling her to return to Sarah's house. This is not just a matter of theological tension; I am left baffled by what this means for God's treatment of my own suffering. Hearing the popular religious slogan that "the blessing is in the breaking" is not comforting when you are Hagar or in a wilderness season of life. Where's Hagar's divine covering and protection? What's her power and self-agency as an enslaved African girl? Why did God send her back to her source of trauma and expose her to pain and suffering once again? I find comfort in Pui-lan's reading of Hagar: "These women complicate history, for they insist that slave girls and prostitutes exist in the same temporality with the master, the mistress, the military and the powerful. These figures disrupt national history, mock the identity formation of a people, challenge sexual normativity, and resist any forms of erasure."[6]

Hagar's encounter with God was a subtle moment of theological and political awakening, revealing her intrinsic worth and understanding of God as intimately connected to the suffering of outcasts. Genesis 16:13 (NIV) says, "She gave this name to the Lord who spoke to her: 'You are the God who sees me,' for she said, 'I have now seen the One who sees me.'" The word *sees* cannot be overlooked. In a world that so often renders Black people and women invisible, Hagar boldly declares her visibility in the eyes of God. The most supreme being in the universe took the time to bear witness to the resilience and resistance of a marginalized, oppressed African woman.

Some of the enemy's most dangerous lies are that we are alone, our suffering is meaningless, and we are not cared about. Through this moment of engaging the Divine, Hagar learned that her story and struggle are known to God. This means we don't need validation from any other source. We don't need our feelings affirmed by anyone else. We have not only been seen but we have been seen by the One who truly matters. This is a form of spiritual currency in a world that tries to convince us that social currency is what's most important. There's no greater comfort than knowing that God is within reach and that nothing we endure is unknown to our Maker. Hagar's story was instrumental in helping me to see myself, a Black woman, within the pages of the Bible.

SPIRITUAL MALPRACTICE

It was in seminary that I was challenged to think about how rape survivors and women who have been sexually assaulted by men may feel when they constantly hear God gendered as male. How does one worship a male deity after being traumatized by a man? How does one love and serve the very thing that nearly destroyed them? If you have suffered at the hands of men time and time again, then why would anyone expect you to find joy in a religion that demands your submission to a male God? Gender relations are complicated, and we don't speak enough about how women are often forced to accept what does not give us psychological and emotional peace and what does not align with our life experiences.

Due to my father passing when I was four years old, I was raised in homes controlled by matriarchs. My childhood friends also lived in female-led households where fathers were not present. From what I witnessed, power was always in the hands of African and Black American women. Yet, they were all bowing down to a male (and, in some contexts, white) God. It wasn't easy to reconcile these incongruences.

Similarly, reading the Bible as a liberation narrative for the poor and oppressed, it becomes difficult to identify God as "Master" and reconcile the Bible's references to "slaves." While these titles are found all throughout the Bible, hymns, and spiritual literature, it's impossible to detach these words from the painful history of the institution of slavery. The brutality of the relationship between the enslaver and the enslaved person should have no place in our spiritual framework. African Americans should not have to relive that trauma through language and imagery when attempting to draw close to God. Upholding the "master-slave" tie does not evoke love, justice, compassion, gentleness, and societal care.

Christ's presence in our lives is meant to be transformative. Belief in his existence should shift us from our addiction to rules to a bond rooted in relationship. If we seek to be like Christ, then we are compelled to fight to change the social conditions around us. We feel compelled to bring social outcasts into the fold of community. We are convicted to do all that we can to bring people closer to healing and redemption. Christ-centered faith is rooted in freedom—our own and that of everyone else. Christianity should not only lead us to *imagine* freedom; it should be the conduit through which we are able to *embody* freedom. We become liberated and are better equipped to help others journey toward freedoms of their own. Our faith should not situate us in a life of bondage; that is the enemy's desire for our lives. Christ did not die for us to be subjugated beings. He endured the cross to secure our wholeness and eternal salvation, liberating us from all forms of oppression.

Many U.S. churches have yet to grapple with how harmful it has been to have Christ historically portrayed as a white man. White men have been the most oppressive group in human history. There is no corner of the globe that has not been colonized or brutalized by white oppressors in search of land, natural resources, political domination, and sexual conquest. Bowing down to a white master and Eurocentric depictions of Christ has truly damaged our psyches. Decolonizing God means that we remove any imprint of white supremacy from our lives of faith.

For me, that does not mean I have to make Christ a Black man. The historical Jesus does not have to be Black for me to see him as Liberator, Redeemer, and Restorer. The State-sanctioned violence that resulted in an oppressed man being executed among criminals is more than enough for me. I relate to the Jesus who fearlessly resisted the Roman Empire and made friends with the rejected of society. While I picture the historical Jesus as a brown-skinned, Middle Eastern man, Christ transcends race.

Yet, I agree with James Cone's argument in his seminal book *God of the Oppressed* that "[Jesus] *is* black because he *was* a Jew. The affirmation of the Black Christ can be understood when the significance of his past Jewishness is related dialectically to the significance of his present blackness."[7] Cone, like many other Black liberation theologians, believed that by being born into a Jewish identity in the context of Roman oppression, Jesus was born into the marginalized Black identity of his day. Jesus takes on modern Blackness because his ethnic and class identity were rooted in subjugation.

Jesus stood and stands in direct opposition to everything white supremacy uplifts. White supremacy seeks to preserve itself, while Christ came to lose himself for the world to be saved. White supremacy is about domination; Christ lived a life of surrender and service. As Jesus said in Isaiah 61:1–3 (NIV):

> The Spirit of the Sovereign Lord is on me, because the Lord has anointed me to proclaim good news to the poor. He has sent me to bind up the brokenhearted, to proclaim freedom for the captives and release from darkness for the prisoners, to proclaim the year of the Lord's favor and the day of vengeance of our God, to comfort all who mourn, and provide for those who grieve in Zion—to bestow on them a crown of beauty instead of ashes, the oil of joy instead of mourning, and a garment of praise instead of a spirit of despair.

So many faith leaders have recklessly misrepresented and inaccurately depicted Christ. These men and women lead churches all over the world, proliferating destructive theology and engaging in spiritual malpractice.

For their own personal gain, they peddle a profit-centered religion indistinguishable from capitalism. This is similar to the Black pastors and white evangelicals who supported Trump and his fascist policies because it opened the door for them to gain money, opportunities, and "a seat at the table." It breaks my heart and simultaneously infuriates me to think about the millions of people worldwide who come to these preachers desperately seeking help and answers to life's hardest questions. Many of them are dealing with the most difficult of circumstances. Prosperity pimps dish out false theology on Sunday mornings to sustain their own lavish lifestyles. How does a "shepherd of God's people" justify extravagance and opulence when their congregants can barely put food on the table and pay their bills?

Theological decolonization demands that we unlearn years of false theology and separate our faith from the traps of capitalism. Some of us don't know the difference between pursuing the American Dream and pursuing a life of faith. We think a relationship with God guarantees us material wealth, financial security, and the absence of problems. We fail to distinguish our spiritual beliefs from our capitalistic aspirations. God does not promise us the American Dream. And if we are being honest, we can admit that the seduction of the American Dream is often in direct opposition to the self-sacrifice, communalism, and life of minimalism that Jesus encourages. We may not be worshipping a molten golden calf like the children of Israel in the book of Exodus, but we have contemporary false gods of our own. Today, those idols might come in the form of job titles, annual salaries, retirement packages, home equity, and designer goods. It's anything that we put our trust and faith in rather than believing in "manna," provision from God to meet our daily needs.

The rejection of Jesus as the Messiah was grounded in an expectation that the Messiah would come in the form of a king. Jesus, as a carpenter, was subjected to first-century classism within the reign of the Roman Empire. He did not adhere to cultural norms related to the Sabbath and cleanliness. In a society that had very rigid understandings about purity and social order, Jesus defied the rules. For us today, this is an open-ended invitation to unravel our conceptions of God as imperialistic.

What shifts when we reimagine Jesus as a political prisoner who was sentenced to death and subjected to cruel and unusual punishment by the State? Or when we envision him as an innocent civilian executed by Roman occupiers? Does that change anything for us? Will how we worship change? What new prayers will we pray? How will we prioritize our lives? Who will we be inspired to become? How does the rejected Christ feel when queer teenagers take their lives because they could not face rejection and alienation from their family members? Would he demand that a ten-year-old girl impregnated through rape carry that pregnancy to full term? Some Americans would rather worship a god that is a merciless dictator than one who is a benevolent friend to the poor and oppressed. Why do so many Christians focus more on eternal damnation than redemption? What do they have to lose by God extending love and empathy to those they don't believe deserve it?

ALCHEMIZING OUR SUFFERING

The story of the prophet Elijah in 1 Kings 19 has always been important to my faith walk. As Elijah struggles with anxiety and depression, he encounters an "angel of the Lord" that is deeply concerned that Elijah gets rest and nourishment for the journey ahead. In his time of despair, Elijah gets a critical lesson into the nature of God. God is not in the wind, earthquake, or fire but in a "soft whisper," "still small voice," or "gentle blowing."[8]

In this biblical passage, God is portrayed as a caretaker who sits by our side and nurses us back to serenity and wellness during life's toughest moments. Elijah is reassured that God is not the source of chaos and confusion in his life, but is instead a peaceful, calm entity whose presence is comforting rather than overpowering. This is a very different portrayal than the "fire and brimstone" overseer presented by many conservatives. Politicians have distorted the image of God to put fear into the hearts of those they seek to control, allowing for manipulation. As we journey toward freedom, we begin to embrace a vision of God radically different than the one historically used to subjugate us. God becomes the loving sojourner who so desperately wants to set us free and see us be made whole.

So often, preachers and everyday Christians try to convince us that God is at the center of our suffering, permitting it for a greater good. The book of Job is used to explain how God allows the devil to harm us but has an ultimate plan for our restoration. This idea suggests that for us to truly be used by God, we must first be broken. This may be the case in some instances; think to the account in Acts 9 of Saul being blinded on the road to Damascus prior to his conversion into the Apostle Paul. God is not one-dimensional and may do or allow things that do not make sense to our limited minds. Let us not forget that the Christian faith is based on the crucifixion of God's Son for the redemption of humanity. But how harmful this way of thinking can be if applied to *all* situations, leaving traumatized people wondering why God willed their abuse, rape, betrayal, loss, accident, sickness, or suffering of any kind.

I once asked a pastor how he reconciles all the suffering that God's people endure, and he reminded me of an often-overlooked Bible verse that says God causes the "sun to rise on the evil and the good, and sends rain on the righteous and the unrighteous" (Matthew 5:45, NIV). Can we be authentic enough to admit that the righteous sometimes experience seasons of inescapable, torrential rain, as well as seasons of drought? Too often, it seems impossible to find shelter from the unrelenting downpours of life. Our faith walk is often corrupted by false teachers who peddle counterfeit hope when we really need radical truth-telling. What spiritual prescriptions have been and continue to be written to shield and heal us from destructive theology? Where can our people go to theologically and strategically learn how to alchemize our suffering?

In various parts of the world, theology has been used to explain and justify the social conditions that people are born into. If you were born into poverty, the argument goes, that must have been God's will for your life. If you were raised in a misogynistic society where women have few to no rights, then God must have situated you in that culture for a reason. These teachings shift responsibility and accountability away from oppressive socioeconomic systems. Instead of fighting to change policies and hold governments accountable, people are led to believe they must surrender to the life and social conditions God ordained for them. For centuries, oppressors have used self-serving, subjugating theology to their own benefit. White enslavers used these teachings to justify the bondage of Africans and forbade them from reading to ensure they would never discover the Bible's ever-present thread of liberation. Men have used it to oppress women, and nations have used it in their justification of colonization and imperialism.

White oppressors trained us to bow down to a meek Jesus with European features. That, however, is not the Jesus I have come to know and love. I serve a Jesus who opens the door for dope boys in crime-infested public housing projects to be redeemed. My overturning-tables-in-the-temple Jesus walked alongside unruly protestors in the streets of Ferguson and Baltimore. He grieves the massacre and forced displacement of Arab people. He weeps with wrongly convicted death row and Guantánamo Bay inmates, making his rounds in prison cells all over the world. In my spiritual imagination, Jesus can be found in all the hospitals, refugee camps, slums, and orphanages of the world, feeding and caring for those in need. He mourns when we mourn and compassionately hears our pleas for healing. We must reclaim the Christ that has empowered and inspired millions to resist slavery, colonization, imperialism, persecution, and imprisonment. This is a theology that has the power to break chains, free captive people, comfort widows, and heal the sick. This is a theology worthy of our devotion.

SEIZING OUR SPIRITUAL POWER

Today, the countless incidents of police brutality have led to an ongoing debate about whether Black lives matter, blue lives matter, or all lives matter. Of course, every human being is precious in the eyes of God. But the Bible uniquely portrays Jesus as the innocent Lamb slaughtered at the hands of the State. The resurrection of Christ is in direct opposition to the brutality of the Roman Empire. Similarly, in Exodus, Pharaoh stands in opposition to the liberation of God's people, and Moses, a community organizer of his day, is tasked with mobilizing the children of Israel out of bondage into freedom.

In story after story, God aligns God's Self with those seeking freedom from the oppressive forces of their day. For me, it is impossible to read about the four hundred years of bondage endured by the children of Israel and not think about the history of enslaved Africans from the shores of West Africa to the colonies of North America. For Black Americans, the United States is our Babylon and Egypt—a site of multigenerational bondage and trauma. If nothing else, African Americans should know that the Bible mirrors their plight and ongoing quest for liberation.

Yet, white evangelicals and Christian fundamentalists have dominated God talk in the United States, making their political agendas synonymous with a Christian agenda. They are coming after body autonomy, gun safety laws, voting protection, educational teachings about race, and so much more. All of it boils down to wanting to maintain societal control, especially over communities of color. They profess to do these things in the name of Christ, misrepresenting what Jesus prioritized and cared about. But their agenda is not a Christian one at all; it is rooted in white supremacy yet veiled as "conservative values."

What do we have to do to reclaim our God from the hands of gun-loving, hateful white nationalists? Pui-lan describes the power of "writing back," which she says "implies an oppositional stance, of claiming the power to narrate, to contest and reconstruct meanings, and to play with language and imagination."[9] We have more tools at our disposal than ever before to "write back" in opposition to a religiosity that is oppressive and archaic. In a world where representation matters so much, we must give voice to the realities ignored and overlooked in the mainstream.

For half a century, hip-hop has been a powerful tool in the hands of Black America to prevent the erasure of the Black struggle and "write back" against white cultural hegemony. Long before Kanye West became a polarizing and offensive figure dishing out internalized racial self-hatred and anti-Semitism, he gifted the world "Jesus Walks" in 2004. The song gained the popularity it did because it presented an Afrocentric, urban image of Christ rarely ever found in mainstream culture. Nearly a decade earlier, Tupac's cover art for *Makaveli—The Don Killuminati: The Seven Day Theory*, which was released two months after he was murdered in September 1996, challenged us to think about how Black men are crucified in society. In 2021, "My Bible" by Nas reassured me that lyricists are still serving as urban disciples and theologians. We need redemption songs now more than ever before. I pray that hip-hop will always have a remnant, a countercultural strand of Afrofuturistic voices, determined to "write back" against white supremacy and resist the urge to "dumb down" for market appeal.

Our generation's decolonizing of God will require our imaginations to be stretched to places previously unknown or even forbidden. If it is helpful to reimagine God as a Black woman, then let us do so. Contemporary artists like Karen Seneferu, who curates an exhibition titled *The Black Woman Is God* virtually and in San Francisco, and Harmonia Rosales, who centers Black women in her recreations of European art, are helping us do just this. Rosales told the *Los Angeles Times* of the piece that made her artwork go viral: "I used this particular image [of Michelangelo's *The Creation of Adam*] to deconstruct the old traditional way of thought.... The original concept here is Michelangelo created the hidden message of a brain but in replacing God here as a black woman, you see a womb."[10] There is no place on earth more protective, life-giving, and nurturing than a woman's womb. And haven't Black women been crucified by empire, having to constantly resurrect ourselves from social death in each generation? While God transcends race and gender, it is helpful for us to hold a vision of the Divine that mirrors the beauty and fortitude of our people.

Through our conversations with one another, we can ask the questions our elders were taught to never ask of God. Trusting that God can handle our seasons of spiritual doubt and anguish, there is room for us to voice anger and frustration. Believing that God will give us enough light for the immediate path that we are on, let's be content with not having all the theological answers. Every day of our lives, we journey with a God that not only loves us but stands alongside us in the fight against injustice. Christ is not only our comrade but also our revolutionary leader in the war against evil, oppression, and enemy occupation.

There is immense power in reclaiming the Jesus that generations of our people have prayed to in their search for wholeness and liberation. The God intended to be a tool of subjugation was recalibrated by freedom seekers, who found in the pages of the Bible a story of freedom and divine love. We too can be guided by a spirituality rooted in deep history and ancestral wisdom. We too should believe that a gracious and merciful supernatural force is at work in our lives. And we too can grasp onto a hope that helps us imagine beyond what we can see. Every aspect of Jesus's story reinforces the fact that God desires to free us from every form of bondage, bring us into the fold of community, and set us on the path to eternal redemption. The more we decolonize our spiritual lives, the more we seize hold of a power that can transform us and the world as we know it.

Conclusion

◆

A Love Letter to the African Diaspora

Dear descendants of Africa,

Time and time again, Black folks have inspired me to take up weapons of intellectual, cultural, and spiritual warfare. Our people are inspiringly resolute. Together, we have built an army powerful enough to bring down these modern empires. Ours has been an enduring quest for survival—constantly morphing and bending in hopes of avoiding harm. While tribalism has so often threatened the success of our resistance, being Black in America constantly reminds us of our collective identity as exiles. A people without a permanent sanctuary. Our resilience has armed us with the tools needed to repurpose our trauma. We are a transcendent people, emerging out of turbulent waters strong enough to overtake us. So many times, I have glimpsed a new future and infinite hope when looking into the eyes of a Black woman, man, or child.

Despite all that we have suffered, Blackness is freedom personified. Our minds house treasured recipes for transformation. Our voices echo the life-saving wisdom of our ancestors. For centuries, there has been an intercontinental obsession with possessing, dismembering, and crucifying our bodies. No matter what oppressors do to undermine our collective progress, we stand steadfast as towers and temples of God's glory. We have filtered out generations of lies meant to confuse, distract, and destroy us as a people. Let us never forget that our resilience is a testament to the fact that God's love, grace, and mercy prevail.

We know that one of the most important journeys we can ever take in life is to the heart of our communal problems. How many times have we sought to find God amid our suffering and heard Holy tears being shed for us? Ask me what is sacred and worthy of divine protection, and I will answer by guiding you back to yourself. You haven't lived unless you have traveled through the depths of Blackness to find joy, pleasure, and redemption waiting for you on the other side.

Black love has always resurrected us, the oppressed, from spiritual death. As we commune, we partake in rituals of healing that free captives from the dungeons of despair and hopelessness. Whenever two or more of us are gathered, salvation is in our midst. As a people, we have laughed ourselves out of psychological bondage. As a people, we have cried and mourned our way into emotional freedom. As a people, we have read ourselves into political awakening. The Underground Railroad continues to run beneath our feet. America has yet to rid the stench of white supremacy from its cultural, political, and socioeconomic fabric. But our ancestral covenant demands that we stay on the freedom trail no matter how blurred and distorted our vision gets.

I write this letter to every Black American heartbroken by the killings of Ahmaud Arbery, Breonna Taylor, Eric Garner, Freddie Gray Jr., George Floyd, Jordan Davis, Michael Brown, Sandra Bland, Tamir Rice, Trayvon Martin, and the countless others whose human dignity was not honored. To those of us who went out into the streets in resistance to our fears of losing our own lives and loved ones at the hands of cops and white vigilantes. To each of us who grew up poor without knowing it and slept to the tune of the American Dream—until that fateful day when we finally realized this country is a source of trauma for millions around the world. Our dreams were so often built on the nightmares being experienced by others.

I write this letter for all the homes shattered by the War on Drugs. How many times I wept while doing prison ministry upon seeing a multigenerational sea of Black men confined to the horrors of the prison-industrial complex. To all the sisters I know who raise fatherless children, refusing to give up on Black men despite all they have endured in the name of Black love. I write this letter for our elders who loved us and prayed for us when we didn't know how to love and pray for ourselves. To each one of us determined to break the chains of generational trauma, resentment, anger, and unforgiveness in our families. Our bodies have carried the weight of so much suffering and brokenness through the years. The time has come for us to finally be healed and restored back to individual and collective wholeness.

Our daughters must be guided to know the true sources of their power and majesty. Our sons must be taught how to love (rather than fear) one another and free themselves from self-destructive notions of masculinity. We must do the heavy lifting of removing every remnant of internalized racism from our bodies and homes. Tragically, it has too often been our own mothers, aunties, fathers, and brothers who have taught us to hate ourselves. Even if it takes a lifetime or many generations, we will heal from the pain of believing that Blackness is inferior. Less beautiful. Less brilliant. Less divine. Less worthy. Less deserving of protection. Less in every way imaginable. We can mend the brokenness that we have been taught to normalize. Freedom will become our new way of life.

Beloved, I pray that you have tasted liberation enough times to know that the world as it is leaves more to be desired. When was the last time you smelled the sweet aroma of Black people cooking up their defiance to every form of bondage? Please do not forsake fellowship with freedom lovers for too long. There will be days and seasons of life when you can no longer imagine freedom. That moment when you no longer take comfort in the promise of God's covering. You have witnessed generations of our people buried with unfulfilled prayers for freedom. I beg you to never stop believing that even the Red Sea will be forced to part to help us make it to the Promised Land.

How hard it has become for us to distinguish between a safe space and a battlefield. Yet, never forget that our movement resurrects every time one of us is publicly lynched by this evil empire. Now and forevermore, it is our duty to make disciples of other Black men and women, baptizing them in a sense of urgency and converting them into prophets, revolutionaries, and village protectors that build locally but stand in solidarity globally.

Aren't we capable of transforming and healing our own generation? Salute to every Black man grooming Black boys fathered by other Black men. We have always been a tribal people. "One can't eat unless we all get fed" kind of people. Sons and daughters of Haitian Revolution leader Toussaint Louverture and Underground Railroad conductor Harriet Tubman, doesn't abolition run through your veins? Don't let them dilute our rage. We are the Joshua generation. We declare the American wilderness cannot be fixed. Cannot be tamed. Cannot be reformed. This barbaric anti-Black America, as we know it, must fall for us to rebuild. But we can't rebuild alone. Our army needs anybody and everybody willing to bring down these apartheid regimes. Our army must sit at the feet of elders, listening and serving more than we are speaking.

I beg you to love yourself and us enough to envision what's possible, valuable, and righteous. They will never be able to understand, because we are relearning our mother tongue. Words of Black love, Black joy, and Black power. Always remember that our angels and ancestors matter more than the oppressor's weapons and demons. I believe we will win because the wrath of God is on our side.

Consider these words my conclusion to a revolutionary, spiritual love letter whose origins date back to the genesis of humanity. To the ancient ruins of Ethiopia and the pyramids of Egypt. But also to the Middle Passage, cotton fields, food deserts, hospitals, courts, prisons, and streets. Can you remember when we reigned, ruled, and waged war against anything that threatened us, our people, our love, and the heirs to our throne? Our land and culture have always been the envy of the oppressor.

But Black love is immortal. It can't be intercepted or annihilated by kidnappers, enslavers, colonizers, or uniformed murderers. Now, let us carry these Afrofuturistic dreams with us to the ends of the earth, as we collectively pen the greatest freedom story ever told in human history. Written in our people's ancestral language of radical defiance and self-liberating faith. Written in the ink of Black resilience, Black resistance, and Black redemption.

Beloved, as I end this letter, please allow me to pray for you and for us. It is the most loving and empowering act I know of as a minister of the Gospel, the Good News. It is my hope that you will meditate on these words and that they will nudge you toward transformation and action. Let us never underestimate the power of prayer and what it means to pray with our feet, as we imagine freedom together.

Dear God,

We come before you knowing that you have always journeyed with our ancestors during times of incomprehensible suffering. For generations, you have walked and wept with us. From Africa to America, you have cradled our people in the palm of Your hands. Through You, we escaped the brutality of slavery. Through You, we triumphantly emerged out of the lion's colonial den and the fiery furnace of apartheid. Through You, we continue to live and breathe amid endless retraumatization. Your Spirit reminds us that our birthright is freedom and not bondage. Reminds us that we are "fearfully and wonderfully made"[1] in Your image. That You knew us before You formed us in our mother's womb.[2] Before we were born, You consecrated us and appointed us as prophets to the nations.[3]

We praise You for planting a warrior's spirit within us and equipping us for resilience and resistance. Most important, we honor and bless Your holy name for the promise of redemption, knowing that the pain and agony of this earth is not the end of our story. Remind us daily that divinity is our inheritance and that a hedge of protection shall be upon us through the ages. Through Christ, You modeled anti-imperial resistance for us. Just as our people were equipped to overcome the colonial stronghold, we will also break free from the grip that the American empire has on us. But we cannot do this alone. We need the power and guidance of the Spirit to lead our people toward the Promised Land.

May You shine Your Light upon this generation of freedom

fighters, intellectuals, ministers, and artists to help our people seize freedom once and for all. Fill us with the same spiritual power that humbled Pharaoh's hardened heart, brought down the walls of Jericho, and emerged out of the tomb. May we break through any barriers that stand between us and our liberation. Equip us to set the captives free. Let us collectively rest and reign in eternal redemption. And continuously remind us that Your Word promises that desecrated lands can be healed: "If my people, which are called by my name, shall humble themselves, and pray, and seek my face, and turn from their wicked ways; then will I hear from heaven, and will forgive their sin, and will heal their land."[4] In Your holy name, I pray. Amen.

In solidarity and Spirit,
Rahiel

Acknowledgments

Jesus has made faith and freedom interchangeable in my life, gifting me *everything* worthy of gratitude. Light and divine love have resurrected me more than once.

This book would not exist without the Pan-African village that has shaped me. My mother, Abeba Habtegaber, made incomprehensible sacrifices as Eritrea dared to imagine freedom. My guardian angels, Brenda Rosser Coleman and Eleanor Grady, engulfed me in lifelong maternal love and nurture. These matriarchs, including my sister Almaz Tesfamariam (who sponsored my entire family in the U.S.), became ancestors as I was writing this book.

My husband, Gideon Msazurwa, and his family have taught me so much about African culture and politics. He nurtures my dreams, sacrifices so I can write/speak, and journeyed with me to this finish line. Our daughter, Zamara, is all the prayers of my life in human form.

My passion for liberation has largely been inspired by my homeland and its people, particularly the Tesfamariam family. Our father, a hero in his own right, groomed eight warriors. My brother Alem, who was the first freedom fighter I ever met, graciously allowed me to tell his story. Members of our community advised me. Others, far and near, have cheered me on for years.

My best friends, DeLise Bernard and Aaron Jenkins, have been the backbone of my adult life. There are no words to describe our sacred, healing bond rooted in unconditional love. Their spouses, Rahsaan and Stephanie, have gifted me boundless generosity, profound conversations, and loving prayers. Yordanos Teklu, Brian Rikuda, and Markëta Howard (deeply grateful for Rashad) have also been instrumental in my journey through unwavering friendship and support. Love to Sammy and Yonathan.

My mentor Bakari Kitwana has enriched me as a thinker, writer, and organizer. He constantly challenges, encourages, and inspires me. As a brilliant editor, he offered infinite input on every page of the manuscript and played an incomparable role in bringing this book to life. I am eternally indebted.

This journey has run parallel with grief. Thank you to the individuals who paid their respects or sent offerings of love. Despite her own grief, my niece Senait Selemun at times cared for my daughter during the editing stage. Bryan Grady helped me navigate the pain of losing our beloved, his mother. Jennifer Tyler, Noma Ndlovu, Jedidah Isler, Aja Byrd, Danielle Moore, Kibwei McKinney, Jeff Dessources, and Damon Jones loved on me (as they have for decades). Eunia Destine, Jovian Peters, Louisa Tatum, and Marsha Campbell Ajayi went above and beyond, as always. Mana Bisseke provided endless care. Hilary Phillips was very generous. Sonya Tennell nurtured me. Kelsie Bonaparte often encouraged me.

Eternal gratitude to my spiritual father, Donald Isaac Sr., who mentored me as a community organizer, licensed me as minister, and always models servant leadership. My spiritual advisors, Tony Lee and Gregory Ellison II, have continuously poured into my life and been steadfast in their love. Michael McBride has been pivotal in my organizing work and ministry. Delonte Gholston nudged me to become a young adult pastor and get ordained. Terrance M. McKinley was my thought partner for years. Chane Morrow played a life-altering role in my faith journey.

Roy Singham, Cosmas Musumali, and Fred M'membe taught me so much about what it means to be a comrade and Pan-Africanist. Their imprint on my politics can be found throughout this book. Ahmad Abuznaid co-led the transformative delegation to occupied Palestine that I write about. Leila Akahloun (who helped me take the leap of faith to relocate to Africa), Nina Hlalo, and Jo Figueroa gifted me sisterhood in Joburg. Lena Green always opened her home to me during my bicontinental years.

Marc Lamont Hill, who mentored me at the start of my public speaking career, thoughtfully provided feedback on every chapter and answered my many questions. Some of the previously mentioned individuals (Delonte, Greg, Rev. Isaac, Jovian, Louisa, Noma, Stephanie) read specific draft chapters, as did my childhood best friend Keonna Carter. I have been blessed with a tribe of big sisters and brothers who have deeply supported me. Like feminist theologian Meggan Watterson, who became my friend, writing partner, and beloved manuscript reader. And Lilakoi Moon (Lisa Bonet), who inspires and lovingly challenges me to be more fierce and free.

My voice has been amplified by many journalists who gave me life-altering opportunities. Denise Rolark Barnes made me editor in chief of the *Washington Informer*. Robert Pierre opened doors that launched my career at the *Washington Post*. Chris Jenkins helped strengthen my journalistic voice, supported my bold ideas, and added "producer" to my résumé. I appreciate everyone who helped me grow and sustain *Urban Cusp*, particularly Ashlee Wisdom (my godsend), Beatitudes Society, Institute for the Future, and Michelle Gadsden-Williams. Without the path that *Urban Cusp* put my life on, this book may not exist.

Gratitude to every university, educator (Andre Willis and Tricia Rose in particular), church, pastor, organization, and individual that informed my thinking, affirmed my calling, and/or invited me to speak. My teachers and principal at Thomson Elementary School laid the groundwork, helping me discover and pursue my love of the written and spoken word. Connie Royster always encouraged me to write. Shaun Derik inspired me to speak more and dream bigger.

Marie Brown, my literary agent and a humble legend, walked this road to authorship with me for a decade. Her belief in me has been ever-present and she has championed for me from day one. Marie was both doula and midwife to the birthing of this book. Forever grateful for her love and faith in me.

Tracy Sherrod believed in me and acquired my book for Amistad, making all this possible. She opened a door that actualized this lifelong dream. Judith Curr supported me every step of the way. Gideon Weil and Abby West, my editors, seamlessly walked me through the process. Their affirmations and commitment to the success of this book have meant the world to me. Gratitude to Maya Alpert and the rest of the HarperCollins team who worked tirelessly on this project. David Jon Walker, a cutting-edge artist, brought my vision for the book's cover to life, which felt like a naming ceremony for my "second born."

While I have sought to take the path of radical inclusion, this will still fall short. For anyone unnamed (family, friends, and sorors) that has deeply blessed my life's journey, I sincerely thank you. May God, the ancestors, and my elders be pleased with "the words of my mouth and the meditation of my heart" (Psalm 19:14, KJV).

Notes

INTRODUCTION: A FREEDOM JOURNEY

1. Larry Buchanan, Quoctrung Bui, and Jugal K. Patel, "Black Lives Matter May Be the Largest Movement in U.S. History," *New York Times*, July 3, 2020, http://www.nytimes.com/interactive/2020/07/03/us/george-floyd-protests -crowd-size.html.

2. Earl Fitzhugh, J. P. Julien, Nick Noel, and Shelley Stewart, "It's Time for a New Approach to Racial Equality," McKinsey Institute for Black Economic Mobility, December 2, 2020, http://www.mckinsey.com/bem/our-insights /its-time-for-a-new-approach-to-racial-equity.

3. Throughout the book, there will be mention of police officer and vigilante killings of Black people. The names of their killers have intentionally been omitted. Using logic similar to not granting fame to mass shooters, I believe that a book on imagining freedom should not memorialize the names of killers who have caused our community deep harm.

4. Catholic theologian Gustavo Gutiérrez founded liberation theology, and his book *A Theology of Liberation: History, Politics, and Salvation* (Ossining, NY: Orbis Books, 1988) is fundamental in the field. I write more about this theology and its founder in chapter 9.

5. First coined by Alice Walker in 1983 to identify Black feminists in her book *In Search of Our Mothers' Gardens: Womanist Prose* (New York: Mariner, 2003).

6. Markham Heid, "Depression and Suicide Rates Are Rising Sharply in Young Americans, New Report Says. This May Be One Reason Why," *TIME*, March 14, 2019, http://time.com/5550803/depression-suicide-rates-youth/.

7. James Baldwin, *Notes of a Native Son* (Boston: Beacon Press, 1955), 9.

8. Tim Elfrink and Fred Barbash, "'These Children Are Barefoot. In Diapers. Choking on Tear Gas,'" *Washington Post*, November 26, 2018, http://www .washingtonpost.com/nation/2018/11/26/these-children-are-barefoot -diapers-choking-tear-gas.

9. "Q&A: Trump Administration's 'Zero-Tolerance' Immigration Policy," Human Rights Watch, August 16, 2018, http://www.hrw.org/news/2018/08/16/qa-trump-administrations-zero-tolerance-immigration-policy.

10. Anna Flagg and Andrew Rodriguez Calderon, "500,000 Kids, 30 Million Hours: Trump's Vast Expansion of Child Detention," The Marshall Project, October 30, 2020, http://www.themarshallproject.org/2020/10/30/500-000-kids-30-million-hours-trump-s-vast-expansion-of-child-detention.

11. Brian Mahoney and Tim Reynolds, "NBA Playoff Games Called Off Amid Player Protests," NBA.com, August 26, 2020, http://www.nba.com/news/bucks-protest-nba-postpones-games.

12. Michelle Alexander, *The New Jim Crow: Mass Incarceration in the Age of Colorblindness* (New York: The New Press, 2010).

13. *The Notebook*, directed by Nick Cassavetes (2004; Burbank: New Line Cinema, 2005), DVD.

CHAPTER ONE: RECLAMATION

1. Alyssa Klein, "Fela Kuti's 'Zombie' Is One of Jay Z's 'Songs for Survival,'" *OkayAfrica*, http://www.okayafrica.com/fela-kuti-zombie-jay-z-songs-for-survival-tidal.

2. Kim Parker and Juliana Menasce Horowitz, "Majority of Workers Who Quit a Job in 2021 Cite Low Pay, No Opportunities for Advancement, Feeling Disrespected," Pew Research Center, March 9, 2022, http://www.pewresearch.org/short-reads/2022/03/09/majority-of-workers-who-quit-a-job-in-2021-cite-low-pay-no-opportunities-for-advancement-feeling-disrespected.

3. Greg Iacurci, "2022 Was the 'Real Year of the Great Resignation,' Says Economist," CNBC, February 1, 2023, http://www.cnbc.com/2023/02/01/why-2022-was-the-real-year-of-the-great-resignation.html.

4. Jill Lepore, "Burnout: Modern Affliction or Human Condition?" *New Yorker*, May 17, 2021, http://www.newyorker.com/magazine/2021/05/24/burnout-modern-affliction-or-human-condition.

5. Sean Illing, "How Millennials Became the Burnout Generation," *Vox*, December 3, 2020, http://www.vox.com/policy-and-politics/21473579/millennials-great-recession-burnout-anne-helen-petersen.

6. The King Center, "The King Philosophy—Nonviolence365," accessed on May 15, 2023, http://thekingcenter.org/about-tkc/the-king-philosophy.

7. Kwok Pui-lan, *Postcolonial Imagination and Feminist Theology* (Louisville: KY: Westminster John Knox Press, 2005), 211.

8. Mark Dery coined the term *Afrofuturism* in 1993 in his essay titled "Black to the Future" in his book *Flame Wars: The Discourse of Cyberculture* (Durham, NC: Duke University Press, 1994).

9. *Afrotopia* is the title of two books, one written by a professor at the University of Gaston-Berger in Senegal named Felwine Sarr and published in 2020, and the other by Wilson Moses, published in 1998.

10. Susan Newman, *Your Inner Eve: Discovering God's Woman Within* (New York: One World, 2005), 7.

11. Ibid., 8.

12. Robin D. G. Kelley, *Freedom Dreams: The Black Radical Imagination* (Boston: Beacon Press, 2003), 88–89.

13. This terminology is used in place of *plantations*. The explanation can be found here: "The Vocabulary of Freedom," Underground Railroad Education Center, accessed on May 15, 2023, http://undergroundrailroadhistory.org /the-vocabulary-of-freedom.

14. Mal'akiy 17 Allah, "Malcolm X: 'Who Taught You to Hate Yourself?'" *New York Amsterdam News*, May 18, 2023, http://amsterdamnews.com /news/2023/05/18/malcolm-x-who-taught-you-to-hate-yourself/.

15. Kelley, *Freedom Dreams*, 14.

16. Benjamin Tetteh, "Beyond the Year of Return: Africa and the Diaspora Must Forge Closer Ties," *Africa Renewal*, September 20, 2020, https://www .un.org/africarenewal/magazine/september-2020/beyond-year-return -africa-and-diaspora-must-forge-closer-ties.

17. Eugene D. Genovese, *Roll, Jordan, Roll: The World the Slaves Made* (New York: Vintage Books, 1976), 210.

18. Ibid.

19. Robert Farris Thompson, *Flash of the Spirit: African & Afro-American Art & Philosophy* (New York: Vintage Books, 1984).

20. Lydia Polgreen, "An Old Journey Forged in Pain; A Remembrance Born to Heal," *New York Times*, September 26, 2004, http://www.nytimes.com /2004/09/26/nyregion/an-old-journey-forged-in-pain-a-remembrance -born-to-heal.html.

21. This quote is from the historical account of "The Maafa," St. Paul Community Baptist Church, accessed on May 16, 2023, http://www.spcbc.com /themaafa.

22. "Maafa," Mount Aery Baptist Church, accessed on May 16, 2023, http:// www.mtaerybaptist.org/maafa.

23. St. Paul, "Maafa."

24. Tyrone Beason, "'Maafa Suite' Mixes Religion, Education, History, Healing," *Seattle Times*, July 16, 2002, http://archive.seattletimes.com/archive /?date=20020716&slug=maafa16.

25. Polgreen, "An Old Journey."

26. Patrick Gathara, "Berlin 1884: Remembering the Conference That Divided Africa," Al Jazeera, November 15, 2019, http://www.aljazeera.com/opinions /2019/11/15/berlin-1884-remembering-the-conference-that-divided -africa.

27. "France Returns 26 Treasures Looted from Benin," Al Jazeera, November 9, 2021, http://www.aljazeera.com/news/2021/11/9/france-hands-back-26 -treasures-looted-from-benin.

28. Joy-Ann Reid, "*Black Panther*'s Glorious Depiction of Wakanda Envisions the Africa of Black Dreams," NBC News, February 18, 2018, http://www.nbcnews.com/think/opinion/black-panther-s-glorious-depiction-wakanda-envisions-africa-black-dreams-ncna849016.

29. Ibid.

30. Elizabeth Schmidt, "U.S. Policy Toward Ethiopia Is a Story of Cynicism and Self-Interest," *Jacobin*, January 22, 2023, http://jacobin.com/2023/01/us-policy-toward-ethiopia-is-a-story-of-cynicism-and-self-interest.

31. Ibid.

32. "Lampedusa Boat Tragedy: Migrants 'Raped and Tortured,'" BBC, November 8, 2013, http://www.bbc.com/news/world-europe-24866338.

33. Morehouse College, "Baccalaureate | The Reverend Michael Anthony Walrond Jr. '93 Speech," YouTube, May 21, 2023, video, 9:09 to 9:35, https://www.youtube.com/watch?v=vHeTwM0s3TE.

CHAPTER TWO: TRAUMA

1. "Working Together to Reduce Black Maternal Mortality," Centers for Disease Control and Prevention, April 3, 2023, http://www.cdc.gov/healthequity/features/maternal-mortality/index.html.

2. Clare Blackwood, "Wall Adjacent to Breonna Taylor's Apartment Grateful for Justice to Have Been Served," *Beaverton*, September 23, 2020, http://www.thebeaverton.com/2020/09/wall-adjacent-to-breonna-taylors-apartment-grateful-for-justice-to-have-been-served.

3. Sarah Maslin Nir, "How 2 Lives Collided in Central Park, Rattling the Nation," *New York Times*, June 14, 2020, https://www.nytimes.com/2020/06/14/nyregion/central-park-amy-cooper-christian-racism.html.

4. Ibid.

5. Steve Almasy, Holly Yan, and Madeline Holcombe, "Coronavirus Hitting Some African American Communities Extremely Hard," CNN, April 6, 2020, http://www.cnn.com/2020/04/06/health/us-coronavirus-updates-monday/index.html.

6. Robert Booth and Caelainn Barr, "Black People Four Times More Likely to Die from Covid-19, ONS Finds," *The Guardian*, May 7, 2020, http://www.theguardian.com/world/2020/may/07/black-people-four-times-more-likely-to-die-from-covid-19-ons-finds.

7. Kim Kelly, "Essential Workers Don't Need Our Praise. They Need Our Help," *Washington Post*, April 30, 2020, http://www.washingtonpost.com/outlook/2020/04/30/essential-workers-dont-need-our-praise-they-need-our-help/.

8. Cornel West, *Race Matters* (Boston: Beacon Press, 1993), 14.

9. Ibid.

10. Joy DeGruy, *Post Traumatic Slave Syndrome: America's Legacy of Enduring Injury and Healing* (Stone Mountain, GA: Joy Degruy Publications, Inc., 2017), 9.

11. "Racial Trauma," Mental Health America, accessed on May 16, 2023, http://www.mhanational.org/racial-trauma.

12. Ibid.

13. Monnica T. Williams, "Uncovering the Trauma of Racism," American Psychological Association, February 13, 2019, http://www.apa.org/pubs/highlights/spotlight/issue-128.

14. Bessel van der Kolk, *The Body Keeps the Score: Brain, Mind, and Body in the Healing of Trauma* (New York: Penguin Books, 2014), 88.

15. "Body," Survivor's Sanctuary, Me Too Movement, accessed on May 27, 2023, http://sanctuary.metoomvmt.org/body/.

16. "Integrative," Survivor's Sanctuary, Me Too Movement, accessed on May 27, 2023, http://sanctuary.metoomvmt.org/integrative.

17. Coleman Barks, "There's Nothing Ahead," in *Rumi: The Book of Love: Poems of Ecstasy and Longing* (San Francisco: HarperCollins, 2005), 9.

18. Cathy Chester, "A Path to Healing: The Wound Is the Place Where the Light Enters You," *Huffington Post*, updated December 6, 2017, http://www.huffpost.com/entry/a-path-to-healing-the-wou_b_7916968.

19. James Baldwin, *The Fire Next Time* (New York: Dial Press, 1963), 112.

20. Ibid., 113.

21. Sunny Fitzgerald, "The Secret to Mindful Travel? A Walk in the Woods," *National Geographic*, October 18, 2019, http://www.nationalgeographic.com/travel/article/forest-bathing-nature-walk-health.

22. Leah Groth, "Frida Mom Postpartum Awareness Commercial Banned From the Oscars as 'Too Graphic,'" Health, February 11, 2020, http://www.health.com/condition/pregnancy/frida-mom-commercial-banned-oscars.

23. Audre Lorde, *A Burst of Light* (New York: Ixia Press, 1988), 130.

24. "Audre Lorde," National Museum of African American History and Culture, accessed on May 27, 2023, http://nmaahc.si.edu/audre-lorde.

25. "Is Cancer Really a 'Battle'?" [Podcast], Dana-Farber Cancer Institute, last modified April 25, 2019, http://blog.dana-farber.org/insight/2019/03/is-cancer-really-a-battle-podcast.

26. Lorde, *A Burst of Light*, 115.

27. bell hooks, *All About Love: New Visions* (New York: William Morrow Paperbacks, 2001), 215.

28. "About," Circle of Mothers, accessed on May 27, 2023, http://www.circleofmothers.org/about.

29. Howard Thurman, *Meditations of the Heart* (Boston: Beacon Press, 1953, 1981), 51.

30. A. L. Roberts, S. E. Gilman, J. Breslau, N. Breslau, and K. C. Koenen, "Race/Ethnic Differences in Exposure to Traumatic Events, Development of Post-Traumatic Stress Disorder, and Treatment-Seeking for Post-Traumatic Stress Disorder in the United States," *Psychological Medicine* 41, no. 1 (January 2011): 71–83, doi: https://doi.org/10.1017/S0033291710000401.

31. Resmaa Menakem, *My Grandmother's Hands: Racialized Trauma and the Pathway to Mending Our Hearts and Bodies* (Las Vegas: Central Recovery Press, 2017), 72.

32. Ibid.

33. *The Shawshank Redemption*, directed by Frank Darabont (1994; Culver City: Columbia Pictures, 1995), DVD.

34. This was the title of Nipsey Hussle's sixth mixtape, released in 2011. It was the sequel to his mixtape *The Marathon*. The marathon theme continued on through the creation of The Marathon Clothing store, The Marathon Agency (a marketing agency), and, posthumously, The Marathon Collective, a cannabis dispensary. The phrase took on new meaning and prominence upon his tragic death.

CHAPTER THREE: CAPITALISM

1. Josef Adalian, "The Most Popular U.S. TV Shows in 18 Countries Around the World," *Vulture*, December 2, 2015, http://www.vulture.com/2015/12/most-popular-us-tv-shows-around-the-world.html.

2. "Obama More Popular Abroad Than at Home, Global Image of U.S. Continues to Benefit," Pew Research Center, last modified on June 17, 2010, http://www.pewresearch.org/global/2010/06/17/obama-more-popular-abroad-than-at-home.

3. Richard Wike, Bruce Stokes, Jacob Poushter, and Janell Fetterolf, "U.S. Image Suffers as Publics Around World Question Trump's Leadership," Pew Research Center, June 26, 2017, http://www.pewresearch.org/global/2017/06/26/u-s-image-suffers-as-publics-around-world-question-trumps-leadership.

4. Anthony Faiola, "A Year After the Capitol Insurrection, the World Still Sees Something Broken in America's Democracy," *Washington Post*, January 5, 2022, http://www.washingtonpost.com/world/2022/01/05/capitol-insurrection-global-american-democrcay-broken.

5. Ibid.

6. Khristopher J. Brooks, "Nearly Three-Quarters U.S. Millennials Live Paycheck to Paycheck, Survey Shows," CBS News, April 28, 2023, http://www.cbsnews.com/news/millennials-paycheck-to-paycheck-financial-status.

7. Andrew Van Dam, "The Unluckiest Generation in U.S. History," *Washington Post*, June 5, 2020, http://www.washingtonpost.com/business/2020/05/27/millennial-recession-covid.

8. Kashmira Gander, "Millennials Are the Most Anxious Generation, New Research Shows," *Newsweek*, May 9, 2018, http://www.newsweek.com/millennials-most-anxious-generation-new-research-shows-917095.

9. Anne Hellen Peterson, "How Millennials Became the Burnout Generation," BuzzFeed, January 5, 2019, https://www.buzzfeednews.com/article/annehelenpetersen/millennials-burnout-generation-debt-work.

10. Annie Lowrey, "Millennials Don't Stand a Chance," *Atlantic*, April 13, 2020, http://www.theatlantic.com/ideas/archive/2020/04/millennials-are-new -lost-generation/609832.

11. Ankur Jain, "Millennials Are Generation Broke—Here's How We Fix It," *Marie Claire*, May 20, 2019, https://www.marieclaire.com/career-advice /a27534694/millennials-generation-broke.

12. Chloe Berger, "Gen Z Is the Most Materialistic Living Generation," *Fortune*, September 14, 2022, http://fortune.com/2022/09/14/how-does-gen-z -define-financial-success-materialism-peace.

13. Amy Langfield, "Today's Teens More Materialistic, Less Likely to Work Hard: Study," CNBC, May 2, 2013, http://www.cnbc.com/id/100699874.

14. Tami Luhby, "Many Millennials Are Worse Off Than Their Parents—A First in American History," CNN, January 11, 2020, http://www.cnn .com/2020/01/11/politics/millennials-income-stalled-upward-mobility -us/index.html.

15. Emily Moss, Kriston McIntosh, Wendy Edelberg, and Kristen Broady, "The Black-White Wealth Gap Left Black Households More Vulnerable," Brookings Institution, December 8, 2020, http://www.brookings.edu/blog /up-front/2020/12/08/the-black-white-wealth-gap-left-black-households -more-vulnerable.

16. Liz Mineo, "Racial Wealth Gap May Be a Key to Other Inequities," *Harvard Gazette*, June 3, 2021, http://news.harvard.edu/gazette/story/2021/06 /racial-wealth-gap-may-be-a-key-to-other-inequities.

17. Isabella Rosario, "When the 'Hustle' Isn't Enough," NPR, April 3, 2020, http://www.npr.org/sections/codeswitch/2020/04/03/826015780/when -the-hustle-isnt-enough.

18. Megan Carnegie, "Hustle Culture: Is This the End of Rise-and-Grind?," BBC, April 20, 2023, http://www.bbc.com/worklife/article/20230417-hustle -culture-is-this-the-end-of-rise-and-grind.

19. Erin Griffith, "Why Are Young People Pretending to Love Work?," *New York Times*, January 26, 2019, http://www.nytimes.com/2019/01/26/business /against-hustle-culture-rise-and-grind-tgim.html.

20. Amy Novotney, "The Psychology of Scarcity," *Monitor on Psychology* 45, no. 2 (February 2014): 28, http://www.apa.org/monitor/2014/02/scarcity.

21. Daniel Keating, "Stress Really Is Killing Us," CNN, April 2, 2017, http:// www.cnn.com/2017/04/02/opinions/stress-killing-us-keating-opinion /index.html.

22. Matthew Desmond, "Why Poverty Persists in America," *New York Times*, April 3, 2023, https://www.nytimes.com/2023/03/09/magazine/poverty -by-america-matthew-desmond.html.

23. Melissa Dahl, "You Absolutely Do Not Have as Many Hours in the Day as Beyoncé," *The Cut*, November 4, 2014, http://www.thecut.com/2014/11 /powerful-people-think-they-control-time.html.

24. Angela Davis, *Women, Race & Class* (New York: Random House, 1981), 5.

25. Patrice Peck, "Hustle Culture Harms Women of Color the Most," *Marie Claire*, November 22, 2022, http://www.marieclaire.com/career-advice /hustle-culture-women-of-color.

26. Ibid.

27. Tricia Rose, *The Hip Hop Wars: What We Talk About When We Talk About Hip Hop—and Why It Matters* (New York: Basic Civitas Books, 2008), 111.

28. Barack Obama, "Jay-Z: The Power of Our Voice," YouTube, October 15, 2012, video, 0:30 to 0:49, http://www.youtube.com/watch?v=cPa76DrWiUE.

29. Michelle Alexander, *The New Jim Crow: Mass Incarceration in the Age of Colorblindness* (New York: The New Press, 2010), 216.

30. Ibid., 215.

31. Ibid., 231–32.

32. Ibid., 232.

33. APB Speakers, "Imagine a New World," YouTube, September 13, 2022, video, 0:33 to 0:42, https://www.youtube.com/watch?v=awtFzgQ_ubU.

34. Ione Gamble, "My Generation Is Obsessed with the Cult of Wellness—But All That Striving to Be Your Best Self Can Be Dangerous," *The Guardian*, June 23, 2022, http://www.theguardian.com/commentisfree/2022/jun/23 /my-generation-is-obsessed-with-the-cult-of-wellness-but-all-that-striving -to-be-your-best-self-can-be-dangerous.

35. Shaun Callaghan, Martin Lösch, Jonathan Medalsy, Anna Pione, and Warren Teichner, "Still Feeling Good: The U.S. Wellness Market Continues to Boom," McKinsey & Company, September 19, 2022, http://www.mckinsey.com /industries/consumer-packaged-goods/our-insights/still-feeling-good-the -us-wellness-market-continues-to-boom.

36. "The Health of Millennials," Blue Cross Blue Shield, April 24, 2019, http:// www.bcbs.com/the-health-of-america/reports/the-health-of-millennials.

37. This quote is from The Nap Ministry's (@thenapministry) bio description on its Instagram profile page, accessed on May 24, 2023, http://instagram .com/thenapministry.

38. This quote and information are from The Nap Ministry website, accessed on May 24, 2023, https://thenapministry.com.

39. Carnegie, "Hustle Culture."

CHAPTER FOUR: MEDIA

1. Meagan Day, "We're Learning More About the Relationships Between Race, Class, and Police Brutality," *Jacobin*, June 23, 2020, http://jacobin .com/2020/06/police-killings-black-white-poverty.

2. Ibid.

3. Ibid.

4. Riché Richardson, "Can We Please, Finally, Get Rid of 'Aunt Jemima'?" *New York Times*, June 24, 2015, http://www.nytimes.com/roomfordebate

/2015/06/24/besides-the-confederate-flag-what-other-symbols-should-go/can-we-please-finally-get-rid-of-aunt-jemima.

5. Jessica Snouwaert, "Aunt Jemima's Logo Has Changed 6 Times, and Its History Is Rooted in Racial Stereotypes and Slavery—Check Out How the Brand Started and Evolved Over 130 Years," *Business Insider*, June 17, 2020, http://www.businessinsider.com/aunt-jemima-history-logo-changed-6-times-rooted-racial-stereotypes-2020-6.

6. Leigh Donaldson, "When the Media Misrepresents Black Men, the Effects Are Felt in the Real World," *The Guardian*, August 12, 2015, http://www.theguardian.com/commentisfree/2015/aug/12/media-misrepresents-black-men-effects-felt-real-world.

7. Ibid.

8. Tamar Lewin, "Black Students Face More Discipline, Data Suggests," *New York Times*, March 6, 2012, http://www.nytimes.com/2012/03/06/education/black-students-face-more-harsh-discipline-data-shows.html.

9. Gabrielle Palmer, "Role of Zero Tolerance Policies in School-to-Prison Pipeline," *Psychology Today*, May 21, 2019, http://www.psychologytoday.com/us/blog/achieving-excellence-through-diversity-in-psychology-and-counseling/201905/role-zero-tolerance.

10. John Gramlich, "The Gap Between the Number of Blacks and Whites in Prison Is Shrinking," Pew Research Center, April 30, 2019, http://www.pewresearch.org/short-reads/2019/04/30/shrinking-gap-between-number-of-blacks-and-whites-in-prison.

11. Ibid.

12. Lynne Duke, "Defense Cites Officers' Fear of Diallo," *Washington Post*, February 23, 2000, http://www.washingtonpost.com/archive/politics/2000/02/23/defense-cites-officers-fear-of-diallo/7cf41086-38c9-4fe5-893a-aa5ae93d06b8.

13. Ibid.

14. Max Ehrenfreund, "What We Know About What Happened in Ferguson," *Washington Post*, November 25, 2014, http://www.washingtonpost.com/news/wonk/wp/2014/11/25/get-completely-caught-up-on-whats-happened-in-ferguson.

15. Laura Westbrook, "Tamir Rice Shot 'Within Two Seconds' of Police Arrival," BBC, November 27, 2014, http://www.bbc.com/news/av/world-us-canada-30220700.

16. Erica Y. King, "Detroit Police Fire 38 Shots in 3 Seconds, Killing Black Man," ABC News, October 5, 2022, https://abcnews.go.com/US/detroit-police-fire-38-shots-seconds-killing-black/story?id=91030791.

17. Mike Brown's killer stated this ("He was just staring at me, almost like to intimidate me or to overpower me") in his grand jury testimony. "Here Is the Full Text of Darren Wilson's Grand Jury Testimony," ABC7, accessed on May 19, 2023, http://abc7.com/darren-wilsons-grand-jury-testimony/410569.

18. Ibid.

19. Marc Lamont Hill, *Nobody: Casualties of America's War on the Vulnerable, from Ferguson to Flint and Beyond* (New York: Atria Books, 2016), 12

20. Ibid., 13.

21. Ibid., 12.

22. Chauncey DeVega, "'He Was Your Average Joe': The Police and the Media Coddle Another White Killer," *Salon*, February 22, 2016, http://www.salon.com/2016/02/22/he_was_your_average_joe_the_police_and_the_media_coddle_another_white_killer.

23. Ibid.

24. Dana Ford, "Who Commits Mass Shootings?," CNN, July 24, 2015, http://www.cnn.com/2015/06/27/us/mass-shootings.

25. Naomi Ishisaka, "How the Media Privileges White Victims," *Seattle Times*, August 15, 2022, http://www.seattletimes.com/seattle-news/law-justice/how-the-media-privileges-white-victims.

26. Ibid.

27. Abbie Vansickle and Weihua Li, "Police Hurt Thousands of Teens Every Year. A Striking Number Are Black Girls," The Marshall Project, November 2, 2021, http://www.themarshallproject.org/2021/11/02/police-hurt-thousands-of-teens-every-year-a-striking-number-are-black-girls.

28. Ibid.

29. Meredith Clark, "Coverage of Black Female Victims of Police Brutality Falls Short: Column," *USA Today*, April 22, 2016, http://www.usatoday.com/story/opinion/policing/spotlight/2016/04/22/police-violence-women-media/83044372.

30. Ibid.

31. Fariss Samarrai, "Study Links Disparities in Pain Management to Racial Bias," UVA Today, April 4, 2016, http://news.virginia.edu/content/study-links-disparities-pain-management-racial-bias.

32. John Eligon, "Black Doctor Dies of Covid-19 After Complaining of Racist Treatment," *New York Times*, December 23, 2020, http://www.nytimes.com/2020/12/23/us/susan-moore-black-doctor-indiana.html.

33. Ibid.

34. Moya Baily, "Bio," accessed on May 19, 2023, http://www.moyabailey.com.

35. Ellen Wulfhorst, "Creator of Term 'Misogynoir' Sees Power in #Hashtag Activism," *Reuters*, June 5, 2020, http://www.reuters.com/article/us-minneapolis-police-hashtagactivism-tr/creator-of-term-misogynoir-sees-power-in-hashtag-activism-idUSKBN23C1F7.

36. "Mammy, Jezebel and Sapphire: Stereotyping Black Women in Media," *The Listening Post*, Al Jazeera, last modified July 26, 2020, http://www.aljazeera.com/program/the-listening-post/2020/7/26/mammy-jezebel-and-sapphire-stereotyping-black-women-in-media.

37. Carter G. Woodson, *The Mis-Education of the Negro* (Illinois: African American Images, 2000), 84–85.

38. "Superstar," Genius.com, accessed May 6, 2023, http://genius.com/lauryn-hill-superstar-lyrics.

39. "Alright," Genius.com, accessed May 5, 2023, http://genius.com/kendrick-lamar-alright-lyrics.

40. Bijan Stephen, "How Black Lives Matter Uses Social Media to Fight the Power," *Wired*, November 2015, http://www.wired.com/2015/10/how-black-lives-matter-uses-social-media-to-fight-the-power.

41. Whitelaw Reid, "Black Twitter 101: What Is It? Where Did It Originate? Where Is It Headed?," UVA Today, November 28, 2018, http://news.virginia.edu/content/black-twitter-101-what-it-where-did-it-originate-where-it-headed.

42. Ibid.

43. Ibid.

44. Heather Brown, Emily Guskin, and Amy Mitchell, "The Role of Social Media in the Arab Uprisings," Pew Research Center, November 28, 2012, http://www.pewresearch.org/journalism/2012/11/28/role-social-media-arab-uprisings.

45. Charlie Hebdo, "The Revolution Will Not Be Televised, It Will Be Tweeted," *Vice*, January 4, 2015, http://i-d.vice.com/en/article/mbe773/the-revolution-will-not-be-televised-it-will-be-tweeted.

CHAPTER FIVE: UPRISING

1. This was a common practice among protestors who, like me, were advised that it was the best method to remedy the burning sensation. Experts have said otherwise: Marla Milling, "The Risks of Using Milk to Soothe Tear-Gassed Eyes; An Expert Says Use Water Instead," *Forbes*, July 21, 2020, http://www.forbes.com/sites/marlamilling/2020/07/21/the-risks-of-using-milk-to-soothe-tear-gassed-eyes-an-expert-says-use-water-instead.

2. Rahiel Tesfamariam, "Why the Modern Civil Rights Movement Keeps Religious Leaders at Arm's Length," *Washington Post*, September 18, 2015, http://www.washingtonpost.com/opinions/how-black-activism-lost-its-religion/2015/09/18/2f56fc00-5d6b-11e5-8e9e-dce8a2a2a679_story.html.

3. Jelani Cobb, "Between the World and Ferguson," *New Yorker*, August 26, 2014, http://www.newyorker.com/news/news-desk/world-ferguson.

4. Julie Bosman and Joseph Goldstein, "Timeline for a Body: 4 Hours in the Middle of a Ferguson Street," *New York Times*, August 23, 2014, http://www.nytimes.com/2014/08/24/us/michael-brown-a-bodys-timeline-4-hours-on-a-ferguson-street.html.

5. Isabel Wilkerson, "Mike Brown's Shooting and Jim Crow Lynchings Have Too Much in Common. It's Time for America to Own Up," *The Guardian*,

August 25, 2014, http://www.theguardian.com/commentisfree/2014/aug
/25/mike-brown-shooting-jim-crow-lynchings-in-common.

6. Ibid.

7. Brent McDonald, "In St. Louis, a Mock Lynching," *New York Times*, November 22, 2014, http://www.nytimes.com/video/us/100000003250178
/in-st-louis-a-mock-lynching.html.

8. Brent McDonald, "A Symbolic Protest at the Old Courthouse," *New York Times*, November 21, 2014, http://archive.nytimes.com/www.nytimes
.com/news/ferguson/2014/11/21/a-symbolic-protest-at-the-old-court
house.

9. Marc Lamont Hill, *Nobody: Casualties of America's War on the Vulnerable, from Ferguson to Flint and Beyond* (New York: Atria Books, 2016), xix–xxii.

10. "Investigation of the Ferguson Police Department," Civil Rights Division, United States Department of Justice, March 4, 2015, http://www.justice
.gov/sites/default/files/opa/press-releases/attachments/2015/03/04
/ferguson_police_department_report.pdf.

11. Ibid.

12. Ñ Don't Stop, "The Mike Brown Rebellion Pt. 1," YouTube, October 21, 2014, video, 1:11 to 1:31, http://www.youtube.com/watch?v=qnprKx1afvM.

13. Kareem Jackson (Tef Poe), "Ferguson Rapper Tef Poe: Barack Obama Has Forsaken Us, But We Will Not Stop Fighting Injustice," *TIME*, September 16, 2014, http://time.com/3330800/tef-poe-ferguson-missouri-police
-militarization-civil-rights.

14. Akiba Solomon and Kristian Davis Bailey, "Michael Brown, One Year Later," *Colorlines*, August 7, 2015, http://colorlines.com/article/michael-brown-one
-year-later.

15. Roxane Gay, "Ferguson Is an Occupation in Plain Sight and Words Aren't Enough to Change That," *The Guardian*, August 14, 2014, http://www
.theguardian.com/commentisfree/2014/aug/14/ferguson-occupation-peace
-calm.

16. Maytha Alhassen, "Faces from Ferguson: Ashley 'Brown Blaze' Yates," *Huffington Post*, updated December 6, 2017, http://www.huffpost.com/entry
/ashley-yates-ferguson_b_6573746.

17. Sheena Jones, "The Man Who Was the Subject of an Iconic Ferguson Photo Has Died," CNN, May 6, 2017, http://www.cnn.com/2017/05/05/us
/ferguson-iconic-photo-death-trnd/index.html.

18. Ibid.

19. "The Preamble," Movement for Black Lives, accessed on May 10, 2023, http://m4bl.org/policy-platforms/the-preamble.

20. Ñ Don't Stop, "The Mike Brown Rebellion Pt. 3," YouTube, October 21, 2014, video, 6:03 to 6:14, http://www.youtube.com/watch?v=qnprKx1afvM.

21. Alhassen, "Faces from Ferguson."

22. "Free Josh," Free Josh Williams, accessed on June 1, 2023, http://www.free joshwilliams.com.

23. Zach Baron, "Jailed Ferguson Protester Joshua Williams Wants to Be Out There with Everyone," GQ, June 5, 2020, http://www.gq.com/story/joshua -williams-ferguson-2020-interview.

24. Ibid.

25. Jim Salter, "A Puzzling Number of Men Tied to the Ferguson Protests Have Since Died," Associated Press, Chicago Tribune, March 18, 2019, http:// www.chicagotribune.com/nation-world/ct-ferguson-activist-deaths-black -lives-matter-20190317-story.html.

26. Ibid.

27. Ibid.

28. Kim Bell, "Protester Featured in Iconic Ferguson Photo Found Dead of Self-Inflicted Gunshot Wound," St. Louis Post-Dispatch, May 5, 2017, https://www .stltoday.com/news/local/crime-and-courts/protester-featured-in-iconic -ferguson-photo-found-dead-of-self/article_072602fb-99f1–531f-aa1c -b971e8b32566.html.

29. Adolph Reed Jr., Class Notes: Posing as Politics and Other Thoughts on the American Scene (New York: The New Press, 2001), 3.

30. Ibid.

31. The People's Plan St. Louis, accessed on June 13, 2023, http://www.peoples planstl.org.

32. Ashley Winters, "Through Action St. Louis, Kayla Reed Aims to Connect Voting to Power for Young People," St. Louis, October 22, 2020, http://www .stlmag.com/news/action-st-louis-young-voters-kayla-reed.

33. Rebecca Rivas, "The Ferguson Movement Is on the Cusp of Revolutionizing Political Power in St. Louis," Riverfront Times, May 6, 2021, http://www .riverfronttimes.com/news/the-ferguson-movement-is-on-the-cusp-of -revolutionizing-political-power-in-st-louis-35478986.

34. Jim Slater, "Bush Latest Ferguson Protester with Political Success," Associated Press, August 5, 2020, http://apnews.com/article/u-s-news-michael-brown -st-louis-politics-racial-injustice-8d71b1b8d25edd627b441fa7f21d23af.

35. Mitch Smith, "Policing: What Changed (and Didn't) Since Michael Brown Died," New York Times, August 7, 2019, http://www.nytimes.com /2019/08/07/us/racism-ferguson.html.

36. "Five Years After Ferguson, Policing Reform Is Abandoned," Equal Justice Initiative, accessed on August 12, 2019, http://eji.org/news/five-years-after -ferguson-policing-reform-abandoned.

37. Earl Fitzhugh, J. P. Julien, Nick Noel, and Shelley Stewart, "It's Time for a New Approach to Racial Equity," McKinsey Institute for Black Economic Mobility, December 2, 2020, http://www.mckinsey.com/bem/our-insights /its-time-for-a-new-approach-to-racial-equity.

38. Tracy Jan, Jena McGregor, and Meghan Hoyer, "Corporate America's $50 Billion Promise," *Washington Post*, August 24, 2021, http://www.washington post.com/business/interactive/2021/george-floyd-corporate-america-racial -justice.

39. David Hood, "Lawsuits Challenge Corporate Diversity Pledges After Floyd," *Bloomberg Law*, April 7, 2023, http://news.bloomberglaw.com/esg/host-of -companies-sued-alleging-unmet-diversity-equity-pledges.

40. Eric Kohn, "Life After Ferguson: Why Ryan Coogler and Ava DuVernay Support Blackout, the Black Friday Boycott," *IndieWire*, November 26, 2014, http://www.indiewire.com/features/general/life-after-ferguson-why -ryan-coogler-and-ava-duvernay-support-blackout-the-black-friday-boycott -67476.

41. Hiroko Tabuchi, "Black Friday Fatigue? Thanksgiving Weekend Sales Slide 11 Percent," *New York Times*, November 30, 2014, http://www.nytimes.com /2014/12/01/business/thanksgiving-weekend-sales-at-stores-and-online -slide-11-percent.html.

42. Walt Hunter, "The Story Behind the Poem on the Statue of Liberty," *Atlantic*, January 16, 2018, http://www.theatlantic.com/entertainment/archive/2018 /01/the-story-behind-the-poem-on-the-statue-of-liberty/550553.

CHAPTER SIX: PAN-AFRICANISM

1. Angel Jennings, "Nipsey Hussle Had a Vision for South L.A. It All Started with a Trip to Eritrea," *Los Angeles Times*, April 7, 2019, http://www.latimes .com/local/lanow/la-me-nipsey-hussle-south-eritrea-south-los-angeles -20190407-story.html.

2. Dan Rys, "Nipsey Hussle on Major Labels: 'We've Been Colonized; Hip-Hop Is Like Africa,'" *XXL*, October 15, 2013, http://www.xxlmag.com /nipsey-hussle-on-major-labels-weve-been-colonized-hip-hop-is-like -africa.

3. Andres Tardio, "Jonah Berger Details Inspiration Behind Nipsey Hussle's $100 Mixtape Idea," *HipHopDX*, October 31, 2013, http://hiphopdx .com/news/id.26044/title.jonah-berger-details-inspiration-behind-nipsey -hussles-100-mixtape-idea.

4. Rys, "Nipsey Hussle on Major Labels."

5. Ibid.

6. Ibid.

7. Ibid.

8. Ibid.

9. Eri-TV, "Interview with Nipsey Hussle Eritrean-American Recording Artist & Entrepreneur," YouTube, May 3, 2018, video, 17:00 to 17:31, https:// www.youtube.com/watch?v=LSjKr7nxiiQ&t=280s.

10. Ibid., 2:59 to 3:50.

11. This phrase is from Matthew 14:7 (NIV) in the New Testament of the Bible.

12. Translated from Spanish to English as rice with chicken.

13. "Correctional Populations in the United States, 2021–Statistical Tables," Bureau of Justice Statistics, Department of Justice, last modified February 2023, http://bjs.ojp.gov/library/publications/correctional-populations-united-states-2021-statistical-tables.

14. Lars Kamer, "Main Destinations of African Immigrants as of 2019, by World Region," June 15, 2022, Statista, https://www.statista.com/statistics/1232898/main-destinations-of-african-migrants.

15. Many South African leaders, rooted in Pan-African and/or Black nationalist ideologies, have called for South Africa to be renamed Azania. The argument is often that most African countries renamed themselves after the end of colonization and South Africa is a colonial, geographical reference point. They argue Azania is indigenous and liberation-centered. Azania is referenced in this book's introduction. To read more, see Darren Taylor, "South African Party Says Call Their Country 'Azania,'" *Voice of America*, February 20, 2014, http://www.voanews.com/a/south-african-party-says-call-it-azania/1855679.html.

16. Walter Rodney, *How Europe Underdeveloped Africa* (Baltimore: Black Classic Press, 1972), 277.

17. Ibid., 277–78.

18. "Azikiwe-Nkrumah Hall," Lincoln University, accessed on June 2, 2023, http://www.lincoln.edu/about/maps/campus-buildings/azikiwe-nkrumah-hall.html.

19. Howard W. French, "Nnamdi Azikiwe, the First President of Nigeria, Dies at 91," *New York Times*, May 14, 1996, http://www.nytimes.com/1996/05/14/world/nnamdi-azikiwe-the-first-president-of-nigeria-dies-at-91.html.

20. John Henrik Clarke, "The Impact of Marcus Garvey," PBS, accessed on June 2, 2023, http://www.pbs.org/wgbh/americanexperience/features/garvey-impact.

21. Ibid.

22. Ibid.

23. "Ghana Trip," The Martin Luther King, Jr. Research and Education Institute, Stanford University, accessed on June 2, 2023, http://kinginstitute.stanford.edu/encyclopedia/ghana-trip.

24. "'The Birth of a New Nation,' Sermon Delivered at Dexter Avenue Baptist Church," The Martin Luther King, Jr. Research and Education Institute, Stanford University, accessed on June 2, 2023, http://kinginstitute.stanford.edu/king-papers/documents/birth-new-nation-sermon-delivered-dexter-avenue-baptist-church.

25. Ibid.

26. Ashley Farmer, "Black Women Organize for the Future of Pan-Africanism: The Sixth Pan-African Congress," Black Perspectives, African American Intellectual History Society, July 3, 2016, http://www.aaihs.org/black -women-organize-for-the-future-of-pan-africanism-the-sixth-pan-african -congress.

27. Ashley Farmer, "Somebody Has to Pay: Audley Moore, Mother of the Reparations Movement," Black Perspectives, African American Intellectual History Society, June 17, 2015, http://www.aaihs.org/somebody-has-to -pay-audley-moore-mother-of-the-reparations-movement.

28. Farmer, "Black Women Organize."

29. Ibid.

30. African Union (@_AfricanUnion), "In #Nigeria he was given the Yoruba name Omowale 'the son who has come home,'" Twitter post, May 25, 2023, https://twitter.com/_AfricanUnion/status/1661602609013174274.

31. Tariq Ali, "Leaving Shabazz," New Left Review 69 (May/June 2011): 157–59, http://newleftreview.org/issues/ii69/articles/tariq-ali-leaving-shabazz.

32. Ibid., 158.

33. Gabriel García Márquez, in "Cuba in Africa: Seed Che Planted," Washington Post, January 12, 1977, http://www.washingtonpost.com/archive /politics/1977/01/12/cuba-in-africa-seed-che-planted/381c98cd-506d -47d8-b8f6–13e013df8c1f.

34. Barbara Ransby, Ella Baker and the Black Freedom Movement: A Radical Democratic Vision (Chapel Hill and London: The University of North Carolina Press, 2003), 348.

35. "SNCC Delegation Travels to Africa," SNCC Digital Gateway, accessed on June 3, 2023, http://snccdigital.org/events/sncc-delegation-travels-to-africa/.

36. "SNCC Delegation," SNCC Digital Gateway.

37. Ransby, Ella Baker, 355.

38. "Why We Say 'Free the Land!'" Malcolm X Grassroots Movement, accessed on June 3, http://freethelandmxgm.org/why-we-say-free-the-land/.

39. Lisa Ryan, "Here's Why Chimamanda Ngozi Adichie Is Wearing Nigerian Brands Almost Exclusively," The Cut, May 8, 2017, http://www.thecut.com /2017/05/chimamanda-ngozi-adichie-wear-nigerian-fashion.html.

40. BETNetworks, "Burna Boy's Mom Accepts His Award For Best International Act Win!," YouTube, June 24, 2019, video, 1:40 to 1:48, https://www .youtube.com/watch?v=qsvCb59TcDk.

41. Yannick Giovanni Marshall, "Out of Pandemic Anti-Blackness, a Case for Pan-Africanism," Al Jazeera, May 6, 2020, http://www.aljazeera.com/opinions /2020/5/6/out-of-pandemic-anti-blackness-a-case-for-pan-africanism.

42. Ibid.

43. Ibid.

44. Ibid.

45. Wabantu Hlophe, "Rhodes Must Fall Everywhere," *Yale Daily News*, April 1, 2015, http://yaledailynews.com/blog/2015/04/01/rhodes-must -fall-everywhere.

46. Noah Remnick, "Yale Will Drop John Calhoun's Name from Building," *New York Times*, February 11, 2017, https://www.nytimes.com/2017/02/11 /us/yale-protests-john-calhoun-grace-murray-hopper.html.

47. Katherine Pomerantz, "The Story Behind *TIME*'s Cover on Inequality in South Africa," *TIME*, May 2, 2019, http://time.com/5581483/time-cover -south-africa.

48. Aryn Baker, "What South Africa Can Teach Us as Worldwide Inequality Grows," *TIME*, 2, 2019, http://time.com/longform/south-africa-unequal -country.

49. Ibid.

50. Kopano Gumbi, "South Africa's Unemployment Rate Rises Amid Power Crisis," Reuters, May 16, 2023, http://www.reuters.com/world/africa /south-africas-unemployment-rate-rises-329-q1-2023-05-16.

51. "The Employment Situation—June 2023," Bureau of Labor Statistics, U.S. Department of Labor, accessed on July 9, 2023, https://www.bls.gov/news .release/pdf/empsit.pdf.

52. Erin Conway-Smith, "South Africa Debates Taboo Question: Was Mandela a Sellout?" *USA Today*, December 14, 2015, http://www.usatoday.com/story /news/world/2015/12/14/nelson-mandela-south-africa-global-post /77272038.

53. "Mineral Resources," Government Communication and Information System, Republic of South Africa, accessed on June 4, 2023, http://www.gcis.gov.za /sites/default/files/docs/resourcecentre/pocketguide/2012/15%20Mineral %20Resources.pdf.

54. Redi Tlhabi, "Black Lives Don't Matter in Xenophobic South Africa," *Washington Post*, March 2, 2017, http://www.washingtonpost.com/news /global-opinions/wp/2017/03/02/black-lives-dont-matter-in-xenophobic -south-africa.

55. "Independent Africa Faces Forward: Hero in History: Kwame Nkrumah," Smithsonian National Museum of African Art, accessed on October 19, 2023, https://africa.si.edu/exhibitions/current-exhibitions/heroes-principles-of -african-greatness/faces/.

CHAPTER SEVEN: SELF-DETERMINATION

1. Janice Gassam Asare, "Our Obsession with Black Excellence Is Harming Black People," *Forbes*, August 1, 2021, https://www.forbes.com/sites /janicegassam/2021/08/01/our-obsession-with-black-excellence-is-harming -black-people/?sh=b56a4222fd99.

2. "United Nations Charter, Chapter I: Purposes and Principles," Article 1,

United Nations, accessed on June 13, 2023, https://www.un.org/en/about-us/un-charter/chapter-1.

3. Nina Totenberg, "The Supreme Court Is the Most Conservative in 90 Years," NPR, July 5, 2022, http://www.npr.org/2022/07/05/1109444617/the-supreme-court-conservative.

4. Ron Elving, "What Happened with Merrick Garland in 2016 and Why It Matters Now," NPR, June 29, 2018, http://www.npr.org/2018/06/29/624467256/what-happened-with-merrick-garland-in-2016-and-why-it-matters-now.

5. Economic Freedom Fighters (@EFFSouthAfrica), "EFF is a radical, leftist, anti-capitalist and anti-imperialist movement anchored by popular grassroots formations and struggles," Twitter post, February 7, 2016, http://twitter.com/EFFSouthAfrica/status/696246781651382272.

6. "Welcome to the Economic Freedom Fighters," Economic Freedom Fighters, accessed on May 28, 2023, http://effonline.org.

7. David Smith, "ANC Youth Leader Julius Malema Thrown Out of Party," *The Guardian*, November 10, 2011, http://www.theguardian.com/world/2011/nov/10/julius-malema-anc-expelled.

8. "2021 Elections Manifesto," Economic Freedom Fighters, accessed on May 28, 2023, http://effonline.org/2021-lgemanifesto.

9. Maya King and Reid J. Epstein, "As Biden Runs Again, Black Voters' Frustration Bubbles," *New York Times*, April 29, 2023, http://www.nytimes.com/2023/04/29/us/politics/black-voters-biden-2024.html.

10. "About Us," When We All Vote, accessed on May 28, 2023, http://whenweallvote.org/about.

11. "Our Purpose," Black Voters Matter, accessed on June 13, 2023, http://blackvotersmatterfund.org/our-purpose/.

12. "Vision for Black Lives," Movement for Black Lives, accessed on May 30, 2023, http://m4bl.org/policy-platforms.

13. "Invest-Divest," Movement for Black Lives, accessed on May 31, 2023, http://m4bl.org/policy-platforms/invest-divest.

14. "Political Power," Movement for Black Lives, accessed on May 31, 2023, https://m4bl.org/policy-platforms/political-power.

15. "Black Panther Party Community Survival Programs 1967–1982," Black Panther Party Alumni Legacy Network, accessed on May 30, 2023, http://bppaln.org/programs.

16. "Community Survival Programs," PBS, accessed on May 30, 2023, http://www.pbs.org/hueypnewton/actions/actions_survival.html.

17. Ibid.

18. John Raphling and Nicole Austin-Hillery, "Poverty, Pandemic, Police Violence: Ongoing Crises Demand the U.S. Address Pervasive Racism," Human Rights Watch, accessed on May 30, 2023, http://www.hrw.org/world-report/2021/essay/poverty-pandemic-police-violence-in-us.

19. Melba Newsome, "There Is a Better Way to Keep Pittsburgh Safe," *Black Pittsburgh*, December 14, 2021, http://blackpittsburgh.com/there-is-a -better-way-to-keep-pittsburgh-safe.

20. Ibid.

21. Ibid.

22. Anna Brones, "Food Apartheid: The Root of the Problem with America's Groceries," *The Guardian*, May 15, 2018, http://www.theguardian.com /society/2018/may/15/food-apartheid-food-deserts-racism-inequality- america-karen-washington-interview.

23. "About Us," Black Church Food Security Network, accessed on May 30, 2023, http://blackchurchfoodsecurity.net/about-us.

24. Bakari Kitwana, "Baltimore Funding Model Challenges 'Nonprofit Indus- trial Complex' Practices," *Colorlines*, August 30, 2018, http://colorlines.com /article/baltimore-funding-model-challenges-nonprofit-industrial-complex -practices.

25. Glennon Doyle, *Untamed* (New York: The Dial Press, 2020), 59–60.

26. Ibid., 61.

27. "Visions of Independence, Then and Now," Africa at 50, Africa Renewal, accessed on May 31, 2023, http://www.un.org/africarenewal/magazine /august-2010/visions-independence-then-and-now.

28. Ibid.

29. "Destiny," Dictionary.com, accessed on May 31, 2023, http://www.dictionary .com/browse/destiny.

30. "Destiny," Oxford University Press, Encyclopedia.com, last modified on May 14, 2018, http://www.encyclopedia.com/literature-and-arts/literature -english/english-literature-20th-cent-present/destiny.

31. Sarah H. Bradford, *Scenes in the Life of Harriet Tubman*, Electronic Edition, Documenting the American South, University of North Carolina at Chapel Hill, http://docsouth.unc.edu/neh/bradford/bradford.html.

32. Victoria Dawson, "Nat Turner's Bible Gave the Enslaved Rebel the Resolve to Rise Up," *Smithsonian Magazine*, September 13, 2016, http://www.smith sonianmag.com/smithsonian-institution/nat-turners-bible-inspiration -enslaved-rebel-rise-up-180960416.

33. "Four More Ways the CIA Has Meddled in Africa," BBC, May 17, 2016, http://www.bbc.com/news/world-africa-36303327.

34. Ibid.; Erin C. J. Robertson, "Here Are Five More Recent Examples of the CIA's Operations in Africa," *OkayAfrica*, http://www.okayafrica.com /five-recent-examples-cias-operations-africa.

35. Staff Reporter, "'I Fear Nothing': Winnie In Her Own Words," *News24*, April 8, 2018, https://www.news24.com/citypress/special-report/remember ing_winnie/i-fear-nothing-winnie-in-her-own-words-20180408.

36. Howard Zinn, *A People's History of the United States* (New York: Harper Perennial Modern Classics, 1980).

37. Assata Shakur, *Assata: An Autobiography* (Chicago: Lawrence Hill Books, 1987), 181.
38. Dan Connell, *Against All Odds: A Chronicle of the Eritrean Revolution* (Trenton, NJ: Red Sea Press, 1993), 70.
39. Ibid.

CHAPTER EIGHT: LOVE

1. Willis Krumholz, "Family Breakdown and America's Welfare System," Institute for Family Studies, October 7, 2019, http://ifstudies.org/blog/family-breakdown-and-americas-welfare-system.
2. Claretta Bellamy, "Kevin Samuels' Death Raises a Simmering Debate Between Black Men and Women," NBC News, May 13, 2022, http://www.nbcnews.com/news/nbcblk/kevin-samuels-death-raises-simmering-debate-black-men-women-rcna28112.
3. Andrew Lawrence, "Taking His Advice Was Like 'Chewing Broken Glass': The Short Life of Dating Guru Kevin Samuels," *The Guardian*, May 13, 2022, http://www.theguardian.com/lifeandstyle/2022/may/13/relationship-guru-kevin-samuels-life-death.
4. Ibid.
5. Kris Putman-Walkerly, "Danny Glover's Social Justice Secret: Organizers Like Barrios Unidos Make the Difference," *Forbes*, May 21, 2021, http://www.forbes.com/sites/krisputnamwalkerly/2021/05/21/danny-glovers-social-justice-secret-organizations-like-barrios-unidos-make-the-difference.
6. Sonia Saraiya, "Viola Davis: 'My Entire Life Has Been a Protest,'" *Vanity Fair*, July 14, 2020, http://www.vanityfair.com/hollywood/2020/07/cover-story-viola-davis.
7. Ibid.
8. Errin Haines Whack, "White Presidential Hopefuls Face 'Woke Litmus Test' on Race," Associated Press, April 24, 2019, http://apnews.com/article/beto-orourke-tim-ryan-politics-ap-top-news-texas-4d4fcf895d7b43279c218c268da0886e.
9. Takim Williams, "#InContext: Cornel West," Human Trafficking Institute, February 22, 2017, http://traffickinginstitute.org/incontext-cornel-west.
10. "Who Taught You to Hate Yourself—Malcolm X," YouTube, June 28, 2016, video, 02:26 to 02:38, https://www.youtube.com/watch?v=sCSOiN_38nE&t=191s.
11. T. D. Jakes, "Real Men Pour In," YouTube, June 19, 2012, video, 21:40 to 21:44, http://www.youtube.com/watch?v=4fTg4FHSSQY&t=3s.
12. Ibid., 21:51 to 22:10.
13. Ibid., 22:15 to 22:34.
14. "The Sapphire Caricature," Jim Crow Museum, accessed on May 26, 2023, http://jimcrowmuseum.ferris.edu/antiblack/sapphire.htm.

15. Michelle Alexander, *The New Jim Crow: Mass Incarceration in the Age of Colorblindness* (New York: The New Press, 2010), 179.

16. Ibid., 180.

17. "Read the Transcript of Kamala Harris's Victory Speech in Wilmington, Del.," *Washington Post*, November 7, 2020, http://www.washingtonpost.com/politics/2020/11/07/kamala-harris-victory-speech-transcript.

18. "Sexual Violence Targeting Black Women," Equal Justice Initiative, http://eji.org/report/reconstruction-in-america/the-danger-of-freedom/sidebar/sexual-violence-targeting-black-women.

19. "About #SayHerName," The African American Policy Forum, accessed on May 26, 2023, http://www.aapf.org/sayhername.

20. "Reps. Robin Kelly, Clarke, Watson Coleman, Fitzpatrick Introduce the Bipartisan Protect Black Women and Girls Act," Congresswoman Robin Kelly, last modified on December 15, 2021, http://robinkelly.house.gov/media-center/press-releases/reps-robin-kelly-clarke-watson-coleman-fitzpatrick-introduce-bipartisan.

21. Elizabeth Wagmeister, "'Surviving R. Kelly' Final Installment Reveals 'Chilling' Details About Abuser's Grooming of Young Men," *Variety*, January 2, 2023, http://variety.com/2023/music/news/surviving-r-kelly-final-part-three-predator-grooming-men-producer-interview-1235477253.

22. Megan Thee Stallion, "Megan Thee Stallion: Why I Speak Up for Black Women," *New York Times*, October 13, 2020, http://www.nytimes.com/2020/10/13/opinion/megan-thee-stallion-black-women.html.

23. "You've Got to Learn," Genius.com, accessed on May 28, 2023, http://genius.com/nina-simone-youve-got-to-learn-lyrics.

24. "Karega Bailey Presents: Radical Gentleness," Bandcamp, last modified on April 2, 2021, http://soldevelopment.bandcamp.com/track/karega-bailey-presents-radical-gentleness.

25. Dear Future Wifey, "Dear Future Wifey, S2, E202: Purpose Partners (Karega & Felicia Bailey)," YouTube, November 18, 2020, video, 30:40 to 30:44, http://www.youtube.com/watch?v=KzMN-zPUhMw.

26. Ibid., 31:09 to 31:19.

27. Ibid., 29:36 to 29:40

28. Ibid., 29:42 to 30:05.

29. Ibid., 31:33 to 31:54.

30. Bakari Kitwana, *The Hip Hop Generation: Young Blacks and the Crisis in African American Culture* (New York: Basic Civitas Books, 2002), 102–3.

31. Martin Luther King Jr., *Strength to Love* (Philadelphia: Fortress Press, 1963), 15.

32. This phrase is a refrain from the African American hymn "There Is a Balm in Gilead."

33. Amanda Barroso, Kim Parker, and Jesse Bennett, "As Millennials Near 40,

They're Approaching Family Life Differently Than Previous Generations," Pew Research Center, May 27, 2020, http://www.pewresearch.org/social -trends/2020/05/27/as-millennials-near-40-theyre-approaching-family -life-differently-than-previous-generations.

CHAPTER NINE: FAITH

1. *Malcolm X*, directed by Spike Lee (1992; Burbank: Warner Brothers, 1993), DVD.
2. Saba Imtiaz, "A New Generation Redefines What It Means to Be a Missionary," *Atlantic*, March 8, 2018, http://www.theatlantic.com/international /archive/2018/03/young-missionaries/551585.
3. Quotation from *A Theology of Liberation* as it appears in "The Case Against Liberation Theology," *New York Times Magazine*, October 21, 1984, http:// www.nytimes.com/1984/10/21/magazine/the-case-against-liberation -theology.html.
4. Kwok Pui-lan, *Postcolonial Imagination and Feminist Theology* (Louisville, KY: Westminster John Knox Press, 2005), 31.
5. Vincent Harding, in Howard Thurman, *Jesus and the Disinherited* (Boston: Beacon Press, 1996), foreword.
6. Pui-lan, *Postcolonial Imagination*, 37.
7. James Cone, *God of the Oppressed* (New York: Orbis Books, 1997), 123.
8. These descriptions of God's nature are found in 1 Kings 19:12. The various translations of the Bible use different wording to describe how God's presence was revealed to Elijah.
9. Pui-lan, *Postcolonial Imagination*, 126.
10. Sonaiya Kelley, "Words and Pictures: Viral Artist Harmonia Rosales' First Collection of Paintings Reimagines Classic Works with Black Femininity," *Los Angeles Times*, September 21, 2017, http://www.latimes.com /entertainment/movies/la-et-cm-harmonia-rosales-the-creation-of-god -reimagined-20170919-story.html.

CONCLUSION: A LOVE LETTER TO THE AFRICAN DIASPORA

1. This phrase is from Psalm 139:14 (NIV) in the Old Testament of the Bible.
2. This is a paraphrasing of Jeremiah 1:5 (NIV) in the Old Testament of the Bible.
3. Ibid.
4. Chronicles 7:14 (KJV) in the New Testament of the Bible.

Index

Index

About the Author

Rahiel Tesfamariam is an award-winning activist, journalist, theologian, and international speaker. A former *Washington Post* columnist, she is the founder of *Urban Cusp*, a cutting-edge online community highlighting faith, social change, culture, and global awareness. Amid the Ferguson Uprising, Rahiel led #NotOneDime, a national economic boycott. For years, she worked in Africa, organizing with Pan-African movements across the continent. Rahiel is a graduate of Stanford University and Yale Divinity School, where she was the inaugural William Sloane Coffin, Jr. Scholar for Peace and Justice. As a generational voice, she has been featured in the *New York Times*, *Forbes*, *Ebony* magazine, and *Elle* magazine and on BET and Revolt TV. *Essence* magazine named Rahiel one of the nation's "New Civil Rights Leaders."

Rahiel.com
Facebook.com/RahielT
Instagram: RahielT
Threads: RahielT
Twitter (X): @RahielT